". . . a smart and valuable book with a strong foundation in theological studies and American history."—**Alan Nadel,** University of Kentucky

". . . opens a window on religion in America today and demonstrates one of the most important cultural influencers in the world—the American movie."—**Andrew H. Trotter Jr.,** Center for Christian Study

". . . an accessible and sophisticated reflection on the interaction and overlap of religion and popular culture."—**Jeffrey H. Mahan,** Iliff School of Theology

". . . should now become one of the standard approaches to studying the epic movie genre."—**Matthew Page,** Faith and Film Critics' Circle, Bible Films Blog

# FILM &
# RELIGION

## An Introduction

## PAUL V. M. FLESHER
## ROBERT TORRY

Abingdon Press
*Nashville*

## FILM AND RELIGION
## AN INTRODUCTION

**Library of Congress Cataloging-in-Publication Data**

Torry, Robert.
  Film and religion : an introduction / Robert Torry and Paul V. M. Flesher.
    p. cm.
  Filmography: p.
  ISBN 978-0-687-33489-6 (binding: pbk., adhesive-notched : alk. paper)
  1. Motion pictures—Religious aspects. 2. Religious films—History and criticism. I. Flesher, Paul Virgil McCracken. II. Title.

  PN1995.5.T67 2007
  791.43'682—dc22

                                                                        2006037351

07 08 09 10 11 12 13 14 15 16—10 9 8 7 6 5 4 3 2 1
MANUFACTURED IN THE UNITED STATES OF AMERICA

*To our students, colleagues, and friends,*
*with special affection for Kerry and Caroline*

# Contents

# Acknowledgments

The authors would like to thank Abingdon Press for publishing this book, and its editor Kathryn Armistead for her patient encouragement and support. Dean Oliver Walter helped create the Religious Studies Program at the University of Wyoming and provided the program a welcoming environment that facilitated its growth. We would also like to thank our friends and colleagues in the English Department and the Religious Studies Program who first encouraged us to teach Film and Religion and then welcomed our discussions about the interpretation of films at the lunch table, in the corridors, and in their offices. In particular, our gratitude goes to those who read and commented on the manuscript at different stages: Caroline McCracken-Flesher, who volunteered her careful expertise over several drafts, and those whose comments on specific chapters enabled important improvements: Cedric Reverand, Quincy Newell, Keith Hull, Susan Aronstein, Christine Stebbins, Janice Harris, Duncan Harris, Elizabeth Hacker, Susan Frye, Andromeda Hartwick, and Kerry Luck. This book is dedicated to all the students who enrolled in our Film and Religion courses over the years and whose comments, observations, and lively suggestions inspired our thoughts, and to our friends and colleagues who helped us persevere in transforming those ideas into written form. Finally, with deep affection we would like to thank our wives, Kerry Luck and Caroline McCracken-Flesher, who helped make life joyful during the long creative process that this book entailed.

# Preface for Teachers

This book began as lecture notes for our course Film and Religion, an upper-level course open to all students, which we have been team-teaching for more than a decade. When we first taught the course, there were no textbooks and no guidelines for teaching such a course, so we set out our own strategy. We began by distinguishing among films that were explicitly based on religion, such as *The Ten Commandments* and *Brother Sun, Sister Moon*, and films that were overtly secular, but which covertly drew upon religious ideas, themes, or characters, such as *The Matrix* and *The Natural*. This distinction quickly fell apart, for we discovered that films that dealt overtly with religious topics often addressed secular, cultural issues (e.g., *King of Kings*), while films that were explicitly secular made the heaviest points on religious questions (e.g., *The Legend of Bagger Vance*).

By wrestling in class week after week with the question of how film uses religion to tell stories and to convey messages, we found that the answer often required us to go outside the film into the social and political culture within which and for which a film was created. That is, films frequently addressed cultural issues under debate in the larger society. Sometimes these issues were of broad national importance, while other times the questions mattered only to a small subsection of society, perhaps as small as the director and his colleagues. Big issue or small, we realized that we needed to ask about each film's cultural context to interpret its use of religion.

This textbook brings together the three areas of knowledge we have found essential for understanding film's use of religion: the films themselves, the religious features that appear in them, and the cultural concerns they address. This book serves as a guide for combining these three kinds of information to reach an understanding of how a particular film or group of films uses religious imagery, characters, symbolism, and so forth. Because of space limitations, it cannot give an exhaustive exploration of each film, but lays out its analyses to indicate avenues of exploration that can profitably be pursued further.

An understanding of this book's organization will help it to be used more efficiently. We have organized each chapter around an issue addressed by a group of films (although sometimes it is a group of one). The chapter analyzes the issue through the investigation of one or two selected films. Many chapters include a vignette or two of related films at the end. Any one of these films may be viewed for the students to follow the chapter's discussion.

The textbook focuses on American major-release films since World War II. This delimited scope enables the chapters to build on each other, especially with regard to cultural concerns. Each chapter's cultural issue may be unpacked in two ways. First, we append a list of suggested readings to the end of each chapter that provides more in-depth discussion. Second, in the chronological section of our course, we like to have the students read a narrative telling of current events to get a broad overview of the many events and concerns of that time in American society. For the book's first two sections, we recommend William Manchester, *The Glory and the Dream: A Narrative History of America, 1932–1972* (New York: Bantam, 1984). Morris Dickstein's *Gates of Eden: American Culture in the Sixties* (Cambridge, Mass.: Harvard University Press, 1997) is good for the 1960s.

While the explicit or implicit use of religion does not seem to make a difference in our film analyses, the explicit use of Scripture does. When a film depicts a Bible story, it usually wishes its portrayal to appear "accurate" to the audience. This is often difficult because most biblical tales are rather short. Even in the Gospels, which comprise entire books devoted to Jesus, most scenes are sketched in little detail; apart from speech, few contain more than a few verses. To see how different films render the biblical text, it is necessary for students to have read the relevant passages or books prior to viewing the film. To understand how a film's adherence to Scripture and its divergence from Scripture interacts to move the film forward and to create a coherent message, we introduce a method of analysis called targumic interpretation in chapter 1. This will be used heavily in chapters 4–8, the chapters dealing with scriptural films.

The book's final section deals with religions other than American Christianity: Hinduism, Buddhism, Judaism, and Islam. For these chapters, students will need an introduction to the religions in order to grasp the basic concepts. The easiest way is to read the relevant chapters in a world religions textbook. Any reputable textbook can be used, but we recommend our favorites: *World Religions Today*, J. L. Esposito, D. J. Fasching, and T. Lewis (New York: Oxford University Press, 2002); and *The New Penguin Handbook of Living Religions*, 2nd ed., John R. Hinnells (New York: Penguin Putnam, 1997).

This textbook draws on our in-class discussions over more than a decade. To give students further perspectives, we offer lists of suggested readings at each chapter's end. We also maintain a blog titled Film and Religion that reflects our developing ideas (http://FilmandReligion.blogspot.com). There we discuss new films, analyze aspects of old films, invite comments, and respond to our readers. If you have any questions, please feel free to come by. Abingdon Press has created a free downloadable guide for this book, which is available at www.cokesbury.com/teachablebooks.

# Introduction

The term "cultural debate" suggests people articulating their views in a straightforward manner. But this is not always the case. Artistic forms of expression—novels, plays, and films, for instance—often use indirection and subterfuge; they may seem to focus on one issue, while actually commenting on another. The film MASH (1970), for example, overtly took place during the Korean War, but its covert topic was the Vietnam War. V for Vendetta (2006) is set in a future Great Britain, yet it speaks to the United States under President George W. Bush. Indeed, film may be the most powerful form of artistic expression used in contemporary culture. A movie can devote not only words but also active visual expression—extended expression at that—to its perspective. Although the cost and length of time it takes to create movies make them unwieldy for short-term issues, films can have an enormous impact on long-term cultural or political debates.

Major cultural debates are often closely intertwined with religious sensibilities, so it is not surprising to find that films frequently express themselves through religious ideas or images, playing to one or both sides of an issue. While religious adherents may choose to disseminate their beliefs through film, as Mel Gibson did in The Passion of the Christ, major-release films are more frequently created by directors and others who exhibit few obvious religious connections. Nonetheless, their films often draw explicitly upon religious characters and stories, and frequently make implicit use of religious symbolism and beliefs in otherwise secular contexts to help make the story and its message effective.

This book aims to help students understand how films use religion to depict their stories and messages, and how they use religion to make points about religious and nonreligious topics within the culture. We use the term "culture" broadly to indicate the arenas of politics, ethics, religion, popular culture, international or military affairs, and so on. Our approach examines the interaction between film and cultural issues and aims to explicate how films use religion in that interaction. This book does not use films to illustrate moral principles, religious ideals, or theological points. While some books take this approach, their neglect of films' cultural context renders them inadequate for our purposes. Nor are we interested in film history as such, or in the more popular genre of works that can be classified under the rubric "the making of. . . ." Finally, we are not concerned with a specific genre of film, but with films of many genres, including detective films, musicals, science fiction, and westerns. There are genres of specifically religious films—the biblical romances and the Roman conversion films of the 1950s and 1960s, for example—but our concern is not limited to them. Instead, we analyze how films use religion in the construction of their narrative, with the goal of understanding in particular how such films use religion to comment upon and interact with current social issues. To accomplish this, our methodology centers on the interplay of two questions.

First, how does a film use religion to convey its story and message? This question aims to analyze the film itself with the intention of understanding the film's narrative, the cultural issues it addresses, and its use of religion. The term "religion" points to any aspect of any religion or any religious phenomena that a film may use to energize its narrative. These may include, but certainly are not limited to, symbols, rituals (real or imagined), theological concepts, religious stories, and themes. Often these are linked to a portrayal of, or allusion to, a religion's founders or heroes—such as Moses, David, Adam and Eve, Jesus, Buddha—or its enemies—such as the Pharaoh who opposed Moses, Pilate and Herod, and even the devil.

Second, what is the cultural issue addressed by the film, and how has it played out in recent, real-world events? This question requires the analyst to turn from the film to the culture it addresses. Here, he or she needs to determine how the issue has been understood by the culture, what different events have shaped that understanding, and what different positions have been taken on it. These are then related back to the film and used to refine the analysis of its action and narrative, seeking to pinpoint the positions it takes on the issue under debate.

In this book's opening chapters, the issues the films address constitute broad-based questions of national importance. But of course not all films show an interest in such large-scale matters. In later chapters, some of the films' cultural questions will be more limited. They may be focused on questions of interest to a particular subset of the nation, or on questions that have not yet risen to the level of national significance. In some cases, films may reflect an issue of concern only to the director or producer and a small group of associates. This does not mean that the film will not be widely accepted by audiences, but that the film's message about a particular issue will be not important in that acceptance.

Our approach, then, relies on these two questions—How does a film use religion? What cultural issue does the film use religion to address?—and the goal toward which they lead a researcher—that of understanding how films use religion to address cultural questions. The investigation of these questions has no techniques specific to it, but instead draws upon methods from many disciplines. When studying the creation, construction, or production of a film, the investigation may draw upon techniques used in the study of prose fiction, plays, painting, and, of course, film. When studying religious phenomena, whether in the film or in the culture, we will draw from the methods of religious studies, as appropriate. And when analyzing the film's cultural context, we may draw from history, political science, cultural studies, and so forth. Thus, our approach is empirical in the sense that we begin with the study of a film itself and let the film determine which methods are used for analysis and how the questions should be refined for more incisive results.

While this approach's flexibility relies heavily on the judgment of the analyst, it has an important advantage over a more defined methodology; it can be applied to any type of film, from any country, about any religion. The approach focuses on the goal of study, rather than on specific means for reaching that goal.

# The Approach of This Book

This textbook applies this eclectic approach to major-release American films after World War II (excepting only the last chapter), a starting point selected because World War II interrupted and then reshaped the development of American culture. Concerns that had been center stage before the war disappeared, and after the war, concerns that had not existed quickly came to dominate the public realm. From 1950 onward, new film genres appeared and old ones disappeared or took on new forms. The technology of film recording and special effects advanced. Most important, society's postwar concerns began to influence film, providing new issues for exploration and comment. By centering primarily on major-release films—those created with the broadest market in mind—this book explores national debates on these new issues.

To give a sense of the variety of American films that make use of religion in the decades from World War II until today, we have divided the book's fifteen chapters into four sections. Chapter 1 is introductory, providing a light-hearted introduction to our methodology by applying it to the problem of Christmas movies. The issue under debate is the meaning of Christmas when the religious meaning supplied by Christianity is ignored, as in most broad-appeal Christmas features.

The book's first section features three chapters on films from the 1950s. These dwell upon two related issues. Science fiction films use religion to explore the dangers and benefits of the atomic bomb, while the Roman conversion films, such as *The Robe* and *Quo Vadis*, examine the Cold War against Communism. *The Ten Commandments*, perhaps the pivotal religious film of the era, brings together both issues.

The book's second section moves into the 1960s and beyond with four chapters on film interpretations of Jesus and his mission. Released in 1961, *King of Kings* continues the emphasis on the atomic bomb and the Cold War, giving the opposite response to the issue from that of *The Ten Commandments*. This is followed by analyses of the antiestablishment, rock-and-roll film *Jesus Christ, Superstar*, the troubling *Last Temptation of Christ*, and the controversial *Passion of the Christ*. From *Superstar* onward, it becomes clear that the concerns of the 1950s no longer hold sway.

The intent of the chapters in the book's third section is to showcase how different film genres make use of religion. From horror films in chapter 9 to science fiction films in chapter 10, we see how these two genres take seriously the notion of religious cosmology and translate it into the modern world. The initial films in these chapters reflect the malaise that the problems of the Vietnam War caused and, finally, in the last film, the country's return to its self-confident, exceptionalist character. In chapter 11, we study films from different genres in which devout religious believers commit crimes and bring scandal upon themselves and their church. We explore how those situations arise and take up the films' question of whether the belief and actions of the believers are invalidated by those crimes. In the section's last chapter, we analyze baseball films and study how religion, faith, and the highest values of sports are covered.

The final section moves away from the Christian emphasis of the films studied up to this point and examines films that draw upon other religions. In chapters 13 and 14, the book focuses on films featuring Eastern religions and Judaism, both of which have found a home (albeit a small one) in the American movie industry. But the book's final chapter explores films based upon Islam. Here, we make an exception to our emphasis on American films, using films from Egypt and Great Britain, because at the time of writing there were as yet no American films knowledgeably and positively making use of Islam or Muslim themes and symbolism. This absence itself poses an important cultural question, one that we lack the space to explore fully.

Films treat religion in so many different ways that this book can only provide a sampling. A few types we have not addressed include angel films, from comedies like *Angels in the Outfield* to more serious treatments like *Michael*; films using medieval religious imagery, like the Holy Grail or the Fisher King, or those centering around the Knights Templar, such as *Indiana Jones and the Last Crusade*, *The Fisher King*, and *The Da Vinci Code*; the apocalypse-averted films, like *Space Cowboys*, *Armageddon*, and *Independence Day*, which continue the nuclear bomb theme but without extensive religious symbolism. Some films combine American ideology with non-Christian religions, such as the three earliest *Star Wars* movies, *Indiana Jones and the Temple of Doom*, and *The Matrix*. These are just a few of the different kinds of films created since the early 1960s that draw upon religion but that are not discussed in this book.

One question often raised by students is whether the authors of a film—the directors, screenwriters, cameramen, actors, and so forth (who is the author of a film anyway?)—intend the meanings we identify in a film. This question is irrelevant to this book's approach. We are interested in interpreting the film itself, not the details of how it was created. In other words, meaning resides in the text, in this case a film, for the simple reason that the text is what we have. We have neither an author to interrogate nor a compelling reason to believe that an author's statements about the text would be any more authoritative than the text itself.

Underlying many of the films discussed in this book, and perhaps the most broadly appearing commonality among them, is the ideology of American exceptionalism, a long-lasting, flexible myth founded on the belief that God chose America to lead the world into an ever-improving future. The myth views American religious history, especially in its Protestant forms, and American political history as intertwined, with religion guiding the nation's political destiny and the nation's political character possessing a divinely ordained purpose. This link between American religion and politics began with the Puritans and, although its importance ebbed and flowed through the nation's history, it reached a high point during World War II and the following decade. It is important to understand the origins of American exceptionalism, and how it remained important, given the power this myth has held from the post-war period until now.

# The Ideological Context of American Film: American Exceptionalism and American Millennialism

Long before it became a nation, America formed the focus of hopes and beliefs of Europeans who came to live here. They believed that America was an exceptional land, and that God gave those who settled here a special destiny. They would build a better society, "a city on a hill" that would enable humanity to fulfill its complete potential, a society that would be a model for the rest of the world. After the nation's founding, American leaders saw the United States as leading in moral improvement, in spreading the gospel, in raising living standards, in pursuing better health care, in striving for equality of rights for women and all members of society—indeed, in seeking out "life, liberty and the pursuit of happiness." From the nation's example, and often with its help, the world would work to achieve what America was already accomplishing. America would be the savior, the savior nation even, of the world.

This is the myth of American exceptionalism, and although we have stated it in secular terms, the myth has deep roots in American Protestant Christianity. Indeed, it is only during the twentieth century that its religious character has become overshadowed by a secular façade. From its origins in Puritan beliefs through to its nineteenth-century incorporation in mainstream Protestantism and even onward into the twentieth century, American exceptionalism has provided the dominant religious understanding of America's place in the world. President George W. Bush's rhetoric about the nation's role in spreading democracy and freedom in the Muslim world echoes what was once a powerful American missionary purpose of spreading Christianity and the American vision across the globe.

The religious character of American exceptionalism still forms the myth's core and provides its strongest imagery. That core comprises a set of beliefs called American millennialism, which at its most fundamental level is concerned with the shape of history. History—that is, time—is not just one thing after another, going on forever; instead, Christian millennialism holds that God has a plan. Human history will reach a climax in the kingdom of God on earth, which according to Revelation 20, will last for one thousand years, that is, a "millennium." Afterward, God will judge all humanity, put a final end to Satan and evil, and then transform the cosmos into a "new heaven and a new earth" (Revelation 21:1).

American millennialism argues that history moves slowly upward toward the presence of God's kingdom. God guides humankind through history, gradually improving the conditions of humanity's existence on earth, in large part by purifying the church and helping it spread God's spirit to an ever-larger number of humans. As human life improves, the church and the world—indeed, all humanity—will gradually enter into the millennium. There will be no radical break between the present age and this future golden age. Believers and nonbelievers will enter the new age together, helping each other. Indeed, many American theologians posited that America had already entered the golden age, or was on the cusp of entering it. Furthermore, many religious thinkers held that the notion of a thousand year kingdom was metaphorical; the utopia of the millennium could last a longer, indeterminate length of time.

Still, even this metaphorical millennium would not go on forever. In the end, Jesus would again appear on the earth to judge humanity, accompanied by a great, apocalyptic cataclysm. Since Jesus' return will come after the millennium, this general understanding of history's shape is sometimes called postmillennialism.

The key to American millennialism is America itself. God would bring his kingdom about by leading a nation—a country of Christian believers— that would show the rest of Christendom the way to God's kingdom. America would be the biblical "city on the hill," lighting the way for the rest of the world. It is here that God would work his improvements first. The "new world" would lead not just toward God's kingdom, but through it toward the "new earth." America was exceptional. Indeed, although the specifics of American millennialist belief changed over the centuries, this belief remained at its core. America would lead the world into the millennial utopia God was bringing about. This belief began with the Puritans even before they arrived in America and dominated American Protestant belief from that time until the latter half of the twentieth century. In the northern United States, it came to be held by nearly all mainstream Protestant churches—Congregationalists, Methodists, Presbyterians, Episcopalians, Disciples of Christ, and even many Baptists (Moorhead, p. xvi).

The one view rivaling American millennialism has been premillennialism, especially in the form of premillennial dispensationalism. This set of beliefs was put into its standard form by the Northern Irish preacher John Darby in the 1830s. It grew in popularity after the Civil War, becoming associated with fundamentalist Christianity after the turn of the century and finding its way into the popular *Scofield Reference Bible* in 1909. The shape of history in premillennialism differs from that found in American millennialism. Instead of humanity steadily progressing upward toward the realization of God's kingdom, humanity is steadily getting worse, going downhill. Although God will bring his kingdom to earth for a thousand years, this will be preceded by long deterioration in humanity's ethical nature, bringing its moral character ever lower. At this decline's nadir, a catastrophic war between good and evil will take place, but to protect the true Christian believers from catastrophe during this war, Jesus will appear in the clouds and take "his people" to heaven before this happens. (This is why it is called *pre*millennialism; Jesus appears *before* the millennium.) In premillennialism, then, there is a separation between the true Christians and the majority of humanity. God is involved with the Christians, but not with the world. Cooperation between Christians and non-Christians does not take place. Thus, true premillennialism is logically incompatible with American exceptionalism and the patriotic belief in the nation's mission to the world. America cannot be leading the world upward toward God's kingdom and going to hell in a handbasket at the same time. Of course, logic does not prevent many Americans from believing in both simultaneously.

The Puritans began the notion of American millennialism when they envisioned themselves in the model of biblical Israel. Just as God through Moses led the Israelites out of Egyptian oppression to a new land, so too in 1630 God was leading the Puritans out of the oppression of England to a new land. Once in the new world, they would establish a new polity. Like Israel, they formed a covenant with God, promising to follow his rules and guidance in exchange for his blessing. Unlike Israel, however, this new

American nation would not receive God's blessing solely for their own benefit. America's divinely guided achievements would ultimately benefit all Christendom, for it would show the way to a more holy union with God.

The First Great Awakening (1734–43) formed another key moment in the development of American millennialism. Jonathan Edwards, the influential Puritan minister and writer, saw the large number of conversions during that period as "the dawning, or at least a prelude, of that glorious work of God," which is the millennium (Edwards, p. 353). Edwards traced the movement toward the millennium as beginning not with the Puritans, but with the Reformation itself. The "Reformation was the first thing that God did toward the glorious renovation of the world, after it had sunk into the depths of darkness and ruin of the great antichristian apostasy" (Edwards, p. 356). Here, Edwards shows his Protestant stripes by seeing the Catholic Church as an apostasy. Until that point the history of the church, and thus the history of humanity, was heading downward, away from God. But with the Reformation, Edwards argued, history began an upward climb toward "the Church's latter-day glory."

America was inseparably part of that climb, for the church's "latter-day glory . . . is to have its first seat in, and is to take its rise from that new world [of America]." Edwards saw God's hand linking America and the Reformation in that America was discovered "about the time of the Reformation, or but little before." This connection is not accidental, he argued, for "God has made as it were two worlds here below, the old and the new . . . two great habitable continents, far separated one from the other. The latter is but newly discovered. . . . This new world is probably now discovered, that the new and most glorious state of God's church on earth might commence there" (Edwards, p. 354).

The nineteenth century gave American millennialism its full character. This was the era of the great American missionary movements, spreading the Christian gospel to peoples around the globe. They were assisted by the century's advances in transportation, communication, and other forms of technology. Steam power, electricity, and the telegraph were all the rage. Indeed, these technological improvements were seen as part of God's plan and as instrumental to the beginning of the utopian golden age. Accompanying this new technology were scientific advances in medicine, improved education, increasing perfection of democratic practices, and the alleviation of poverty. In 1893, the popular Protestant theologian Josiah Strong extolled the tie between Christianity and secular advances. Scholar James Moorhead characterizes Strong this way:

The kingdom, said Strong, "does not mean the abode of the blessed dead, but a kingdom of righteousness which he [Christ] came to establish on earth." Abandoning the false distinction between secular and sacred, the church would discover that it must use secular instrumentalities as well as religious ones to achieve its ends. Once the church "employs the methods demanded by modern civilization, she will mightily hasten the millennium." Or as he explained in another passage, "Science, which is a revelation of God's laws and methods, enables us to fall into his [God's] plans intentionally and to co-operate with him intelligently for the perfecting of mankind, thus hastening forward the coming of the Kingdom." (Moorhead, p. 91)

This union of the sacred and the secular was an important component of American millennialism by the late nineteenth century. God was going to bring not just the church but all humanity into his kingdom. The sacred and the secular were conjoined. Secular advances helped spread God's word, and often Christians themselves were the ones helping along advances in the secular areas of society. In the early decades of the twentieth century, even advances in business practices, often under the banner of "efficiency," were adopted by Christian activists in their efforts to hasten "the coming of the Kingdom." Indeed, "Millennialist expectation about the coming of God's kingdom and Enlightenment optimism about the triumph of reason," writes Amanda Porterfield, "became intertwined in the mind of many Americans during the nineteenth century" (Porterfield, p. 45).

The joining of secular and sacred was possible because, as Moorhead indicates,

The great modernizing forces—the Enlightenment, independence from the British Crown, democratization, and the market revolution—did not arrive in America as strident opponents of traditional religion. By contrast to their impact in much . . . of Europe, these changes possessed no sharp antiecclesiastical or heterodox edge, forcing persons to choose between the new order and faith. In fact, much of the initial thrust toward a *modern* America came from the Protestant churches, which prospered and enjoyed considerable cultural eminence. (Moorhead, p. 18. Italics added.)

We should not think that the joining of sacred and secular in millennialist thought meant that Christians believed God had forgotten the question of sin and punishment. Far from it. But "[t]he postponement of the final judgment assured the temporal interval necessary for the gradual evangelical conquest of the world, the fulfillment of America's providential mission, and the triumph of secular progress. Postmillennialism assured that the golden age would be a rational continuation of the best features of the present; its synergism enlisted the effort of the saints to create that future" (Moorhead, p. 17).

By the twentieth century, it became increasingly difficult to assert religious belief against the growing dominance of the secular notion of progress. Between the two world wars, mainstream Protestantism developed a more liberal bent. Although it held onto its concept of building God's kingdom, the ongoing process of building and improvement became the goal. It dropped the notion there would be an end—a physical return of Christ, with an accompanying apocalypse—that would follow God's utopian age. America was still exceptional, but that status would continually lead the world into an ever-improving future. God's kingdom would not be pushed aside for a new heaven and a new earth. It is unclear whether this change was even perceived by the congregants of these churches, let alone followed. American popular religion continued to believe in the notion of judgment and a divinely ordained end.

# Analyzing Scripture Films

One feature of this textbook remains to be introduced, namely, its approach to film adaptations of the Bible. The obvious question to ask about any movie portrayal of a biblical story is whether it is accurate. The inevitable answer is no. Critics of all religious stripes point out events and statements left out of, or added into, the film. Even the synopses and casual descriptions of Scripture-based films found in catalogs and on the Internet routinely indicate that the film is "not very accurate." Since Scripture is important to many Christian believers, this inaccuracy is seen as insulting. Indeed, every Jesus film released for the popular market since 1950 has been picketed by Christian groups, usually evangelical or conservative, because of its divergence from the biblical text and thus its inaccurate depiction of Jesus. The only Jesus film that conservative Christians widely hailed as accurate, the 2004 *The Passion of the Christ*, makes so many changes and additions to the biblical story that the claim of accuracy is patently false.

The scholarly world has not done much better than the popular media in coming up with a way of analyzing the relationship between a Scripture film and Scripture. There are a variety of methods, usually falling under the names of "midrash" or "intertextuality," that have been applied but that have accomplished little more than finding a more academic way of stating the obvious—that the films follow the scriptural story at some points and ignore it at others. What is lacking is a means to evaluate the importance of those similarities and differences, a way to identify what that mix means in a particular film.

In chapter 1, we introduce a new way of addressing this problem, one that begins rather than ends with the recognition of difference between the original story and its film adaptation. Our approach derives from the ancient Jewish translations of the Hebrew Bible called *targums*, which combine exactingly accurate renderings of the Hebrew text into Aramaic with additional material. These additions can be as small as a word or two or as large as several paragraphs. Their presence changes the meaning of the literal translation and thus gives the entire passage a new message, one that can be faithful to the original text and yet at the same time alter it significantly. This problem also appears in film renderings of Scripture and has interfered with scholarly attempts at analysis.

The paradox of fidelity and infidelity applies to any film treatment of a text from which it wishes to derive authority. Of course, many films are adaptations of books, short stories, plays, or other literary works. But most films wish to be seen as artistic works in their own right and do not attempt to borrow the authority of the original text, often because the original text has no significant authoritative power.

One type of literature modern films have deemed authoritative is beloved children's books, such as *How the Grinch Stole Christmas*, or just beloved books in general, such as *The Lord of the Rings*. Chapter 1 uses *The Grinch* to explicate this targumic method, illustrating both how it works and how it can be analyzed. The method will then be used in the later analyses of *The Ten Commandments* and the Jesus films.

# Suggested Readings

Jonathan Edwards, *Some Thoughts Concerning the Revival* (1743). Citations from *The Great Awakening*, C. C. Goen, ed. (New Haven: Yale University Press, 1972).

Richard T. Hughes, *Myths America Lives By* (Urbana and Chicago: University of Illinois Press, 2003).

George M. Marsden, *Religion and American Culture* (Fort Worth, Tx.: Harcourt Brace Jovanovitch, 1990).

James H. Moorhead, *World without End: Mainstream American Protestant Visions of the Last Things, 1880–1925* (Bloomington: Indiana University Press, 1999).

Annabel Patterson, "Intention," in Frank Lentricchia and Thomas McLaughlin, *Critical Terms for Literary Study* (Chicago: University of Chicago Press, 1990), pp. 135-46.

Amanda Porterfield, *The Transformation of American Religion: The Story of a Late Twentieth-Century Awakening* (New York: Oxford University Press, 2001).

Earnest Lee Tuveson, *Redeemer Nation: The Idea of America's Millennial Role* (Chicago: University of Chicago Press, 1968).

# Christmas Films: The Search for Meaning

The appearance of *The Nativity Story* in 2006 highlights the absence over the previous six decades of major-release Christmas films that focus on the Christian story of Christmas. No films have emphasized the importance of the birth of the baby Jesus, of Mary and Joseph camping in a stable, or of the visits by shepherds or wise men. Even the classics, such as *It's a Wonderful Life* (1946) and *Miracle on 34th Street* (1947), ignore the Nativity. To be sure, such scenes are portrayed in films, but these films are not Christmas movies, rather lives of Christ, such as *The Greatest Story Ever Told* (1965), *Jesus of Nazareth* (1977), or even *The Life of Brian* (1979). More significant, in these films, the meaning of Jesus' birth comes from the larger narrative of his life; they do not dwell on the meaning of his birth as such. It turns out that the only general-audience features dealing with the Christian holiday are TV productions that include pageants, such as *The Greatest Christmas Pageant Ever* (1983) and *A Charlie Brown Christmas* (1965).

Christmas films fall into two categories, both ostensibly nonreligious. Either they focus on nonreligious subjects to elevate the importance of the holiday—such as *The Polar Express* (2004), *The Nightmare Before Christmas* (1993), and *Miracle on 34th Street*—or they poke fun at it. Some of these films, like *Bad Santa* (2003), use ridicule, while others, such as *Earnest Saves Christmas* (1998) and *Home Alone* (1990), still emphasize the holiday's importance despite their humorous approach.

The films that aim to raise Christmas's importance often center their plots on its meaning. If Christmas does not derive its significance from the Christian story, why celebrate it? If the birth of Jesus is not its meaning, then what is? Many films address this problem head on. Some feature a character who doubts the holiday's importance or denies its relevance altogether. These involve the secular mythology of Christmas, with people who need reassurance about the existence of Santa Claus, the elves, and the reindeer. Several films focus on the possibility that Christmas may not happen because Santa's midnight present delivery from the North Pole cannot take place. Whether threatened by weather, as in *Rudolf, the Red-Nosed Reindeer* (the 1964 TV production featuring Burl Ives), or by hatred, as in *Olive the Other Reindeer* (1999), these films end with Christmas taking place or with the doubter's belief in Christmas being restored.

Underlying the problem of providing a secular meaning for Christmas has been the increasing commercialism of the holiday. If it is not about the birth of Jesus, then it must obviously be about the buying and giving of presents. Indeed, the season's secular mythology—centered on a Santa whose main job is giving presents—seems designed just for that purpose. But if Christmas is about presents, then in reality the main beneficiaries of Christmas are not the individuals who receive gifts, as Caroline McCracken-Flesher observes, but the companies from which those items are purchased. Santa the toy-giver provides a smoke screen for crass commercialism. Indeed, while each child will receive a few toys, the exchange of tens of millions of dollars for those toys will enrich many stores and manufacturers. Such a message is simply *not* an acceptable meaning for Christmas, so the implication that the exchange of gifts makes the givers poorer and the companies richer must be avoided at all costs.

This creates a narrow path for Christmas films. They must deemphasize the commercial aspects of the holiday even as they avoid straying too close to the Christian meaning of Christmas. The 1967 cartoon version of *How the Grinch Stole Christmas!* addresses this tension by attacking commercialism head on. Based on Dr. Seuss's 1957 book, *How the Grinch Stole Christmas*, the cartoon's plot is driven by the Grinch's belief that Christmas is about presents and the holiday's other secular trappings. The story's climax shows this to be wrong.

The cartoon's derivation from the book raises an important question, namely, does the cartoon give a different meaning from the book? The quick answer is that the cartoon differs from the book in significant ways.

The problem is how to analyze that difference. This chapter introduces a method for such investigation—based on the ancient, Jewish practice of Bible translation called *targum*—which will enable us to differentiate between the meaning of a written story and the meaning of its filmic presentation.

# Ancient Biblical Translation and Modern Film Interpretation

When directors make a film based upon a book, they must address the question of how the film will relate to the book, particularly if the book is well known. How closely does the film need to follow the book? The choice they make will shape how audiences see the relationship between the book and the film. If the link between the two is close, then the book—if well-known or authoritative—will help authorize the film. That is, the film will draw upon the book's authority. If the link is loose, then the film will stand on its own. The first film of the Harry Potter series, *Harry Potter and the Sorcerer's Stone* (2001), for example, followed the book's story quite closely, relying on it for authority. Although it could not incorporate every scene from the book into the film, the scenes present varied little from the book. By the release of the third film, *Harry Potter and the Prisoner of Azkaban* (2004), however, the Harry Potter films were a phenomenon in their own right, no longer depending on the books for their popularity. The director therefore took more liberties with the story and the setting.

The film *Clueless* (1995) represents the opposite choice. Although based on Jane Austen's 1816 *Emma*, situated in a small English village, the film relocates the novel to late-twentieth-century urban California, leaving behind any direct claim to the book, although audience members who have read Austen will recognize key elements.

The cartoon version of *How the Grinch Stole Christmas!*, like the first Harry Potter film, follows its book quite closely, but it also departs from the original story. How can we identify and analyze those changes and the ways in which they alter the cartoon's meaning from that of the book? What makes this task difficult is a paradox. On the one hand, the cartoon's changes are hidden. On the other hand, because we view the entire cartoon, those changes are hidden in plain sight. We need an analytical method that enables us to understand the interpretive effects of hiding changes in plain view.

The method that addresses this circumstance is called targumic interpretation. Historically speaking, a *targum* is a rendering of a book of the Hebrew Bible/Old Testament from Hebrew into the language of Aramaic, sometime between the second and ninth centuries CE. Targums have an unusual character; they translate the Hebrew text in a highly literal fashion, yet at the same time add new material into the literal rendering. These additions could be as small as a word or two, or a short phrase; or as long as a sentence, a paragraph, or even several paragraphs. This was because the writers of the targums, known as targumists, were not satisfied with producing literal translations. Often a straight rendering of the Hebrew text left aspects of the story unexplained, or, even worse, created inappropriate or immoral implications about biblical heroes or heroines, or even worse, about God. At other times, a straight translation left intact a story that seemed to have no relevance to present circumstances.

The targumists placed the additions carefully, inserting the units into the translation without disturbing it—skillfully interweaving added words and phrases into the literal translation. This means that this additional material was hidden within the text—*visibly* hidden in plain sight. Targums, like films, were presented; they were read aloud in the synagogue service. If people were not intimately familiar with the Bible's *Hebrew* text, which is why they had a translation in the first place, most targumic additions would pass unnoticed. They were simply understood as part of the original text, hidden by their audience's assumptions.

To illustrate this point, let us try an experiment. Read the English translation of a targumic version of the Adam and Eve story below without opening a Bible. Which words did the targum add?

> And to Adam he said: "Since you have heeded the voice of your wife and have eaten of the tree concerning which I commanded you, saying: 'You shall not eat of it,' the earth will be cursed on your account. In pain will you eat the fruits of its harvest all the days of your life. . . . You will eat bread from the sweat from before your face until you return to the earth, because from it you were created; because you are dust and to dust you are to return. But from the dust you are to arise again to give an account and a reckoning of all that you have done." And the man called the name of his wife Eve because she was the mother of all the living. And the Lord God made for Adam and for his wife garments of glory, for the skin of their flesh, and he clothed them. (Targum Neofiti to Gen. 2:17, 19-21 [McNamara])

If you identified the sentence-long addition of "But from the dust you are to arise again to give an account and a reckoning of all that you have done," then you did well. Why was this added? Without it, the translation's previous sentence might imply that since Adam will only return to the dust, that there is no resurrection, and hence no afterlife or Judgment—key Jewish beliefs.

But did you identify the smaller additions? The targum to Genesis 2:17 adds "In pain will you eat *the fruits of its harvest.*" (The italics indicate the addition, and will do so throughout the book.) Otherwise, the translation reads "you will eat of it," with "it" indicating "the ground." The targum to Genesis 2:21 inserts "Lord God made for Adam and for his wife garments *of glory,* for the skin *of their flesh.*" Where the Hebrew text reads "garments of skin," the targum has added two words, dividing the simple description into two phrases, but unless a reader knows the original text exactly, the addition is hidden and difficult to identify. Of course, the additions hidden in plain sight do not always escape notice, as we shall see.

Whether or not the targum's audience could have identified the additional material, the additions have an impact beyond their mere presence. Even when a targum translates exactly the original text, the additions nonetheless can change the original text's meaning, for they import external concerns into that text. In other words, at the moment of a targum's composition, those external concerns comprise part of the context within which the original text resides. The insertion of this external context into the literal translation does not make the translation less literal—indeed, the entire original text is present in the targum; instead the additions make the targum into a new text, one which combines the original with elements of its context from the targum's time of creation. The targum text now constitutes a translation that carries a context with it, one that can alter the original's meaning even though it alters none of its wording. Let me explain.

It is widely understood that meaning depends on context. For example, the 1974 disaster film *The Towering Inferno* featured people trapped in a burning skyscraper, playing upon the urban fear of being trapped in a common, everyday structure. Imagine what the reaction to the film would have been if it had been released after the destruction of the World Trade Center towers in 2001. It would be seen as a meditation on the immense tragedy of that day, but one in which the victims escape their fate. Meaning, then, is created by the contemporary cultural context. Thus when an object—in this case a film or a book—is studied, two things need to be taken into account. The first is the object itself, and the second is the context in which it appears. This context may be textual, social, ecological, or something else altogether. Although the context is often overlooked, a change in context can transform the entire meaning of the object—as would the hypothetical change regarding *Towering Inferno*.

Additions placed into targumic translations not only bring their own meaning, but they function as context. It is a context that was fixed at composition and imported into the targum itself. As context they provide a new setting for understanding the exact translation, and hence can alter its meaning. Similarly, when a text appears in a new setting—such as a film, TV show, novel—it acquires new material and the meaning of the story changes.

---

*Rules of Targum*
Primary Rules

    Rule 1: When translating or presenting the original text, do so exactly.
    Rule 2: When adding material, integrate it smoothly into the translation.

Secondary Rules

    Rule 3: A large addition may be placed at the beginning or end of story to ensure that the new context is clear.
    Rule 4: An addition may be drawn from or imitate related material elsewhere in the work.
    Rule 5: A word may be substituted for one in the original, without disturbing the surrounding translation.
    Rule 6: Occasionally some of the original may be ignored or left out. The translation smoothly adapts to this loss.

---

# The Targumic Adam and Eve

To examine how a few additions can alter a text's original meaning, let us now turn to a longer example, that of the targumic rendering of the Adam and Eve story from Genesis 2–3. The targumic version of the entire story appears in this book's appendix. We will here discuss only key passages from the story. As we work through the story, we will refer to the Rules of Targum given in the table. The main characteristics of the targumic interpretation are given by the primary rules, while the secondary rules cover less frequent yet relevant features.

This story's central plot is well known. God creates a man, Adam, and places him into the Garden of Eden. God makes Adam the gardener and instructs him not to eat from the Tree of the Knowledge of Good and Evil. When God notices that Adam is lonely, God tries to solve this problem first by creating animals, and then by creating a woman, Eve. A snake persuades Eve to eat from the tree of knowledge. She persuades Adam, and they both eat. God punishes the three characters for this violation and casts Adam and Eve out of the garden.

As we saw in the verses cited above, the targum provides a highly literal translation of this story. Most of it follows Targum Rule #1, namely, when the targum translates, it does so literally. There were a few small insertions (Rule #2), but these were woven into the translation so they did not stick out. The first addition that changes the tale's meaning appears in Genesis 2:15, accomplished with the addition of only two Aramaic words. Following Targum Rules #1 and #2, it hides the two words in plain view, with no accompanying linguistic alterations to indicate they are not original.

> And the Lord God took Adam and had him dwell in the Garden of Eden to toil *in the Torah* and to observe its *commandments*. (Targum Neofiti to Gen. 2:15 [McNamara])

The Hebrew text characterizes Adam's task as that of a gardener; he must "work" the garden "and keep it." The targum's two added words change the object of his efforts. His task no longer focuses on the garden, but on God's "Torah and . . . its commandments"—that is, on the Torah that God created for humanity's moral guidance. Since God's charge here establishes the story's central theme, the addition of these two words changes not only the sentence, but the entire two-chapter story.

The emphasis on Adam keeping the Torah appears again in Genesis 3:15. Here, the Hebrew text contrasts the children of the snake with the woman's children. The two will alternate in supremacy, but, according to the carefully interwoven verse in Targum Neofiti, that alteration will depend on following the Torah.

> And I will put enmity between you [i.e., the snake] and the woman and between *your sons and her sons. And it will come about that when her sons observe the Torah and do its commandments they will aim at you and smite*

*you* on your head and *kill you. But when they forsake the commandments of the Torah* you will aim and *bite him* on his heel *and make him ill.* (Targum Neofiti to Gen. 3:15 [McNamara])

Adam's failure to follow the Torah has serious consequences for him, yet it is not the end of the story. Although God kicks humans out of Eden, there will be a people in the future who will follow God's Torah, namely, the people Israel. This is made clear in the following addition, which follows Targum Rule #3, namely, that large additions may be placed at the end of a story to reinforce the targum's understanding of its meaning.

*Numerous nations are to arise from him [i.e., Adam], and from him shall arise one nation who will know to distinguish between good and evil. If he had observed the commandments of the Torah and fulfilled its commandment he would live and endure forever like the tree of life. And now, since he has not observed the commandments of the Torah and has not fulfilled its commandment, behold we will banish him from the Garden of Eden.* (Targum Neofiti to Gen. 3:22 [McNamara])

The presence of this addition confirms the hints that have already appeared. The story about Adam concerns his failure to follow the Torah. The test was not simply about eating the forbidden fruit, but about doing God's will as expressed in his commandments. The punishment for not following Torah is banishment, as can be seen from the addition, and death, as is made clear in the translation itself. In the future, triumph will come to the people who follow the Torah, namely, the Jews themselves; they will "live and endure forever like the tree of life."

Further examples of targumic interpretation could be studied, but the main point is now clear. The method allows the targum faithfully to present the original text; yet by inserting additional material and making other changes, the targum imports a new context for the faithful representation and hence changes its meaning. When noticed, they are given authority by their association with the original material. The same process works in the creation of films from written stories.

# Film as Targum

The one difference between transforming a written story into a targum or a film is that a targum has the choice of whether to add material while a film does not. Books and films engage their audience in different ways. Both depend on visualization, on the audience having a picture of the story. Books rely on their readers to create the visualization themselves from a few descriptive comments. (In children's books, a few sketches aid this task.) Films, by contrast, depict their own visualization and leave little to the audience's imagination. They must present clothing styles, character expressions, the weather, details of a setting, and so on. A key difference between a book and a film, then, is that each reader visualizes a book in his or her own way, while a film forces its entire audience to see the same thing.

The creation of a film from a written story often follows the targumic process, at least with regard to the two primary rules. When films follow the story's narrative, they do so as closely as possible; when they add elements to the story, they seamlessly weave them into the story so as not to interrupt the story's flow.

What governs how closely the film of a book follows the targumic procedure is whether its creators intend the film to draw upon the book's cultural authority. If the text has a high status in the culture, such as the Bible, a film will likely take care to follow it closely. Similarly, if the story is well known and well loved by its readers, the film is more likely to follow the text closely. This is particularly true for children's stories, such as *Winnie the Pooh and the Honey Tree* (1966), *The Polar Express* (2004), and *Harry Potter and the Sorcerer's Stone*.

To understand more fully how targumic additions influence a story, let us think about how they affect its narrative elements. To keep it simple, we shall discuss only the basic elements of characterization, plot, and setting.

First, characterization centers upon an individual's personality and motivation, which are often indicated by facial expressions, body movements, the sound of the voice, and so on—all of which a film may add using the targumic process. Motivation indicates a person's purposes or goals. There are things they wish to accomplish, whether it is developing a musical talent, getting a girlfriend or boyfriend, finding a good job, or just eliminating the enemy in front of them. Similarly, goals may derive from events of a character's past life, reactions to present circumstances, or desires for the future.

*The Grinch* develops characters through two main strategies: narration, where a voiceover describes a person's mood, motivation, and so on; or interaction with other characters. In the latter, aspects of a character are not merely described, but are demonstrated by how the character responds to others.

Second, interaction between characters serves to move along the story's plot. Indeed, a plot often focuses on the conflict between two or more characters and their goals. For instance, a frequently used plot mechanism is a love triangle, where two men try to get the same woman. The various means by which they aim to accomplish this, interacting with the woman and each other, moves the plot forward. Another aspect of plot development, one that the targumic process often supplies, is that of cause and effect. In a story, why does a character perform a particular action or have a particular idea? Targumic additions often supply causes or inspirations, especially if missing in the original.

Third, perhaps the least noticed yet most important kind of additional material establishes the setting. If scenes take place outside, what is the weather? If inside, what is the lighting? Are buildings, furniture in good repair or heavily worn? What country and time period do they come from? Are they rich and luxurious, poor and rough, fashionable or tasteless? What about clothing? Colorful or drab? Worn or new? Dirty or clean? While these elements often go unsaid in a written story, in a film they must be targumically supplied.

All of these decisions must be made by a film's creators. The choices affect the film's plot, character interaction, and setting—ultimately reshaping its meaning.

# A Targumic Analysis of *How the Grinch Stole Christmas!*

What stands out in a first viewing of the 1967 cartoon of *How the Grinch Stole Christmas!* is how close it is to the 1957 book. Almost every word of Dr. Seuss's poem is in the film, in keeping with Targum Rule #1. A closer look confirms this impression; all but thirty-six words of the book appear in the cartoon—twenty-nine words are missing (all from p. 42 of the book), while seven are changed. The missing words are in keeping with Targum Rule #6, while the changed words fit with Rule #5. Most of the changed words are transition words, such as "and." The most meaning-laden are two words on page 46, where the book's "And he puzzled three hours" is changed to "And he puzzled and puzzed (*sic*)." So, apart from seven changed words, the cartoon faithfully reproduces every word it takes from the book.

The book's drawings are not quite so exactly replicated. While every drawing is represented in the cartoon, the details have frequently been changed. On pages 6 and 7, the exact drawing of all the toys and games does not appear as such in the film, but most of its elements appear in different frames of the extended scene where the Grinch imagines the toys and their noise. These small variations from an exact rendering of the book are quite in keeping with the secondary rules of the targumic process.

The most obvious additions are the songs, which are placed without interrupting the story's original text, keeping its flow moving without a blip. This appears most clearly in the placement of "Welcome Christmas," which appears first at the beginning of the cartoon, before narrator Boris Karloff reads the story's opening words. The next two times, the song is sung where the story mentions the Whos singing. The first of these follows the lines:

> They'd stand hand-in-hand. And the *Whos* would start singing!
> They'd sing! *And they'd sing!*
> AND they'd SING! SING! SING! SING!

The last of the song's performances is not sung, but read by the narrator. This is at the end of the story, after the last word of Seuss's tale. Thus the song frames the original story, in accordance with Targum Rule #3, providing an introduction and ending, as well as illustrating relevant moments. The songs introduce new words to interpret the story, but they also accompany added visual scenes. These scenes introduce the *Whos* as a independent group within the story. Instead of first presenting the *Whos* through the Grinch's imagination—as happens in the book—the film shows the *Whos* as themselves, overexcitedly celebrating Christmas.

Most of the additions to the story help develop character, especially that of the Grinch. While much of the Grinch's character development takes place in interaction with other characters, his personality begins to emerge at his first appearance, when he is by himself. The book's audience first notices the Grinch's wide range of grimaces and frowns. Even when he smiles, it is an "awful" smile, to match the "wonderful, awful idea" he has to stop the *Whos'* Christmas. The cartoon matches these expressions with small, unpleasant habits. At the cartoon's opening, where the book simply has the Grinch leaning on a wall in front of his cave, the cartoon gives him a long blade of grass, which he twiddles like a cigarette, and then munches like a cow chewing its cud.

These small additions help pave the way for the Grinch's reaction to the noise he expects the *Whos* to generate. Rather than allowing the book's repetition of "NOISE! NOISE! NOISE! NOISE!" to be sufficient, the cartoon inserts its first large addition to describe the toys, instruments, and games that will generate that noise. And of course, since it is a film, those items will be shown in action producing the noise. The added poem is as follows:

> And they'll shriek squeaks and squeals
> Racing round on their wheels.
> They dance with jing-tinglers tied onto their heels.
> They'll blow their floo-floobers.
> They'll bang their tar-tinkers.
> They'll blow *Who*-whoobers.
> They'll bang their gar-dinkers.
> They'll beat their trum-tookers
> They'll slang their sloo-slonkers.
> They'll beat their blum-blookers
> They'll wang their *Who*-wonkers
> And they'll play noisy games like zu-zither-karzay,
> A roller-skate type of lacrosse and croquet.
> And then they'll make ear-splitting noises deluxe
> On their great big Electro-*Who*-kardial-schnooks.

While this large insertion describes the *Whos* and the noise they make while having fun with their presents on Christmas morning, its location in the story enhances the Grinch's motivation for hating Christmas, thus affecting the meaning of the unchanged aspects of the story.

The added poem's "hidden" character comes from Targum Rule #4, that is, additions may be constructed like related material elsewhere. One of the trademarks of Dr. Seuss's writing is his wonderful made-up words, even though none appears in the 1957 *Grinch* book. The made-up names of toys and noisemakers, placed here as an insertion, are like related material elsewhere. This use of Seussian style helps this large addition hide in plain view.

Despite all of these added elements, most of the cartoon's characterization of the Grinch takes place when he interacts with his dog, Max. This happens in another set of additions. In the book, Max does not appear until page 15, where the Grinch ties the reindeer antler to his head. In the cartoon, however, Max shows up first in a scene corresponding to page 4, and remains the Grinch's on-screen companion until the story's end.

Max trots out to keep the Grinch company while he looks down the mountain toward *Who*-ville. His character as the Grinch's faithful sidekick is immediately clear as he stands beside the Grinch and wags his tail. This is the moment when we might expect a master to reach down and pat the dog's head. Instead, the Grinch picks up Max by the scruff of his neck and growls his discontent into Max's face. Then he brings their two faces together, shoving his eyes into Max's—as only cartoon figures can. When the Grinch lowers Max from his face, he continues to hold him by his neck and then drums his fingers on Max's head. Rather than the Grinch being a loving master, he uses the dog as an outlet for his anger and hatred. The true character of a man is shown by how he treats his dog, and here the Grinch begins to stand out as someone who abuses his dog.

The abuse continues as the Grinch's song is inserted after his "wonderful, awful idea." If any doubt remained about the Grinch's character, the first line of the song clears it up: "You're a mean one, Mr. Grinch." While the song, sung by Thurl Ravenscroft (the voice of Tony the Tiger), goes on to detail the Grinch's terrible nature, the visual antics reveal just how poorly the Grinch treats Max. After grabbing Max by the tail and dragging him into the cave, the Grinch sets him to work by making him pump the sewing machine. The Grinch then glares his disgust at Max when Max's tail gets caught in the sewing machine. Max's struggle to stay balanced while holding the too-heavy mirror, again indicating his misplaced devotion to the Grinch, results in a rough pull and a shove. In a visual transition to the Grinch tying on the reindeer horn, an added scene shows Max finally realizing that something bad is happening and he runs and hides under the bed. The horn is too heavy, and the scene's additional material depicts Max as unable to stand straight. It is practicality, rather than concern for his dog, that prompts the Grinch then to cut branches off.

But the depths of the Grinch's disdain for Max have not yet appeared. The sleigh ride down the mountain—all added by the cartoon—reveals the Grinch's total lack of concern. When the sleigh runs over poor Max and, wagging his tail, he decides to enjoy a ride on the back, the Grinch mercilessly pulls him back to the sleigh's front. When Max becomes terrified at the heights and the speed of the sleigh and clings to the Grinch in fear, the Grinch, grimacing in disgust, pushes him off. When the song starts again, to accompany the Grinch's stealing of the *Whos*' Christmas things, the Grinch continues to treat Max poorly by throwing large bags and rugs onto Max and crushing him.

When the Grinch finishes taking the *Whos'* Christmas, the cartoon finally shows the only scene of the Grinch's mistreatment of Max found in the book, where Max is forced to pull the loaded sleigh to the top of Mt. Crumpit. Up to this point, all the scenes of the Grinch mistreating Max have been added into the story. Clearly, the cartoon emphasizes the Grinch's mean character through his treatment of Max.

The film targumically enhances a third figure, Cindy-Lou. In the book, Cindy-Lou appears only in the four-page scene where she wakes up and asks, "Santy Claus, why, *Why* are you taking our Christmas Tree? WHY?" The cartoon gives her several earlier appearances. Although we don't learn her name, we recognize her in the "Why?" scene because she is the only *Who* who has been portrayed as an individual. She puts her head into the middle of a wreath on page 1 (this is substitution, Rule #5); she swings between her parents during the singing; and she is the cute kid who receives a strawberry in the Russian-doll sequence of covered dishes. By focusing these scenes on Cindy-Lou, rather than different *Whos* each time, the cartoon develops her character.

Additions enhance the plot as well as develop characters. Some plot enhancements indicate cause and effect. They show why something happens or why someone has an idea. The scene where the Grinch forms the idea to take the *Whos'* Christmas provides a good example of this kind of targumic enhancement. In the book, the idea arises out of nothing. In the cartoon, while the Grinch is talking and thinking, he absentmindedly backs Max into a snowdrift. When Max comes out, his head is covered with snow so that it looks as if he has a white beard and stocking cap. As the Grinch stares at Max, he has the idea of imitating Santa Claus and stealing the *Whos'* Christmas things. Another cause-effect addition comes at the start of the Cindy-Lou scene. Why should Cindy-Lou wake up at that precise moment, especially since she did not wake through the Grinch's earlier antics? Her waking was caused by a tree ornament that fell off the tree and then rolled to the bed where Cindy-Lou was sleeping.

# The Meaning of Christmas

While the above additions show how changes help character development and enhance the plot, a larger addition at the end of the story emphasizes the Grinch's transformation into a believer in Christmas. In the book, when the Grinch realizes that Christmas does not come from a store, that it "means a little bit more!" he simply turns around and brings back all the

Christmas toys, trees, and food. His acceptance into *Who* society is shown in the last page where "He Himself . . . ! The Grinch carved the roast beast."

The cartoon augments this ending by adding a crisis at the moment when the Grinch has his change of heart. In the cartoon, the Grinch has his realization while the loaded sleigh is teetering on the top of Mt. Crumpit. Directly following his change, the sleigh begins to slide down the slope toward the cliff. The Grinch immediately leaps toward the sleigh and tries to pull it back, but unfortunately, the sleigh is too heavy and has too much momentum. Not only does it continue on its way, but it pulls the Grinch and Max along with it to their apparent doom. Just as all seems lost, the narrator speaks the passage from the book:

> And what happened *then* . . . ?
> Well . . . in *Who*-ville they say
> That the Grinch's small heart
> Grew three sizes that day!

The narrator continues without stopping into the following addition:

> *And then, the true meaning of Christmas came through*
> *And the Grinch found the strength of ten grinches, plus two.*

As the narrator utters the word "strength," the Grinch suddenly finds a new strength within himself and saves the sleigh, lifting it above his head. So in a targumlike manner, the cartoon adds new words and a new scene, carefully fitted into the depiction of the original and altering the original's meaning, even though none of the words themselves is changed.

This is then followed by another addition, one targumically hidden from the viewer by being interwoven with the original text and by being packed with Seussian nonsense words.

> And *now that* his heart didn't feel quite so tight,
> He whizzed with his load through the bright morning light
> *With a smile in his soul he descended Mt. Crumpit,*
> *Cheerily blowing Who-Who on his trumpet.*
>
> He rode into *Who-ville*, he brought back their toys,
> *He brought back their floof to the Who girls and boys,*
> *He brought back their snoof and their tringlers and fuzzles*
> *He brought back their pan-tookers, their dafflers and wuzzles.*
> *He brought everything back! All the food for the feast!*
> And he . . .

These two larger additions emphasize two points. First, the Grinch was truly transformed when he finally understood the true meaning of Christmas. By showing him nearly sacrificing himself and then finding a new strength within himself to save the sleigh, the cartoon emphasizes the Grinch's character as a new person. Second, the addition emphasizes that the Grinch brought back everything he took by giving a list of toys that segués into the food for Christmas dinner. The list functions to suggest that by bringing everything back, the Grinch has made a complete restitution.

So what is the meaning of Christmas? The book provides an answer that starts in the negative:

> "Maybe Christmas," he thought, "*doesn't* come from a store."
> "Maybe Christmas . . . perhaps . . . means a little bit more!"

Christmas does not come from a store; it is not presents, decorations, or food. So what is it, if not that? The Grinch hints "perhaps . . . a little bit more." This answer is positive, but it completely lacks content. More what? The book does not say. The acceptance of the Grinch into the Christmas feast hints at community, fellowship, and perhaps friendship, but that is not articulated. By leaving open the answer in this way, the cartoon allows each member of the audience to give his or her own answer.

The cartoon also leaves open the meaning of Christmas but, in true targumic character, provides an addition at the end to help guide the audience toward its point. After the last line of the poem is read, the narrator recites a stanza from the *Whos'* song:

> Welcome Christmas, bring your cheer
> Cheer to all *Whos* far and near.
> Christmas day is in our grasp
> So long as we have hands to clasp.
> Christmas day will always be
> Just as long as we have we.
> Welcome Christmas while we stand,
> Heart to heart, and hand in hand.

While the song gives no major insights into Christmas's meaning, it indicates that it is about human togetherness and friendship. As long as humans (*Who*-mans?) have one another and relate to each other "Heart to heart, and hand in hand," then the cheer of Christmas Day will be in effect. So Christmas is about friendship and togetherness, about human kindness toward each other. This is a nice message, sort of a warm fuzzy approach to meaning, and one that certainly fits with the book. But it is not a strong message.

# The Grinch in Christian Imagery

The Grinch story focuses on the Santa Claus Christmas rather than the Christian Christmas. Despite this lack of obvious religious content, Dr. Seuss's tale does not ignore Christianity altogether. Indeed, the success of the story, from the book onward, hinges on its underlying Christian narrative. This narrative is that of conversion, the process by which someone who stands outside a religion changes and becomes a member.

Christian doctrine requires people to convert in order to become members of the church. People are not born Christians; they must make a decision to join. In some Christian traditions, baptism—originally, adult baptism—is the ritual that formalizes and celebrates the decision to convert. In other traditions, baptism (usually of infants) must later be reaffirmed through the rite of confirmation. American Evangelical Christianity has long emphasized the transformative process that accompanies—indeed inspires—conversion. An individual does not join a church as if he or she were joining a stamp collectors club. Instead, persons must recognize that they have led a sinful life, show remorse for their deeds, and decide to turn away from that life and to follow a new life centered around the worship of God. This is often referred to as a "second birth," or as being "born again."

Conversion is followed by social acceptance. Individuals join the church, where, even if they had committed a crime, the church community forgives them and treats them according to their new character.

Evangelical Christianity encourages individuals to share the details of their conversion, transformation, and forgiveness as part of its public evangelizing activities. This is called "giving witness." These stories, commonly called conversion narratives, follow a standard formula: first, I was a terrible sinner; second, I was born again; third, now I am where I belong, in the Christian church. No matter what life experiences a person underwent on his or her spiritual journey, the story takes this standard shape.

The plot of *How the Grinch Stole Christmas!* takes the shape of a conversion narrative: first, the Grinch shows how terrible he is by stealing the Christmas things; second, he has a conversion experience when he realizes the true meaning of Christmas; third, he joins the community (of *Whos*) when he returns the toys, and is, presumably, forgiven. The popularity of Seuss's Grinch story stems in part from its character as a familiar conversion narrative, which is so widely recognized within American culture that even people who have rejected Christianity or have no Christian background at all subconsciously recognize and respond to its logic. The tale would not be as effective in a Hindu or Buddhist culture, where conversion is not a religious goal. It is a Christian aspiration that communicates best within a Christian society.

In the book and the cartoon, the Grinch begins outside *Who* society. His misunderstanding and hatred of Christmas keeps him outside a society made up of those who know the meaning of Christmas, until he finally realizes Christmas's meaning. While the book just takes this scenario as read, the cartoon makes a bigger deal of the conversion. What if the Grinch is faking? The additional words and scene where the Grinch saves the loaded sleigh ensure that he is not. The Grinch has a true conversion, one that supplies the "strength of ten grinches, plus two," enabling him to rescue the sleigh.

Another version of the story, the 2000 film *Dr Seuss' How the Grinch Stole Christmas* starring Jim Carrey, reshapes this narrative by placing a large addition at the film's beginning, in accordance with Targum Rule #3. In this narrative, the Grinch begins within *Who* society, where he is delivered to adoring parents like other *Who* boys and girls. However, he has problems fitting in and eventually, while still a child, is driven out. The adult Grinch lives on Mt. Crumpit outside *Who*-ville. Meanwhile, it becomes clear that the *Whos* themselves no longer understand the true meaning of Christmas. They think it is about presents, presumably about *giving* them, but definitely about *buying* them.

The film makes the Grinch into a social critic. Indeed, before he converts, the Grinch is a prophet, and an unpopular one at that. Although he does not know the true meaning of Christmas, he knows the *Whos* no longer grasp it, even though they celebrate the holiday. His actions among the *Whos* are quite in keeping with those of Old Testament prophets, who often used outrageous actions and angry words to get the members of Israelite society to realize their sins and failings. Recall Hosea's marriage to a prostitute, Elijah's extreme fasting, and Isaiah's prophesying naked.

The Grinch's speech as he leaves the *Who*-bilation denounces the *Whos* for their greed and avarice. He knows they throw away much of what they receive because he lives at their garbage dump. The final prophetic act is his taking of all the Christmas things. It is then and only then that the *Whos* realize they have held to the wrong meaning of Christmas. As the ancient Israelites sometimes worshiped foreign gods that led them away from the true God, so too the *Whos* focused on the presents, which led them away from the true meaning of Christmas. It takes the Grinch's actions and the questions of Cindy-Lou to inspire her father, Papa Lou, finally to declare that the true meaning of Christmas is "my family." There is no need for presents, decorations, trees, or food to celebrate Christmas. It is Lou's statement that brings realization to all the assembled *Whos* and enables them to sing joyously. Then, as in the book, the joyous singing causes the Grinch to realize the meaning of Christmas and to convert into a "believer." In other words, the film switches from the targumically added plot featuring the Grinch as a prophet and reverts back to the original conversion narrative. He brings back the toys and shows remorse by saying, "I'm sorry." The *Whos* forgive him and welcome him back; he even acquires a family when Martha May declares her love for him rather than the mayor.

So the film adds a prophetic narrative to Seuss's tale. And, in the realm of cause and effect, the Grinch's prophetic role causes the *Whos* to return to the true meaning of Christmas. That allows them to sing, which causes the Grinch's conversion, which in turn allows him to be reestablished within *Who* society. Since it had been the *Whos*' loss of Christmas's true meaning that had driven him out in the first place, it is fitting that their return to the proper understanding brings him back in. The film thus ends with the same unity depicted in the book and the cartoon.

# The Problem with Presents: Consumption and Production

So if Christmas is not about the birth of Jesus, what is it about? Many Christmas films, as mentioned in this chapter's introduction, focus on presents and usually feature Santa Claus. Moreover, films that focus on presents ironically express the point that Christmas is *not* about presents. This negative statement about what Christmas is not is then followed by a struggle to provide a positive definition of Christmas, which usually proves to be more difficult. Christmas may be about family, friendship, and human relationships, as in the Grinch cartoon and film. It may be about the "spirit of giving" and followed by the actions of giving, as seen in film versions of Charles Dickens's *A Christmas Carol*.

The rejection of presents as the meaning of Christmas stems from commercialism. Economically, the Christmas season is when most retail stores determine whether they will have a profit or lose money for the year. Richard Feinberg of the Purdue Retail Institute says that Christmas accounts for "up to 40% of annual sales but more importantly up to 75% of all profit." Christmas functions to ensure the success of capitalism; it is the holiday of consumption and of profits. Clearly corporate profit is no basis for a holiday; who wants to celebrate the holiday of "help these companies make money"? So while Christmas films reject consumption as the meaning of Christmas, the role of consumption remains problematic.

In the book version of *The Grinch*, the Grinch returns the presents to indicate his conversion. In the cartoon version, the Grinch actually puts his life at risk and is transformed all so he can save the presents and return them to the Whos. Most ironically, in the 2000 film version of *The Grinch*, it is the Whos' agreement with Papa Lou's declaration that he does not need presents, only his family, that ultimately causes the Grinch to return the missing presents. In other words, because they realize that they do not need presents, they get them back. If the Whos had not had this revelation, then the Grinch would not have returned the presents.

The issue of presents in Christmas films goes deeper than the rather superficial question of getting presents. These films display an anxiety about consumption and production. In the 2000 version of *The Grinch*, the Whos do not produce, they only consume. They buy, buy, buy! But they are never shown as making anything. Indeed, that differentiates the Grinch from the Whos, for he is shown making his present for Martha May as a child, and later, as an adult, he fills his cave full of mechanical devices that he has constructed from the Whos' garbage (he even recycles!). As the film reaches its climax, the Grinch is shown building his rocket-powered sleigh out of junk. So the Grinch produces while the Whos consume. They view Christmas as the biggest moment of consumption.

In *The Nightmare before Christmas*, the problem of production and consumption is played out in a different way. When the residents of Halloween Town take over Santa's production (and delivery) tasks, they produce the wrong kind of toys, ones that are scary and harmful rather than what the children wished for. When the toys are delivered, their odd character makes them poorly received. The children do not want them. The situation is one in which the entire Santa process takes place successfully, but since the wrong Santa delivered the wrong items, which were made by the wrong "elves," the final step of consumption failed. It takes the real Santa, of course, to set things right.

Anxiety about production and consumption likewise appears in films more closely aligned to other Santa-oriented themes. Those that focus on the possibility that Santa may not deliver the toys, like *Rudolf the Red-Nosed Reindeer*, are struggling with the problem that consumption may not take place. Those that wrestle with the matter of the belief in Santa, like *Olive, the Other Reindeer*, are worried that the production may not even happen—if there is no Santa, there is no producer.

In the end, it becomes clear that when the Christian meaning of Christmas is taken away, American culture lets its economic concerns come through, consciously or unconsciously. The worries about presents and about Santa serve to cloak society's anxiety about consumption and production, the very backbones of the USA's capitalist society. While Christmas films explicitly deny this holiday is about consumerism, their construction reveals that those concerns lie just below the surface.

# Vignettes

## *Dr Seuss' How the Grinch Stole Christmas* (2000)

This film, starring Jim Carrey as the Grinch, shows that the targumic method of film-making describes not only a film's relationship to the original story but also to prior films of that story. The film version adopts many of the innovations that the cartoon version introduced into the story, including the songs, the near-loss of the sleigh, and some of the added wording. As discussed in the chapter's body, the film's large additions—following Targum Rule #3 at the start of the story—contribute a prophetic element to the conversion narrative, indicating the Whos have lost their understanding of Christmas, even as they celebrate it.

The repertoire of characters has been expanded, as have the roles all characters play. Indeed, the conflict about Christmas and motivations for actions comes not from general attitudes, but from specific interactions between individuals. The Grinch saves the sleigh, for instance, because

Cindy-Lou is on top of it. His hatred of Christmas is not a general antipathy but derives from the (future) mayor's ridiculing him for his gift to Martha May. In the end, his conversion into a Christmas believer actually enables him to win Martha May away from the mayor, so the Grinch gets a "present" too—and changes a love triangle into a pair.

## A Christmas Carol

Charles Dickens's *A Christmas Carol* has been produced on film and in cartoon many times. The most notable versions are probably *A Christmas Carol* (1951), starring Alistair Sim as Scrooge; the version *Scrooge* (1970) with Albert Finney; *Mr. Magoo's Christmas Carol* (1962); *Scrooged* (1988) with Bill Murray; and the hilarious *A Muppet Christmas Carol* (1993) with Michael Caine. All of these produce the story using the targumic method of hidden interpretation, citing Dickens's story exactly (and sometimes previous film versions) and interweaving their own additional material with it.

Versions of *A Christmas Carol* wrestle with the issue of consumption, like other Christmas films. As in the book, Scrooge exploits his customers' poverty so they cannot consume. In other words, he consumes the wages of their production. He pays his employees so little, they lack sufficient funds to consume well; Bob Cratchit's family is too poor to afford even a decent Christmas meal. But in the movies, after Scrooge's conversion into a Christmas believer, he helps others consume. Even before he gets out of his pajamas, he starts buying food and gifts for the Cratchit family. He raises Bob's salary so the family can consume more. In the end, Scrooge becomes known for keeping Christmas well, by which the film means that he gives away money. He "produces" it—rather than taking it—so that others may consume.

## The Polar Express (2004)

Before this film's release, the book *The Polar Express* was well known among young children and their parents for its elaborate illustrations as well as its story about the young boy who has his doubts about Christmas removed by traveling on the train to meet Santa Claus. The symbol of his restored belief is a small bell whose sound can only be heard by people who believe in Santa. The targumic character of the movie, which expands the story far beyond the book's rather simple tale, is obvious.

Still, one of the film's selling points was that every scene in the book was recreated in the film.

Even though *The Polar Express* retains its gentle children's story, the added materials that extend its images into narrative scenes transform it into a tale about consumption and production. One of the characters is a boy so poor that he has never received a gift at Christmas—he has never consumed. He does not feel that he belongs with the other children and so sits alone in the rear car. When the train arrives at Christmas Square, he is afraid to get out with the other children.

When the two other main characters try to persuade him to come out, the car is accidentally separated from the train and rolls away, traveling through a vast industrial complex where the elves make all the toys. Santa and the elves are the producers (and deliverers), while the children are the consumers. But lost among the factories, the children are overwhelmed with production and in danger of missing Santa's appearance, and thus gaining or restoring their belief in him. Luckily this does not happen. The older boy meets Santa and has his doubts removed. The younger poor boy returns home at the end of the film to find his first Christmas present.

# Suggested Readings

Paul Davis, *The Lives and Times of Ebenezer Scrooge* (New Haven: Yale University Press, 1990).

Bruce Chilton and Paul V. M. Flesher, *Introduction to the Targumim* (Peabody, Mass.: Hendrikson, forthcoming).

Richard Feinberg, "Notes on Holiday Retail Spending," November 15, 2005. Purdue Retail Institute (University of Indiana) at: http://news. uns.purdue.edu/html3month/2005/051115.FeinbergHoliday.html.

Paul V. M. Flesher, "The Resurrection of the Dead and the Sources of the Palestinian Targums to the Pentateuch," In: *Handbuch der Orientalistik. Judaism in Late Antiquity*, Part 4, *Death, Life-After-Death, Resurrection & The World-to-Come in the Judaisms of Antiquity*, A. J. Avery-Peck and J. Neusner, eds. (Leiden: E. J. Brill, 2000), pp. 311-31.

Paul V. M. Flesher, "Targum as Scripture," in: *Targum and Scripture: Studies in Aramaic Translation and Interpretation in Memory of Ernest G. Clarke*, P. V. M. Flesher, ed. (Leiden: Brill, 2002), pp. 61-75.

Caroline E. E. McCracken-Flesher, "The Incorporation of *A Christmas Carol*: A Tale of Seasonal Screening," *Dickens Studies Annual* 24 (1996): 93-118.

M. McNamara, *Targum Neofiti 1: Genesis*, The Aramaic Bible 1a (Collegeville, Minn.: Liturgical Press, 1992).

Dr. Seuss, *How the Grinch Stole Christmas!* (New York: Random House, 1957).

Robert R. Wilson, *Prophecy and Society in Ancient Israel* (Philadelphia: Fortress, 1980). See esp. pp. 21-88.

# Ultimate Destruction and the Cold War in the 1950s

# CHAPTER 2

# Religion, Science Fiction, and the Bomb

People usually try to make sense out of a new idea, fact, or experience by placing it in relationship to what they already know. If the new experience or fact overwhelmingly changes the world as they understand it—a tsunami or hurricane destroys their city, ethnic cleansing dislocates hundreds of thousands of their fellow citizens, or war devastates their country—people may turn to religion and its worldview for the explanation a powerful god provides. If the experience is terrifying, religion may provide comfort not found elsewhere.

World War II brought about enormous destruction, devastation, and death. Both the winners and the losers had to come to grips with the considerable changes the war's events caused. Among the main combatants, the United States of America was in the unusual position that none of the war had been fought on American territory, apart from the distant waters of Pearl Harbor. It did not have to deal with the physical destruction of its country, although it did have to come to grips with the death of many young soldiers.

When the United States dropped the atomic bomb on the cities of Hiroshima and Nagasaki to end World War II, it opened a Pandora's box of problems. The weapon's power to destroy property and human lives was the stuff of nightmare visions; never before had such massively devastating power existed in human hands. Fundamentalist Christianity, with its premillennialist theology about the cataclysmic end of time, emphasized the apocalyptic significance of this new technology.

The bomb brought about not only a general concern with advanced technology in U.S. popular culture but also an intense preoccupation with the apocalyptic implications of the devastating new weapon. The reason for this is not difficult to discern. For the first time in history a technological means existed that could produce the devastating effects associated with the eschaton. Descriptions of cataclysms on a geological scale, such as those found in the biblical book of Revelation, suddenly took on new immediacy. Revelation 6:12 was just one verse that seemed to prophesy the destructive power of nuclear weaponry. "Behold, there was a great earthquake; and the sun became black as sackcloth, the full moon became like blood . . . the sky vanished like a scroll that is rolled up, and every island and mountain was removed from its place." For interpreters of biblical prophecy, the atomic bomb's destructive power provided the means by which this vision of judgment and annihilation would be achieved. The bomb's creation was thus seen as indicating the rapid approach of the prophesied, apocalyptic end time.

Premillennialist interpreters saw the coming apocalypse in negative terms. As Paul Boyer points out, for such interpreters of prophecy, America had fallen away from its Christian foundations and would not be spared the imminent general destruction. Salvation has no nationalistic biases, they argued, and the sinful America would be destroyed. But those steeped in American millennialism saw a positive side. Several mass-market films from the early- to mid-1950s consider one benefit of apocalypse to be the means by which America would accomplish the national destiny imagined by Puritan writers in their account of the role of the New World in the unfolding of a divinely guided historical process. The United States would provide humankind's ultimate salvation.

At first, 1940s and 1950s science-fiction films dealing with the bomb and other World War II technological advances seem to feature secular themes. Films such as *The Thing* (1951) and *Them* (1954) made literal and symbolic references to the bomb, atomic energy, and radiation. These saw atomic power as the cause of some monstrous invasion force like the giant ants in *Them* or as an attribute of mutation, such as *The Thing*'s killer-plant being, which is located by the radiation it emits.

A deeper look at some of these science-fiction films, however, reveals that they drew upon Christian themes, stories, and theologies in their wrestling with the changes the new technology brought about. This chapter will examine two such films, *When Worlds Collide* (1951) and *The*

*Day the Earth Stood Still* (1951). These films approach America and the atomic bomb's destructive powers not through a simplistic exercise of linking prophetic symbolism to current events, but through the theological structure of the puritan equation of the American New World with the ancient Israelite Promised Land. This structure enables these films to see America's possession of the atomic bomb's apocalyptically destructive power as an indication of its special role in the furthering and even saving of humanity. To understand how this is articulated, we must begin by explaining puritan belief and its underlying logic of typology.

# America: The Promised Land

When the Puritans came to America in 1630, they understood their arrival in the New World as the fulfillment of a divine promise in the narrative of history. The historian Sacvan Bercovitch provides a succinct description of this crucial aspect of puritan belief. The central idea of the puritan enterprise in the new world is that the Puritans understood themselves to be God's elect, a group ordained to create in America a New Jerusalem. As Bercovitch writes, "The New England settlers . . . discovered in their migration God's call to His redeemed, and world redeeming remnant" (p. 61). Cotton Mather, the seventeenth-century puritan preacher, celebrates this migration of God's elect as an act of profound spiritual and historical significance:

> It hath been deservedly esteemed one of the great and wonderful works of God in this *last age*, that the Lord stirred up the spirits of so many thousands of his servants . . . to transport themselves . . . into a *desert land* in America . . . *in the way of seeking first the kingdom of God*. Surely of *this work*, and of *this time* it shall be said, *what has god wrought?* (Bercovitch, p. 49)

Indeed, for the Puritans, history revealed the working of the Spirit: it was the narrative experienced in the time of God's eternal design beginning at the creation and proceeding to the end of time in the second coming of Christ and the judgment of humanity. Thus, historical events in the present were, like those recorded in the Bible, filled with the signs of divine intention. Indeed, they were to be read as a continuing scripture themselves. Just as Puritans believed that the Bible could be interpreted correctly only by those who read with the eye of faith and confirmed belief, so they brought to their interpretive work a firm belief in the divine significance of the puritan enterprise in America:

> The perceiver . . . had to identify with the divine meaning of the New World if he was to understand his environment correctly. He had to "cast his account" as an American, and his "conclusion" had to balance private and corporate redemption in the context of American destiny. (Bercovitch, p. 114)

Central to the puritan method of scriptural interpretation was a mode of reading called *typology*, which aimed to reveal the connections between the Old and New Testaments. The approach is relatively simple. While the events depicted in the Old Testament were accepted as literally true, they also functioned as prefigurations of the incarnation and soteriological purpose of Jesus. That is, they comprised models for later events in God's plan of salvation. For example, Moses constitutes both an actual historical figure who delivered the Israelites from Egyptian bondage and a *type* who prefigures what is termed the *antitype*. In this function, the Puritans considered Moses to be the type for Jesus, the antitype, who delivered Christian believers from the bondage of sin. Jesus as antitype is a more perfect realization of what is anticipated in the preceding type. He is a greater Moses. Thus, history as recorded in the Old and New Testaments is a movement from type to antitype and traces the development of God's salvation narrative as it moves toward its ultimate end in the prefigured incarnation.

The Puritans, with their understanding of history following the death of Christ as a *continuing* series of events with divine meaning, saw their own historical role through the lens of typology. They believed themselves to be the New Israelites, and the New World was the antitype of the biblical Promised Land, a land filled with millennial promise. In Bercovitch's words:

> They were not only spiritual Israelites. . . . They were also, uniquely, American Israelites, the sole reliable exegetes of a new, last book of scripture. Since they had migrated to another "holy land," as Thomas Tillam hymned upon his first sight of Massachusetts—"the *Antitype* of what the Lord's people had of old". . . . [T]hey were a "second, more glorious Israel" . . . [and] they inhabited the earth's millennial fourth quarter "to which that blessed promise truly's given. . . . " (Bercovitch, p. 113)

To state this claim more succinctly: The Puritans believed themselves to be the antitype of the ancient Israelites, the Chosen People. They left England in an exodus across the ocean just as the Israelites left Egypt in an exodus across the desert. With God's favor, they would establish a New World in America as the Israelites had formed a new nation in Canaan.

This idea of American exceptionalism, the belief in America's special character and destiny, has remained a deeply held American belief. Several of the films we will study are informed by this concept of a special American destiny of profound historical and spiritual importance. In this chapter, it functions as a means of dealing with the potentially catastrophic problems of the atomic bomb and the Cold War, while later on it will respond to the aftermath of the Vietnam conflict.

# When Worlds Collide

*When Worlds Collide* appeared in American theaters in 1951, providing its audience with a depiction of total annihilation. In this film a runaway star rushes toward earth on a collision course as a group of scientists and engineers race to complete a spaceship that will save a small number of people by taking them to the star's single orbiting planet. The film's religious resonances begin with the opening shot, in which an ornate Bible opens to Genesis's account of Noah and the ark. This presiding motif, marking the parallel between Noah's purpose and that of the film's protagonists, again suggests the eschatological implications of modern technology in the religious imagination of the early Cold War period. Indeed, the biblical reference, perhaps more than simple metaphor, may prefigure the overtly typological emphases of *The Ten Commandments* released five years later.

The film's primary effect is its creation of a sense of rapidly elapsing time as the small group of workers tries to complete the ship before the earth is destroyed by the speeding star. Again and again we hear the voice on the camp's public address system begging the workers to "hurry, hurry." Above the calendar whose pages we see falling away is a sign reading "Waste anything but time. Time is our most valuable material." In the progress of the star toward earth and in the struggle to complete the rocket ship before its arrival, two complementary actions are marked by the falling calendar pages. Each day brings the runaway star closer to its collision with the earth and brings the rocket ship closer to completion.

The ship will be launched in literally the final moments of earth's existence. Thus, the religious resonances supplied by the film through its initial reference to the Noah story sharpen our appreciation of its emphasis on the duality of the apocalyptic scenario: salvation of an elect requires the utter annihilation of an unsaved remainder. The countdown to the removal of the chosen survivors to a new world is also the countdown to apocalyptic destruction.

*When Worlds Collide*'s religious references derive from the apocalyptic implications of modern technology, notably the atomic bomb. This can be more clearly seen when we look to certain of its significant narrative and visual details. In the 1933 Philip Wylie and Edwin Balmer novel from which the film is adapted, the approaching planet (changed to a star in the film) is simply named Bronson A, after the astronomer who discovered it. In the film that name is changed to *Bellus*, a word suggesting *bellum*, the Latin word for war. The windowless, stubby-winged design of the spaceship and the fact that it is launched from a track suggest the V-1 (ramjet-powered) terror weapons launched by Germany against England in World War II. Early in the film there is a scene in the United Nations as Dr. Hendron, the leader of those who will build the rocket, attempts to convince an unbelieving international audience that the world is in fact doomed to destruction with the advent of *Bellus*. The United Nations refuses to take any action, and Hendron with his chosen followers, having a clear-sighted understanding of what must inevitably happen, works alone to provide the means of salvation for some.

Consider these details from the perspective of the early years of the Cold War, the Korean conflict, and the anxious inauguration of the arms race between the United States and the Soviet Union. This perspective reveals how the film makes use of religious motifs to see in the horrors of nuclear warfare the saving feature central to traditional imaginings of apocalypse. If the apocalyptic imagination envisions an ultimate and utter destruction, that destruction serves as the means by which the old world passes away and a "new heaven and a new earth" come into being.

It is in this context that the film, with its constant referral to Zyra as the "new world" offering hope to the survivors of the catastrophe, alludes to the American founding myth that Bercovitch sees as a constant feature of the political and religious thought of the United States. If the Puritans saw the New World as the site of a "New Jerusalem," the safe harbor of God's "New Israelites" who have escaped the corruption of the old world as the original Israelites escaped Egypt, then the film's depiction of young Americans borne safely to a new world amidst the destruction of the old reimagines that myth in the context of Cold War fears of an inevitable nuclear holocaust. Through its employment of a modern form of the myth of American election, the film offers a hopeful, if tough-minded, vision of the outcome of a nuclear war. Only a remnant, even of Americans, survive. The vision of disaster propounded here doesn't offer a wish-fulfilling vision of war without terrific losses. It does, though, in its characterization of the survivors, depict a group of young, intelligent, healthy, and good-looking Americans—the image of an American future safe from any further threat. If war is to be terrible, the recompense for such horror takes the form traditional to imaginings of the Apocalypse. Those elected to survive do so on a new world. Here, the vision of the American New World in its realized ascendancy as celebrated in the Puritans' millenarian vision is represented in the vernacular of science fiction by the actual new world of Zyra. If destruction must come, it will lead past the horror to an American New World free of threat and able to realize its utopian promise.

It is important to note that this vision of the new American beginnings takes place in a specific moment of the arms race. In 1951, the United States was hurrying, as the characters in the film hurry, to complete a complex technological project imagined to be crucial to American survival. After the 1949 Soviet atomic bomb test, the short postwar period of American arms superiority came to a premature end. President Truman had been assured by his advisors that the Soviets would not have the bomb for at least a decade. When he was informed of the test, he is quoted as saying, "Now we have no more time." Thus, the historical actualities of the period, the sense of diminishing time and the race to deal with what was viewed as the imminent threat of Soviet hostilities, are reflected in the film. Indeed, the response to the Soviet test was to begin the development of the hydrogen bomb in an attempt to regain American superiority in weapons of mass destruction. This project was begun in 1950, and the first test of an American hydrogen bomb occurred at Bikini atoll in November 1952. In this race to complete the hydrogen bomb, the weapon was deemed strategically crucial as both a potential deterrent to war and, should war occur, a weapon vastly more destructive than the atomic fission bomb.

*When Worlds Collide* was released precisely in the midst of the hydrogen bomb's development. This time period is reflected in the dual implications of the film's rocket. On the one hand, we have noted that the ship bears a resemblance to the German V-1 aerial bombs of World War II. On the other hand, when the film combines this visual feature with the role of the ship as a vehicle of salvation, its meaning as a reflection of the hopes and anxieties of the film's specific historical moment stands out. Just as the hydrogen bomb was a weapon whose destructive power was viewed as a means of potential "salvation," either as threat or in actual use, so the rocket in the film comes to suggest the more drastic of these possibilities, at the same time both weapon and ark, destruction and salvation. In the linked countdown the film emphasizes, this double significance is again underscored. That the film synchronizes the arrival of *Bellus* with the completion of the rocket down to essentially the last moment links the two together thematically. Each is the figure of the other in a complex image of salvation in destruction.

In view of the film's portrayal of *Bellus* as a star that will serve as a new sun for the inhabitants of Zyra, it is important to recall that at the time the hydrogen bomb was often explained by using the power of the sun as an example of its mechanism. As *Time* magazine reported in its January, 1950 edition, "The sun's energy is generated by the same process of nuclear fusion that will supply the hydrogen superbomb." *Newsweek* in February of the same year explained, "The sun, in sober fact, is a kind of hydrogen bomb." It is in this typical means of explaining the mechanism of the hydrogen bomb that the film's changing *Bellus* from the book's planet into a sun becomes obviously significant. That *Bellus* will both bring terrible destruction and provide life-supporting light and warmth for the inhabitants of Zyra is perfectly in keeping with the dual focus of the film's apocalyptic themes. Just as the biblical book of Revelation promises a "new heaven and a new earth" following the destruction it predicts, so the survivors in the film will reside on a new planet beneath a new sun. Such a reference to the decidedly positive aspects of an apocalyptic event depicted through the language and imagery of science alters importantly the vision of a technologically effected apocalypse as predicted by those who saw atomic weapons as means of divine judgment from whose wrath only the Christian elect would be delivered. Here the puritan view of an American New World is subtly reinstated to depict an aggressively nationalist view of such an event. The utopian Zyra—as an Edenlike site of a new beginning, as the postapocalyptic new world beneath a new heaven—combines traditional images of America's New World promise. If America was to provide humankind with a new beginning free of the constraints of old Europe, and if it was to be a land of millennial promise, *When Worlds Collide* uses the language of science fiction to renew that traditional and comforting vision in the face of Cold War anxieties.

# The Day the Earth Stood Still

*The Day the Earth Stood Still* is often considered anomalous among the genre films of the early Cold War because it avoids a simplistic us-versus-them vision of international tensions. In the film, Klaatu, the wise and benevolent alien, arrives on earth to warn all its belligerent inhabitants that their behavior will not be tolerated by the advanced interplanetary society he represents. If earthlings, who have recently begun to develop the technology to pose a threat to other planets, eventually export their violence by means of space travel, the earth will be utterly destroyed in an act of self-defense. The film thus seems to condemn Americans and all other participants in the Cold War as a dangerously violent threat to interplanetary peace.

While at one level the film thus suggests that the United States does not differ from the other nations reprimanded by Klaatu for their violent behavior, the context of the early Cold War allows us to read the film at a metaphorical level. In this reading, the film imagines the potentially beneficial results of the use or threatened use of nuclear weapons in dealing with the international tensions of the early 1950s. Klaatu's warning that the exportation of human violence beyond the boundaries of the earth will lead irreversibly to the total destruction of the planet includes a description of the role of his giant robot, Gort, in the implementation of this policy. As Klaatu explains, his people have developed this race of robots as police and given them the permanent and inviolable mandate to meet any act of violence with total destruction of the perpetrators. This threat of instant and complete retaliation has, Klaatu informs his listeners, utterly eliminated war from the interplanetary society he represents. He asks earth to renounce violence and join that community.

What is important to understand when interpreting the film is the state of the Cold War in the early fifties. The Korean conflict, begun the year before the release of *The Day the Earth Stood Still*, provided the first major test of President Truman's new policy of "Containment." By 1947, Soviet expansionism had become a serious concern. The Soviet Union was consolidating its control over the nations of Eastern Europe that had been entrusted to its care. Instead of allowing free elections and political self-determination for these countries, the Soviet Union assumed an iron control.

The United States and its allies were worn out from years of fighting, and they lacked the strength to do more than utter protests through diplomatic channels. President Truman recognized this state of affairs when he proposed the Truman Doctrine in 1947. He saw that despite the efforts of the past decade, the world was now divided into two camps.

> At the present moment in world history nearly every nation must choose between alternative ways of life. The choice is too often not a free one.
>
> One way of life is based upon the will of the majority, and is distinguished by free institutions, representative government, free elections, guarantees of individual liberty, freedom of speech and religion, and freedom from political oppression.
>
> The second way of life is based upon the will of a minority forcibly imposed upon the majority. It relies upon terror and oppression, a controlled press and radio, fixed elections, and the suppression of personal freedoms. (Bernstein and Matusow, p. 255)

Truman proposed to "contain" Communism in general and the Soviets in particular within the nations they now controlled and to prevent them from insinuating their ideology into any other nations. This resulted in the Marshall Plan, which helped restore the economic health of the Western European nations, and the establishment of the North Atlantic Treaty Organization (NATO) military alliance between Western Europe and the United States. It also explained the United States' continued support of the nationalist forces in China against Mao's communists.

In 1950, Truman's doctrine of containment took American armies into South Korea to confront communist aggression there. Although early in the fighting President Truman had threatened the use of atomic weapons to deal with the invasion, he backed off in the face of the disapproval of U.S. allies who emphasized the Soviet capacity to enter the conflict with atomic weapons of their own. At the time of this film, combat in Korea continued solely with the use of conventional weapons.

Seen in this context, *The Day the Earth Stood Still* takes on a more complex and less benevolent meaning. Klaatu's speech to the people of earth is a clear version of the policy of containment, with one essential difference: his people have embraced the strategy of the utter annihilation of aggressors, while the United States had retreated from the use of atomic weapons in its attempt to prevent the expansion of Communism in Korea.

The role of Klaatu as an alien Christ is thus not to bring a message of peace and love but rather, as in Matthew 10:34, "a sword." As a Christ figure, and thus a representative of certain and benevolent wisdom, Klaatu not only supports in his message the concept of containment but insists upon the version abandoned by the Truman White House. He maintains that peace can only be maintained by the will to use, at the slightest provocation, the full power of devastating weaponry. In the final minutes of the film, Klaatu finally gives his message. As he speaks, the camera pans over the faces of the international group of scientists assembled to hear him. Prominently included in the group are the representatives of the Soviet Union and the People's Republic of China. In this pointed allusion to the actual world outside the fictional realm of cinema, *The Day the Earth Stood Still* emphasizes its connection to the realities of the Korean conflict and the problem of dealing with current and future communist expansionism. Although in reality—and despite the arguments of General Douglas MacArthur, who advocated using the radiation from a number of atomic explosions along the Chinese border to prevent troop movement—the Korean conflict and all later attempts at containment were conducted without the use of nuclear weapons. One central reason for such restraint was, as we have seen, the fear of response by the Soviets, who were armed with atomic weapons of their own. The world of Hollywood film maintained for some time, despite the realities of Soviet atomic capability, a fantasy born of the brief period in which only America possessed the bomb. It continued to imagine the ultimately positive results of apocalypse. If Revelation pictures the destruction of the wicked and the end of the current world, it also imagines the salvation of the just, and the creation out of destruction of "a new heaven and a new earth."

It is from this perspective that the Christlike role of Klaatu in *The Day the Earth Stood Still* becomes clear. If the Christ of the eschaton, in his role as judge of the living and the dead, brings both destruction and salvation, the end of the old world and the beginning of the new, this film in its historical context constitutes less a chastisement of warlike humanity by an advanced alien intelligence than a "divine" endorsement of the moral necessity of the American policy of containment.

Yet, this is containment not as practiced by the Truman administration in Korea, but as a commitment to perform what Truman would not. It rests completely on the determined will to use the most fearful weapons available to punish expansionist activity. Indeed, Gort the robot "policeman" serves as the emblem of precisely such an unwavering will. The race of robots of which he is an example has, as we have noted, been given the mandate utterly to destroy an aggressor. This policy calls for no delay, no stages of escalation, no half measures. To inaugurate hostilities is to be destroyed, and the robots, having been provided the power massively to punish aggression, cannot do otherwise, nor can they be reprogrammed. To consider Klaatu's Christlike role in the historical context of the film is to see beneath the surface chastisement of human violence to discover a more disturbing message: *The Day the Earth Stood Still* actually targets the contemporary lack of will to respond to communist expansion in the manner prescribed by Klaatu. Through Klaatu's parallel with Jesus, the film evokes Christ the eschatological Judge as imagined by those for whom the atomic bomb signaled the advent of the end times, but with an uncharacteristically nationalistic emphasis. This Christlike alien's wisdom advocates the will to use utterly devastating force as do the robot policemen of the enlightened interplanetary confederacy: without hesitation or moral uncertainty. In the film's view, that will—whether or not it leads to the actual use of nuclear weapons—constitutes the only means of assuring a lasting peace, namely, the millennial peace imagined by Christian prophecy.

In its promotion of the will to protect and sustain international peace through the threat to employ nuclear weapons, *The Day the Earth Stood Still* transforms in a disturbing fashion the optimistic view of an American historical mission as formulated by nineteenth-century American millennialism. This doctrine, as we have seen, held that the United States should disseminate throughout the world democratic and progressive ideals derived from Christianity understood as a liberal force. As a model for the rest of the world, America would thus take a leading role in a historical process of spiritual (and thus social and political) enlightenment, leading ultimately to the establishment of a millennial era characterized by worldwide peace and the realization of human potential. Indeed, when Klaatu describes for his young human companion Bobby the utopian conditions of his home world, a place where the abolition of war has allowed a flourishing of technology devoted to peaceful and life-enhancing purposes, the film describes precisely the vision of the future foreseen by nineteenth-century American millennialism.

# Vignette

## The Conquest of Space (1955)

Another science-fiction film of the early fifties, *The Conquest of Space*, develops a religious theme. Here commander Samuel Merritt—the leader of an expedition to Mars, the first interplanetary voyage undertaken by humanity—begins in the midst of the trip to fear that space travel may be a blasphemous invasion of God's realm. As his anxiety deepens he several times nearly destroys the ship and crew, one of whom is his own son. Merritt's religious obsession is countered by the faith that develops in his son Barnet during the voyage. Initially uninterested in space travel and wishing only to return to earth and his wife, Barnet comes to appreciate the necessity of human expansion into space if humanity is to overcome the dangers of overpopulation and dwindling natural resources. In a theological discussion with his increasingly agitated father, Barnet counters Merritt's fear of blasphemous human presumption. He argues that the fact of space travel becoming possible just as the need for land and resources is reaching a crisis should be understood as a sign of divine providence.

The film, of course, favors the son's theological position. From portions of dialogue we come to understand that after a series of wars, the world has been united under a benevolent international government, and the makeup of the crew (although commanded by an American) suggests an era of peace and cooperation. From the perspective of this enlightened culture, Merritt's religious fears represent a dangerous return to outmoded theological error. Indeed, given the early explanation of "space fatigue" by a physician aboard the space station from which the Mars expedition departs, we can see Merritt's condition is a form of madness. Such dangerous religious mania threatens not only the crew but the very future of mankind. God's blessing upon the mission becomes clear near the end of the film. Having been deprived of water by an act of sabotage by Merritt, the crew faces death as they await the proper date to lift off and successfully reach earth. On Christmas Day snow falls, and the crew is saved. This providential event thus supports Barnet's enlightened theological understanding of God's plan for human expansion into space.

# Suggested Readings

Sacvan Bercovitch, *The Puritan Origins of the American Self* (New Haven: Yale University Press, 1975).

Barton J. Bernstein and Allen J. Matusow, *The Truman Administration: A Documentary History* (New York: Harper and Row, 1966).

Paul Boyer, *By the Bomb's Early Light: American Thought and Culture at the Dawn of the Atomic Age* (Chapel Hill: North Carolina University Press, 1985).

Paul Boyer, *When Time Shall Be No More: Prophecy Belief in Modern American Culture* (Cambridge: Harvard University Press, 1992).

Robert Torry, "Apocalypse Then: Benefits of the Bomb in Fifties Science Fiction Films," *Cinema Journal* 31:1 (Fall, 1991): 7-21.

# CHAPTER 3

# Making Rome Christian

After World War II several films dealing with the contrast between pagan Roman culture and Christianity appeared, including *Quo Vadis* (1951), *Salome* (1953), *The Robe* (1953), *Demetrius and the Gladiators* (1954), and *Ben Hur* (1956). Addressing the conflict between the spiritual and ethical values of Christianity and Roman militaristic imperialism, these films feature a virile fighting man—usually a Roman soldier, but sometimes a gladiator or a bandit—from the first-century Roman Empire who ultimately converts after significant contact with the Christian community. Many of these films include a contact between the protagonist and Jesus, Peter, or Paul, while others include a female lead—who either is a Christian or becomes a Christian—with whom the protagonist falls in love. This loose collection of films makes up the genre of Roman conversion films. *Quo Vadis* and *The Robe* constitute the strongest works and in many ways represent the epitome of this genre.

The Roman conversion film is set at a particular historical moment: that of the first years of Christianity, when both Peter and Paul appeared in Rome. The emphasis of these films derives from the depiction of a historical turning point of profound significance: the moment when Christianity, which will of course under Emperor Constantine (324 CE) become the favored religion of the Roman state, endures its troubled beginnings in the heart of the pagan world. The two films we will deal with, *Quo Vadis* and *The Robe*, derive much of their significance from the sense of historical inevitability arising from this precise temporal setting. Their concern is the representation of the conflict between the old world of the pre-Christian Roman Empire and the reformulation of that empire with the eventual acceptance of Christianity. As we will suggest below, this theme of the redefinition of empire, through the movement toward an ideal state governed by Christian ethics and belief, resonates powerfully in the early years of the Cold War, the period following the American ascendancy to world power following the defeat of Nazi Germany and Japan. In the aftermath of these victories it was clear that the United States, rather than the old European colonial powers such as Great Britain and France, had become the preeminent force in international affairs. The New World had come militarily, politically, and culturally into its own.

This shift from the old to the new, from the past to the future, marks in these films a narrative suggestive of utopian possibility, an ideologically attractive way of thinking about American power as the means of a beneficent transformation of the world—just as these films imply that the Christianizing of the Roman Empire constituted just such a transformative event. Both films are set in the first years of the Jesus movement and take place largely in Rome. This is the Rome of the emperors Nero (*Quo Vadis*) and Caligula (*The Robe*), both of whom, regardless of actual historical fact, have become symbols of the worst excesses of imperial Rome, tyrannical autocrats of grotesque cruelty. The films locate their narratives in a world ruled by the capricious power held by such men in order to introduce into such an evil empire the utopian possibility represented by the Christian revelation. The films thus stage a conflict between an old world and the promise of a new, a conflict made compelling through an emphasis upon the act of conversion. In each of these two films, a powerful Roman figure, the agent and beneficiary of imperial military and political power, is converted to the new religion, an act with severe consequences, but one that embodies an historical inevitability the significance of which will be important for our understanding of the films within their historical context: the initial years of the Cold War. The fact that Rome will, following the rule of Constantine, accept Christianity as its state religion and thus allow for its spread throughout the Roman world governs our certainty in witnessing the struggles of the convert protagonists that whatever horrors they must endure, they are the vanguards of an inevitable future—a new empire ruled by Christian ethics and belief.

This idealistic version of Christian Rome is significant in that it seeks to locate in the renovated Roman Empire the type of an equally idealized America as an inevitably arisen global power in the aftermath of World

War II. The voice-over introduction to *Quo Vadis* depicts the evil of an as yet unconverted imperial Rome.

> This is the Appian Way, the most famous road that leads to Rome as all roads lead to Rome. On this road march her conquering legions. Imperial Rome is the center of the Empire and undisputed master of the world. But with this power inevitably comes corruption. No man is sure of his life; the individual is at the mercy of the state. Murder replaces justice. Rulers of conquered nations surrender their helpless subjects to bondage. High and low alike become Roman slaves, Roman hostages. There is no escape from the whip and the sword. That any force on earth can shake this pyramid of power and corruption, of human misery and slavery seems inconceivable.

# Christianity: The Harbinger of Freedom

The depiction of the Roman Empire as the enslaver of the earth, challenging the ethic of freedom and love represented by Christianity, is common to both films. Neither film shows great interest in the theological niceties of Christian doctrine; Christianity in each film, like the Judaism of *The Ten Commandments*, has primarily a political and ethical value. It is the religion of human freedom that will oppose and ultimately convert the Roman state. Indeed, in *The Robe*, Emperor Tiberius forcefully equates the new religion with the human desire for freedom as he meditates upon the significance of Marcellus's experiences in Judea:

> When it comes, this is how it will start. Some obscure martyr in some forgotten province. Then madness infecting the legions, rotting the Empire. Then the finish of Rome. . . . This is more dangerous than any spell your superstitious mind could dream of. It is man's desire to be free. It is the greatest madness of them all.

That the theme of slavery versus freedom is thus emphasized in the two films is highly significant at the end of World War II and the beginning of the Cold War. The United States had been instrumental in the defeat of Nazi Germany and its allies by overcoming the authoritarian, militaristic governments that had aimed at widespread conquest. However, the beginning of the Cold War immediately after the defeat of Germany and Japan involved the United States in another, prolonged struggle against a new set of totalitarian regimes: initially the Soviet Union as it extended its power over much of eastern Europe, and after 1949 the People's Republic of China that would back the communist regime of North Korea in the conflict erupting in 1950. From the perspective of the United States, these conflicts, both armed and otherwise, would mark the coming decades as a contest between the powers of freedom as represented by the liberal democracies of the West against the "enslavement" effected by the Marxist states. This struggle between "freedom" and "slavery," in which the United States saw itself as the beacon of genuine progress and democratic principles, is clearly defined by Dwight Eisenhower in a speech given during the 1952 presidential campaign. Eisenhower described the United States as

> [T]hreatened by a great tyranny—a tyranny that is brutal in its primitiveness. It is a tyranny that has brought thousands, millions of people into slave camps and is attempting to make all humankind its chattel. . . . Latvia and her million people. Estonia and her million and a quarter, and Lithuania and her more than twice that number. Poland and her twenty-five million. . . . East Germany and her more than seventeen million. East Austria with her two million. . . . (Bernstein and Matusow, p. 294)

In keeping with Eisenhower's depiction of a world rapidly succumbing to communist enslavement, the Republican Party's 1952 campaign platform advocated not the mere containment of communist expansion but, as argued by the soon-to-be Secretary of State John Foster Dulles, a dedication to the "liberation" of those who had fallen beneath the communist yoke.

If *Quo Vadis* begins with its account of Roman enslavement of the world, *The Robe* opens in Rome's slave market as Marcellus competes with Caligula for the purchase of two women slaves. In this initial scene, we are introduced to Demetrius, the Greek slave whose attempt at escape is foiled by Marcellus, and whom Marcellus buys to save him from Caligula's desire to make him a gladiator. Similarly, in *Quo Vadis* Vinicius convinces Nero to turn over to him Lydia, the hostage whom he desires and whom the Christian Plautius and his wife consider their daughter. Vinicius falls in love with Lydia and she is ultimately instrumental in his conversion to Christianity, as Demetrius is to the conversion of Marcellus. The centrality of the issue of slavery and the reformation of Marcellus and Vinicius, both of whom under the influence of Christianity turn against the idea of people as possessions, maintains throughout each film the emphasis upon the new religion as a force in opposition to Rome as the enemy of human freedom.

It is the relationships between each soldier and a Christian that brings about their conversion. Vinicius falls in love with Lydia, and the two are married by Peter before being sent to the arena to suffer the wrath of Nero. Marcellus comes to regard Demetrius as an equal and risks his life to rescue his former slave from Caligula's torturers. Indeed, both Demetrius and Lydia represent the power of Christianity as the power of freedom and enlightenment that will have a redemptive effect on Marcellus and Vinicius. On the one hand, it is literally beneath the cross upon which Jesus is dying that Demetrius is given the power to declare his freedom from Marcellus, denouncing him as the representative of a vicious Roman imperialism:

> You crucified him! You, my master! But you freed me. I'll never serve you again, you Roman pig. Masters of the world, you call yourselves. Thieves! Murderers! Jungle animals! A curse on you! A curse on your empire!

On the other hand, it is Demetrius who liberates Marcellus from his madness and superstition when he, in a surprisingly modern manner, informs Marcellus that he has not been cursed by the robe but is the victim of a potent guilt over his part in the crucifixion: "You think it's his robe that made you ill, but it's your own conscience, your own decent shame. Even when you crucified him, you felt it. The spell isn't in his robe. It's in you—your heart and your mind."

This view of Christianity as the source of liberation derives from the nineteenth-century ideas of American millennialism, but it has nothing to do with first-century Christianity. The Christianity of Jesus and Paul was not against slavery; it was an accepted part of the world. Jesus never protested against or condemned the enslavement of human beings. Paul counsels slaves not to protest against their status. In 1 Corinthians 7:21, he writes, "Were you a slave when called? Do not be concerned about it." This is because the freedom of Christianity is spiritual rather than physical, "For whoever was called in the Lord as a slave is a freed person belonging to the Lord" (1 Cor. 7:22).

The notion that slavery is wrong consolidated during the Enlightenment. In America, its beginnings lie in the Declaration of Independence, which states, "We hold these truths to be self-evident, that all men are created equal." But of course, many of the Declaration's signers were slaveholders themselves or viewed the institution of slavery as acceptable. It was not until the nineteenth-century abolitionist movement that America's African slaves were seen as having the right to be free. The abolitionist movement was essentially religious. It was part of the American millennialist upward push for the improvement of all Americans' lives, not just an elite few selected by God. Even though the Bible explicitly supported the holding of slaves, abolitionism won out (with the help of the Civil War); American millennialism's identification of Christianity and human freedom thus became woven into American Christianity's understanding of itself.

# The Transformation of Violence

If the Christian influence upon Marcellus and Vinicius redeems them from their participation in a system discriminating between master and slave, it will allow each of them as soldiers to redirect their skill at arms toward the purposes of liberation rather than enslavement. Both protagonists, as Roman officers, begin as willful participants in the imperial violence of the system they serve. Vinicius has returned to Rome, having for years killed in the service of the empire. He enthusiastically recounts, to Lydia's horror, his experience in Britain where the enemy "threw themselves upon our swords," and mocks Lydia's bodyguard, Ursus, when he asserts that "killing is a sin." Ursus's statement invokes the pacifism of early Christianity, and each film will attempt to deal with this aspect of Christianity while avoiding an outright condemnation of violence. One way *Quo Vadis* deals with this question is through the character of Lydia's bodyguard. As a bodyguard and a Christian he is obviously in a complicated situation. He is sworn to protect Lydia, yet he is firmly opposed to killing. It is of course not long before the film employs him to support the idea of justified "Christian" violence when, in the aftermath of his rescue of Lydia, he kills the brutal champion wrestler in a desperate struggle. While Ursus apologizes to Vinicius for the death of his associate, the film clearly supports the necessity of the act. Indeed, his defeat of this murderous champion of the arena clearly implies the superiority of justified violence to the immoral kind practiced by the Roman establishment.

*The Robe* deals with the question of Christian violence in another, perhaps less convincing, manner. Marcellus's conversion to Christianity begins when he returns to Judea as a spy for Tiberius. Hoping to find and destroy the robe, which the emperor's superstitious physicians say has cursed him, Marcellus is also assigned by Tiberius to gather the names of the Christian subversives he encounters in his search. Marcellus, though, begins to be persuaded by the Christian revelation as he interacts with the members of the Jesus movement in Judea. He is introduced to Christian morality and a sense of community through the guidance of Justus the weaver and the other members of the Christian group.

In light of this experience, Marcellus the soldier remains a soldier, but his attitude toward the use of force has changed, the purposes of violence have been redefined. When the Roman legionaries murder Justus in their attack upon the Christians gathered to hear Peter speak, Marcellus intervenes and saves the Christians when he defeats the officer in charge of the Romans in single combat. Rather than simply killing the officer in his moment of triumph, Marcellus spares his life. Later, when Demetrius is captured by Caligula, Marcellus and a contingent of Christians arm themselves to go to his rescue. Again, despite the significant amount of swordplay in each of these episodes, the Christian fighters do not take a single life; they merely overpower their opponents. *The Robe* thus deals with the question of Christian violence by avoiding the act of killing, albeit in a rather strained and unrealistic way.

As is made clear in Marcellus's oath to Peter ("From this day on, I'm enlisted in his service. I offer him my sword, my fortune, and my life. And this I pledge you on my honor as a Roman."), the film wishes to redefine the role and duties of a Christian soldier. Peter's implied acceptance of the oath suggests that Marcellus's martial skills are useful to the Jesus movement. Just as the crippled Miriam is not cured of her deformity but made to think differently about it, so Marcellus does not become a pacifist but is given a new attitude toward the arts of war. His actions after conversion are in the service of his new Christian values. While the taking of life is not condoned, violence is judged by the use to which it is put. When, as a servant of the Roman Empire, Marcellus directs the crucifixion of Jesus, the act serves as a symbol of the evil and injustice of all imperial violence. Having suffered for his sin, Marcellus as a redeemed Christian soldier fights not to enslave and murder the innocent, but to protect and free those threatened by the powers he used to serve.

Marcellus and Vinicius represent the initial Roman converts to a Christianity that, with an eye to the future Christianization of the Roman Empire, underscores the progressive nature of the new religion. We see in Marcellus, whose sympathy for Demetrius is such that he pays a small fortune for the slave to rescue him from the gladiatorial arena, a man whose ambivalence toward Roman imperial values disposes him ultimately to embrace Christianity. He finds in his conversion a set of beliefs to embody his dissatisfaction with the old world and to provide him with a motive for the actions through which he becomes the model of the new Christian soldier who fights against those who enslave and murder the innocent. In Vinicius we see a more radical conversion. Out of love for Lydia he allows her to practice her religion, but he persists in seeing it as fit only for the disempowered. Even though the two are married by Peter just before their torment in the arena, Vinicius resists conversion until his prayers are apparently answered when he prays to God that Ursus defeat the bull attacking Lydia.

# Miracles

The progressive nature of Christianity is indicated in another way in these films through their handling of the supernatural aspects of the new religion. As we have noted, neither film deals to any significant degree with the more supernatural elements of Christian faith, and this lack contributes to the films' emphasis upon the progressive, political elements of that faith. This is especially true in *The Robe*. Whereas *Quo Vadis* simply omits almost completely any reference to the miraculous, *The Robe* tends to downplay the supernatural in favor of a "progressive" psychological understanding of certain events. For example Marcellus's "madness" after the crucifixion is explained by Tiberius's superstitious physicians as a curse placed on Marcellus by Jesus' robe. He feels, of course, the terrible burning when he puts the robe on as he returns from Calvary, and he screams to Demetrius to take it from his shoulders. On his return to Rome Marcellus is tortured by memories of the crucifixion and falls into an obsessive suicidal despair. He is advised by the physician at Tiberius's court that he will regain his sanity when he locates and destroys the robe. It is clear in this sequence that Tiberius regards his physicians as superstitious fools, and that his main reason for sending Marcellus on his quest is to gather information about the Jesus movement. As he says, he will use a madman against madmen, whose condition, the "real madness," he diagnoses as the "desire for freedom" that will topple the empire as he knows it. In this sequence the question of the magical is thus subtly shifted to that of the ethical and political.

This theme continues when Marcellus returns to Judea. Although we hear from Justus the story of Jonathan, whose leg was cured by Jesus, the emphasis falls on the "miracle" of a charitable and redeemed perspective rather than on supernatural intervention. When Jonathan gives the donkey Marcellus has given him to another child who is crippled as he once was, we see the cure most importantly as psychological and spiritual. In such acts of charity the social world is redeemed. This point is made again in the testimony of Miriam, the young crippled woman who, as Justus the weaver states, was once bitter and depressed. When Marcellus marvels at her joy despite her condition and notes that Jesus did not cure her of her physical malady, she responds that he did indeed effect a cure: "[H]e had done something even better for me. He'd chosen me for his work. He'd left me as I am so that all others like me might know that their misfortune needn't deprive them of happiness within his kingdom."

Later, when Marcellus finds Demetrius and commands him to destroy the robe, Demetrius informs Marcellus that he has not been cursed but is the victim of his own conscience: "You think it's his robe that made you ill, but it's your own conscience, your own decent shame." After he has been rescued from Caligula's dungeon, where he has been mercilessly tortured, the seemingly dying Demetrius is cured by Peter of his wounds, much to the anger and chagrin of the Roman physician who accuses Peter of the use of illegal magic. Like Jesus' cure of Miriam, this healing is not depicted on screen but rather behind the closed door of Demetrius's chamber. Whereas the film allows us to imagine here a supernatural intervention, it does not insist upon it. And while we may see in the physician's anger the demonstration of Christian faith as a supernatural power superior to pagan medicine, his accusation of illegal magic again introduces the theme of progress. This is not the "magic" of pagan imagination, the film contends, but something superior to what the Roman physician can imagine. While we may posit the miraculous, the film's handling of the cure leaves open the option that Demetrius has been aided by Peter in a recovery effected by the physical and psychological benefits of faith. The Christian cure, as in the case of Marcellus's casting off of madness when the power of forgiveness alleviates his guilt, whether or not we choose to see a "miracle," is an element in the progressive nature of Christianity. It is part and parcel of the world to come with the victory of the new faith over the brutality and superstition of the old.

In these films, then, the emphases upon conversion, upon the embracing of an ideology of freedom and a progressive, therapeutic new faith—

the ultimate success of which is guaranteed in the eventual Roman con-version to Christianity—work to underscore the contemporary signifi-cance of each narrative in the context of the early Cold War.

# The Dictators

While these films are opposed to the sort of Roman imperialism to which Vinicius and Marcellus initially contribute, neither film opposes all that Rome represents. It is not the powerful, militarily and politically successful state that these films denounce, but rather Rome under the rule of Nero and Caligula—emperors who have been castigated in (Christian-influenced) history as monsters, as madmen whose absolute and arbitrary exercise of power dramatically portrays the loss of Roman virtue associ-ated with the republic before its collapse. That a pre-Christian Rome was not without virtues is made clear in the examples of Romans like Petronius, who ultimately so displeases Nero that he chooses to commit suicide rather than be killed by his emperor. While Petronius dies a pagan, he is clearly sympathetic to the religion his nephew will ultimately adopt, and he argues against Nero's plan to blame the burning of Rome on the Christians. Just as his nephew has fallen in love with a captive, Petronius has fallen in love with a slave who chooses to die with him. This sympathetic portrait of Petronius, as well as the examples of Marcellus and Vinicius in their conversions, marks the rule of Nero and Caligula as essentially antiprogressive. Caligula is drastically worse than the intelligent and reasonably enlightened Tiberius as represented in *The Robe*, and Nero's decadence contrasts powerfully with the besieged virtue of Petronius, his elder.

Indeed, it is important to note that while Marcellus is opposed to the cruelty and madness of Caligula, he readily reaffirms his loyalty to the empire when Caligula demands it. It is not the Roman state, whose potential for enlightenment is implied in the conversion of aristocrats like Marcellus, that is condemned. Marcellus remains loyal to the state but refuses to denounce Christ. He says:

> If the empire desires peace and brotherhood among all men, then my king will be on the side of Rome and her emperor. But if the empire and her emperor wish to pursue the course of aggression and slavery that have brought agony and terror and despair to the world . . . then my

king will march forward to right those wrongs. Not tomorrow, Sire. Your majesty may not be so fortunate as to witness the establishment of His kingdom. But it will come.

Here Marcellus manifests his dedication to a future Rome, one that will accept Christianity as its state religion. As he and Diana march off to execution at the end of the film, a lap dissolve shifts them from Caligula's court to a scene in which the two walk upward in a gentle incline with a blue sky and white clouds behind them. While this image suggests their entry into the kingdom of God, it also suggests the forward, progressive march of history. By conflating these two implications the image marks history as a slow but ultimately triumphant passage toward utopian possibility, that of Christian Rome and, more significant, that of the United States as viewed from the film's idealistic ideological perspective as a just and enlightened "empire."

In this context it is worth recalling specifically the role of "new Rome" imagined for the United States by its founders. The new American republic's idea of its historical status and mission was, as we have seen, profoundly influenced by the concept of an American new Israel as a light to the world. Combined with this was the concept of the United States as a nation that would enact and preserve the freedom and virtues of the Roman republic. As Robert Bellah reminds us:

> Roman classicism dominated the surface symbolism of the new republic. Its very terminology was Latinate, the words "republic," "president," "congress," and "senate" being Latin in origin and clearly distinct from the terminology from their British counterparts. The great seal of the United States bears two Latin mottos, *e pluribus unum* and *novus ordo saeclorum.* . . . Though even the Virgillian reference of the latter should not blind us to the biblical level of meaning that it also carries. George Washington, the Cincinnatus of the West, went to his inauguration by passing under arches of laurel. Greco-Roman classicism dominated the architecture and much of the art of the early republican period. (Bellah, p. 23)

That the films recognize the positive aspects of the Roman Republic and look forward to a Christianized Rome, predicted in the conversions of their central characters, defines the rule of emperors Caligula and Nero as aberrations, wrong turns that merely delay the inevitable progress mandated by history. In doing so the films address, in a dramatic fashion, the ideological struggles of the Cold War. While the confirmation of

American military and political power after World War II appears as the outcome of a progressive historical design, this optimistic nationalism faced a serious problem in the threatened spread of Communism in the postwar world. Communism disputed American belief in the national myth by which it saw itself as a progressive and redemptive world power. Marxists, of course, believed Communism to be such a redemptive historical force, one with its own faith in the historical necessity of its ultimate triumph. Each film deals with this ideological contest in its depiction of the abuses to human freedom and dignity enacted by imperial power. In Caligula and Nero we are given the type of the dictator in a period that had seen the rise and costly defeat of Hitler's Germany and that had still to face the threat of a communist menace personified in Stalin. The memory of Hitler and the reality of Stalin, director of a police state the absolutist terrors of which would essentially define Communism for Cold War Americans, add a powerful resonance to the films' portrayals of Caligula and Nero. As ruthless dictators feared by their own people and devoted to the world enslavement that each film depicts as the goal of Roman power, these figures obviously exploit the horrors of contemporary history by suggesting the dictatorial regimes and imperial ambitions of the defeated Hitler and, more to the point, of Stalin, who died the year The Robe was released. The defeat of Nazi Germany and the onset of the Cold War struggle against Communism mark the context of the American assumption of preeminent military and political power in the "free world." Just as Marcellus and Vinicius take up the progressive, Christian struggle against the evil empire of Rome under the dictators, the United States in World War II and in the Cold War understood its role to be that of leading the free world in resisting the enemies of true historical advance. If the films exploit our knowledge of the inevitable Christian triumph over pagan Rome, that certain future victory serves as the type of an equally inevitable American defeat of its totalitarian opposition.

In *Quo Vadis* the distinction between the benign reformation advanced by Christianity and a supremely misguided and apocalyptic version of progress is characterized by Nero's desire to remake Rome according to his perversely utopian vision of a radical improvement. When Nero burns Rome in order to clear a space for his newly designed city, to be named Neropolis, the film depicts the horror of such an apocalyptic method of procuring the future. The holocaust of Rome ablaze recalls the ashes of Europe and the revolutionary designs of the communist world. The Christian alternative to such apocalyptic fury finds its historical reenactment in a United States eager to assert its Christian credentials in the midst of the ideological contest of the Cold War. In 1954, for example, the phrase "under God" was added to the pledge of allegiance, and two years later, "In God We Trust" became the national motto. Nero's totalitarian ambitions embraced an apocalyptic enthusiasm for murder and destruction, but his misguided "utopian" vision was doomed to failure, and the genuine utopian ambitions of the Christian Romans were guaranteed victory. In the same way—the films may be understood to imply—the subsequent, violent utopian ambitions of the communist world would not survive the ascendancy of the just New Rome, the United States depicted as the defender of freedom and progress.

# Vignettes

## *Ben Hur* (1959)

Although a Roman conversion film, *Ben Hur* largely abandons the earlier films' attempts to justify the ideas of a benevolent empire and justified military violence. The main character, Judah Ben Hur, is a wealthy and influential Jew in Jerusalem during the time of Jesus' young manhood and eventual ministry. Judah is not particularly anti-Roman at first; in fact, one of his closest childhood friends had been Masala, a Roman officer who, as the film begins, has just returned to Judea to assume an important military post. When Masala asks Judah to spy for him against his own people, however, the conflict lying at the heart of the narrative begins. Masala has Judah's mother and sister unjustly condemned to prison for an attack upon the Roman governor, and he sends Judah to suffer as a slave on the Roman galleys. When Judah saves the life of the Roman general Arius during a battle, he is delivered from service on the galleys, brought to Rome, and officially adopted by Arius.

Judah, of course, famously returns to Judea to defeat Masala in a chariot race in which Masala is mortally injured. The discovery, though, that his mother and sister have contracted leprosy while languishing in a Roman prison keeps Judah's anger and desire for revenge strong. He refuses to accept Roman citizenship, and plans to lead a revolt against the Roman occupation.

He has, however, met Jesus, who gave him water on his agonized march in chains to the sea and slavery, and he now hears of Jesus' message of

love and forgiveness, a message that ultimately converts him and van-
quishes his desire for warfare and vengeance. As he says, "His [Jesus']
words took the sword from my hand."

In several ways, *Ben Hur* looks forward to the antiwar sentiments of
*King of Kings*, released two years later. Judah is, like Vinicius and
Marcellus, the heroes of the earlier conversion films, a manly figure,
strong, skillful with weapons, and, of course, a masterful charioteer. Here,
though, Judah's martial abilities are seen as useful to the Christianity he
ultimately will espouse. Although he comes to abhor the Roman Empire
no less than do Vinicius and Marcellus, the film does present the idea of
a future just empire so important to the political interests of those earlier
Cold War epics. The film, although allowing us the satisfaction of
Masala's violent death, clearly opposes Judah's desire for armed rebellion,
suggesting that to engage in violence will make Judah no better than
Masala, who had been corrupted by Roman cruelty. The film's final image
of Judah's mother and sister, both of whom are healed of leprosy by Jesus,
expresses *Ben Hur*'s understanding of a therapeutic Christianity that will
bring peace through the abandonment of war and violence.

## Demetrius and the Gladiators (1954)

In 1954, following up on the success of *The Robe, Demetrius and the
Gladiators* was released. This film's plot testifies to the popularity of the
conversion narrative. Here, Demetrius, the Christian slave who was
instrumental in the conversion of Marcellus in *The Robe*, is condemned
to gladiatorial training and combat for interfering with Caligula's attempt
to find the robe of Jesus. Caligula believes that the robe will give him
eternal life and the power to resurrect the dead. Demetrius, believing that
Lucia, a young woman he loves, has been killed resisting the advances of
a fellow gladiator, loses his faith in Jesus and becomes a violent performer
in the arena. His prowess attracts Messalina, Claudius's wife, and through
her influence, Demetrius is freed and made a tribune in the Praetorian
Guard.

Pursuing an affair with Messalina, Demetrius slips further into nihilistic
hedonism until he is made aware by Peter that Lucia has survived. When
Caligula tests the robe by killing a prisoner and attempting to resurrect
him, Demetrius is outraged and attacks the emperor, who punishes him
by sending him again to the arena. Demetrius, his Christian faith restored,
refuses to fight, but is saved when the Praetorian Guard, sympathetic

to his plight, rise up and kill Caligula. Claudius is made emperor, and he promises that Christians will not be molested as long as they pose no threat to the state.

As this summary of the plot suggests, this is a film concerned with the theme of resurrection. Caligula, wishing to be an immortal god, seeks the robe of Jesus for its "magical" properties, and makes his grotesque attempt to restore life to the man he has had murdered. Condemning Caligula's superstitious ignorance, this film, like *The Robe*, downplays the miraculous to suggest that the power of Christianity lies in its ability to effect a spiritual and ethical resurrection. Lucia's "resurrection" for Demetrius when Peter shows her to be alive promotes Demetrius's own overcoming of the "death" of despair and disbelief to once again embrace Christianity. The ascension to power of Claudius, who promises not to persecute Christians, suggests the eventual reformation of Rome given such thematic and ideological weight in *The Robe*.

# Suggested Readings

Robert N. Bellah, *The Broken Covenant: American Civil Religion in Time of Trial* (New York: Seabury Press, 1975).

Barton J. Bernstein and Allen J. Matusow, *The Truman Administration: A Documentary History* (New York: Harper and Row, 1966).

Gerald E. Forshey, *American Religious and Biblical Spectaculars* (Westport, Conn.: Praeger, 1992).

# CHAPTER 4

# The Ten Commandments and America's Fight against Tyranny

T he problem with the Roman Conversion films is that the liberation of the enslaved—that is, the evolution of the empire into
Christian Rome—belongs to each film's future; it does not take
place during the film itself. Cecil B. DeMille's 1956 *The Ten
Commandments* transformed this anticipated future into cinematic reality.
By focusing on Moses' liberation of the enslaved Israelites from Egypt,
DeMille's film told a story of actual liberation, one that resulted in a new
nation for former slaves. DeMille thereby created perhaps *the* pivotal
movie for the use of religion in American postwar film.

*The Ten Commandments* is an epic film into which DeMille crammed
thousands of actors and innumerable details of action, architecture, and
plot. At times, the mass of detail threatens to overwhelm the audience. But
when the viewers can rise above this flood of visual information, the overall message appears straightforward. The film portrays the liberation of the
Israelites from oppression by Egypt and their foundation as a new nation
under God's law. This nation is governed by the "Law of Freedom"—
indeed, as Moses tells Dathan before the Golden Calf, "There is no freedom without the law"—and stands in opposition to the "tyranny" of Egypt.

---

* For this chapter read Exodus 1–20, 24, 32–34; Numbers 12–16, 20–25; Deuteronomy
31–34.

To ensure that the audience understood that God's Law of Freedom in opposition to tyranny was not simply an issue for ancient times, Director DeMille himself opens the film by stepping onto an empty stage and giving an introductory speech. He tells the audience that "this same battle continues throughout the world today." In this way, he reveals the true identity of the film's protagonists and antagonists. The oppressive Egyptians stand for the Soviet Russian Communists, while the liberated, God-fearing Israelites point to America.

To understand how the ancient story of Moses and the Israelites' liberation from Egypt links to the 1950s Cold War between the United States of America and Russia, we need to take several steps back. We need to see how *The Ten Commandments* uses Scripture to authorize its cinematic tale, and how it changes, reshapes, and adds to the biblical text to make it speak to the concerns of 1950s Americans.

# Authorizing the Film: Targumization and Authentication

As we pointed out in the first chapter, targumic interpretation is the primary means by which films draw upon the authority of an original text or story. Given the medium's visual character, it must add information to any tale told in words. If the film also wants to be seen as authoritative—as a true representation of that story—it must smoothly interweave this additional material with the details of the original story. This is necessary if the film is to appear authoritative to viewers with even a minimal knowledge of the original text.

*The Ten Commandments* draws extensively upon the two primary Rules of Targum, combining faithfulness to the biblical book of Exodus (in the King James Version even!) with a willingness to bring in nonbiblical material, often a considerable amount. These it weaves into a unified story. This takes place primarily in the film's second act, once Moses returns to Egypt and the plagues begin, but also at the start of the first act, where the earth's creation and Moses' birth are related. The secondary Rules of Targum are also in play. The most obvious is Rule #3, which observes that large additions may be placed at the beginning of the story to provide the context for the more faithful material that follows. Since the first act is nearly all added to the biblical story, the rule certainly applies. But *The Ten Commandments* also uses the other secondary rules, those of substitution, borrowing from other parts of the text, and leaving out story elements.

While the targumic method of hidden interpretation is the key mode of bringing the original's authority to a film, it is not the only mode. A group of related techniques, which we will call "authentication," complement targumization. Authentication is the practice of claiming to adhere to the original and its historical or cultural context, whether explicitly or implicitly.

*The Ten Commandments* uses two types of explicit authentication. The first links the films to the original texts through an explicit claim of identity. *The Ten Commandments* explicitly claims Scripture's authority twice: in the opening speech given by Director DeMille, and in the opening credits that indicate that the film was created "in accordance with the ancient texts of . . . The Holy Scriptures"—with the last three words being prominently displayed on the screen by themselves.

The second approach to explicit authentication comes from the claims of historical accuracy to the time and place of the film's setting. In *The Ten Commandments* this takes place by filming "on location," which it indicates in the opening credits by claiming, "Those who see this motion picture . . . will make a pilgrimage over the very ground that Moses trod more than 3,000 years ago." Historical authentication also comes through the use of historical information. Both DeMille's opening speech and the opening credits claim that the film draws upon information filling in gaps of the biblical story found in ancient sources, such as Philo Judaeus, Flavius Josephus, Jewish exegetical Midrashim, and Eusebius, as well as making reference to the recently discovered and highly publicized Dead Sea Scrolls.

Since few audience members were familiar with these sources, the claim itself is more important than how the sources were actually used, as Melanie Wright observes. The film draws mainly personal names and general ideas from these texts while ignoring more extensive details. For example, *The Ten Commandments* uses Josephus's story about Moses' expedition to conquer Ethiopia (*Jewish Antiquities* II:238-53), but leaves out most details, including Josephus's story of Moses' marriage to the Ethiopian princess.

The main form of implicit authentication DeMille uses is archaeology. It provides verisimilitude—the filmic appearance of reality—with regard to architecture and interior decoration, dress, and tools of occupations (such as those of scribes). Even reconstructions of ancient building techniques appear when Moses is erecting Sethi's pylon. DeMille makes no explicit claim of authenticity for archaeology, but his extensive use of it enhances the film's accurate portrayal of ancient Egypt.

*The Ten Commandments'* use of targumic hidden interpretation functions implicitly to enhance the film's authority. Many of the film's verbal additions to its scriptural base, for instance, are cast into language imitating the biblical text, in the version most familiar to the audience, namely, the King James. Thus the opening narration draws from Exodus 1:13-14, "So did the Egyptians cause the children of Israel to serve with rigor. And their lives were made bitter with hard bondage." This is then followed by a paraphrase of two clauses in Exodus 3:7, 9, "And their cry came up unto God. And God heard them." And the narration concludes with sentences imitating KJV English style, "And cast into Egypt, into the lowly hut of Amram and Yochabel, the seed of a man upon whose mind and heart would be written God's law. . . ." This follows Targum Rule #4, which states that an addition may imitate related material.

Another use of Rule #4 also helps implicitly authenticate the film. *The Ten Commandments*, although based on the Old Testament books of the Pentateuch, draws passages from other parts of the Bible, even the New Testament, and places them into the speech of the narrators or characters. This is a use of proof text familiar to American Christians, used often in preaching and biblically based exposition, where a passage is taken without citing its context and given a meaning that fits with the speaker's point but not necessarily with the biblical writer's intention, as far as it can be inferred. Moses' description of his encounter with God at the burning bush includes a reference to the first verse of John's Gospel. Moses says, "[God] revealed his word to my mind. And the word was God." The second sentence of this quote comes from John, where "word" would be capitalized as "Word," for it refers there to Jesus who accompanied God the Father in heaven before his birth to Mary. The use of this proof text transforms it into a statement about the Christian character of Moses' interaction with God.

# Characterization and Plot: The Targumic Influence

Most of the material that the film adds to the Exodus story functions in a targumlike manner. Sometimes the additions are so large that it is impossible to miss them, while other times they are interwoven with passages that faithfully follow the text. While the latter confuse the viewer and provide the impression that more scenes and dialogue adhere closely to the story than actually do, the former, even though usually recognized by the viewer, change the meaning of the sections that follow the biblical story in a literal manner.

One technique appearing frequently in the film is to use scriptural language in the narration at the start of key scenes. Act II, for example, opens with Exodus 4:19-20. The film's introductory narration likewise begins with a literal quotation of Genesis 1:3 and then brings in a phrase from Genesis 1:26. Following Targum Rule #2, however, this initiates an interweaving of biblical verses with lines original to the film (shown in italics). For the audience, the presence of the biblical citations authorizes the nonbiblical material.

> And God said, "Let there be light." And there was light. (Gen. 1:3) *And from this light God created life upon earth.* And man was given dominion over all things upon this earth. (Gen. 1:26) *And the power to choose between good and evil. But each sought to do his own will because he knew not the light of God's law. Man took dominion over man. The conquered were made to serve the conqueror. The weak were made to serve the strong. And freedom was gone from the world.*
>
> So did the Egyptians cause the children of Israel to serve with rigor. And their lives were made bitter with hard bondage. (Ex. 1:13-14) And their cry came up unto God. And God heard them. (Ex. 3:7,9) *And cast into Egypt, into the lowly hut of Amram and Yochabel, the seed of a man upon whose mind and heart would be written God's law and God's commandments. One man to stand alone against an empire.*

*The Ten Commandments*'s targumic approach can be more fully illustrated by looking at the character of Dathan. In Scripture, Dathan does not show up until Numbers 16, where he plays a minor role in a rebellion against Moses well after the end of the action portrayed in *The Ten Commandments*. In the film, by contrast, he plays a major role as a challenger to Moses' leadership after the Israelites leave Egypt and as rival with Joshua for the affections of Lilia. Since Dathan's role in the film is created without support from Exodus, it is not surprising that much of his time on-screen is simply added without reference to the text. However, there are key scenes—the Israelites at the Red Sea and the Golden Calf scene—that carefully weave Dathan into them so that he seems to be an authentic participant in the eyes of the viewers. Let us look briefly at the Red Sea scene.

When the Egyptian chariots appear over the hill to destroy the Israelites trapped against the sea, Dathan rises up to challenge Moses. Although this scene in *The Ten Commandments* does not include all the information from Scripture, what it does contain, it represents fairly accurately. Below is a list of the key actions and dialogue accompanied by their scriptural references:

| | |
|---|---|
| [Chariots come over hill and people crowd at sea's edge. | Exodus 14:10 |
| Dathan: "Was it because there are no graves in Egypt that you took us away to die in the wilderness?" [Scared cries from the crowd.] | Exodus 14:11 |
| Moses: "Fear not! Stand still and see the salvation of the Lord." | Exodus 14:13 |
| [Fire pillar appears between Israel and Egypt.] | Exodus 14:19 |
| Crowd member: "The pillar of fire!" | — |
| Aaron: "It is the breath of God." | Based on Isaiah 11:4; 32:33 |
| Moses: "Gather your families and flocks. We must go with all speed." | Based on Exodus 12:32-33 |
| Dathan: "Go where? To drown in the sea? How long will the fire hold Pharaoh back?" | — |
| Moses: "After this day, you will see Pharaoh's chariots no more." | Exodus 14:13 |
| Dathan: "No! You'll be dead under them." | — |
| Moses: "The Lord of hosts will do battle for us. Behold his mighty hand." | Exodus 14:14 |
| [Moses stretches out his hands, the wind blows and the sea parts. Shots of crowd reaction.] | Based on Exodus 14: 16, 21 |
| [Sea appears as a wall on right and left.] | Based on Exodus 14:22 |

As can be seen from the second column, most of the remarks and action come from Scripture, primarily from the story itself in Exodus 14, but there is some dialogue from elsewhere. Dathan makes three comments, the first of which appears in the story, while the other two are original to the film. The important observation here is that Dathan's comments are set up so that each one precedes a biblically based command by Moses (all quite literal) and makes it appear as if Moses responds to Dathan—even though in Scripture the comments from Exodus 14 form part of a single, uninterrupted speech. *The Ten Commandments* thus portrays Moses arguing with Dathan before the crowd—both aiming to persuade the crowd to his own view—rather than Moses preparing the Israelites for God's action of parting the sea. The weaving together of Scripture with additional remarks has the effect of authorizing Dathan's presence in the scene.

In Scripture, the line from Exodus 14:11 is assigned to no one in particular; it is simply a comment from the crowd. By assigning it to Dathan, the remark no longer represents the feelings of the crowd but rather the thoughts of this individual. It is the viewers' knowledge of this individual that enables them to interpret it and Dathan's actions opposing Moses in general. Most of the audience's knowledge about Dathan comes from all the additional scenes in the film's first half that have no connection to Scripture. Dathan is a rival for Lilia's attentions against Joshua and wins by blackmailing her (in what today we would term sexual abuse and even implied rape). He was already well known as a stool pigeon and an informant before he sold his information about Moses' identity. Dathan consistently showed himself more interested in profiting from the Egyptian overlords than in considering the welfare of his people. Given his promise to the overseer to bring back the people to Pharaoh, the audience already knows that despite the meaning of the words he utters in this scene, he is not thinking about what is good for the Israelites, but about what is good for the Egyptians, namely, a return of the Israelites to slavery.

It is common in the targumic method for a story to have a large addition at the beginning to set up the characterization and context for the remainder of the tale, which is adhered to much more faithfully (Rule #3). This holds true for *The Ten Commandments*, in which most of the first act constitutes an addition to the biblical story. Most of what is new to the story in this large addition is character development and plotting that helps the audience understand the tale later on. The development of the different characters' personalities and motivations is shown through their interaction. To enable the clear comparison of individuals, the film sets up groups of three individuals in which two people compete for the attentions of the third. Consider the two love triangles, the one in which Moses and Rameses compete for Nefretiri, and that in which Joshua and Dathan compete for Lilia. This romantic approach to telling biblical tales—the genre of biblical romance—has become a convention in the few biblically based films since World War II. DeMille used it himself in *Samson and Delilah* (1949), and it appeared as well in *David and Bathsheba*

(1951)—two of the few biblical films made between World War II and the release of *The Ten Commandments*. A less contentious triangle, but still important for fleshing out personalities, is that between Nefretiri and Sephora for the love of Moses.

The first act's dominant rivalry is that between Moses and Rameses for the attention of Pharaoh Sethi. While Rameses is clearly jealous of Moses for Nefretiri's preference of him, Sethi adds to the rivalry when he starts making statements about how the next pharaoh should be chosen by deeds rather than by blood—a notion which everyone else, including Moses, finds unthinkable. Moses' apparent achievements in these two rivalries cause Rameses' great hatred of him. When Moses' successful completion of the tasks of conquering Ethiopia and building Sethi's city (which had been transferred to him after Rameses' failure) are added into the mix, Rameses' loathing of Moses becomes overwhelming.

While the large addition to the story may at first appear to be put into *The Ten Commandments* just for entertainment purposes, further consideration indicates that it has a more important role. One of the purposes of targumic additions is often to explain questions that the new text's author knows, or assumes, the audience will ask. For example, how does God harden Pharaoh's heart? As it stands in Scripture, Pharaoh appears as an automaton into which God reaches and controls his reaction. Not only is that an unsatisfactory answer to this question for a modern audience, but it also makes boring drama. It would be equivalent to God pushing a button and Pharaoh doing what God wants. Much of the large addition develops Rameses' personality and motivations so that the plot itself reveals why Rameses refuses Moses' request. Part of Rameses' refusal stems from his ownership of the slaves and the wealth they represent, but much of it stems from the hatred of Moses he developed in the competition for the attentions of his wife-to-be, Nefretiri, and of his father, Sethi. It also stems from his atheism, which he indicates when he accuses the priests of inventing the gods for their own purposes of power, and from his fear of ridicule by slaves and by other nations. Finally, the taunts of his wife drive him to attempt the ultimate punishment of the slaves by killing their firstborn males.

This brings us to another important question for a modern, American audience. In the last of the plagues, God kills all the firstborn males of Egypt. Why would God kill all these innocent people, most of whom had nothing to do with Pharaoh or with slavery? Does not that action make God cruel and unjust? The answer given in *The Ten Commandments* is that Pharaoh's own decree determines the nature of the last plague.

Moses says in his penultimate interview with Pharaoh, "If there is one more plague on Egypt, it is by your word that God will bring it." Later, when Nefretiri tells Moses what Rameses decreed, Moses says, "Out of his own mouth." Thus, in a "let the punishment fit the crime" way, God turns Rameses' punishment onto the Egyptians, thus resulting in the death of all their firstborn. The killing of the firstborn sons may be unjust, but it is Rameses' fault, not God's.

Once God gives Rameses the power to decide the final punishment, Moses has no more involvement. Nefretiri comes to the slave compound to save Moses' son Gershom by sending him back to Midian. Moses cannot return the favor by saving Nefretiri's son. He tries to explain and she does not believe him. Like Rameses, she does not understand the difference between Moses' actions and those of his God. She blames Moses personally for her son's death, and she instigates Pharaoh's military attack on the fleeing Israelites. These provide human motivations for the plot developments in the film. It is not God controlling events so much as it is the interaction of people whose character and motivations were formed long before.

The rivalry between Moses and Rameses portrayed in the film presents Moses as almost oblivious to the competition. He is content with his place and sees no reason—and has no expectation—to supplant Rameses from his. Where Rameses is jealous and plotting, Moses is content and guileless. He does not play petty politics to influence Sethi's opinion of himself or others but rather lets his actions speak for themselves. He carries out his assigned tasks—such as conquering Ethiopia and building the city—with a sense of duty and love. As he says, he builds the city for the "love of Sethi." In the end, he is quietly and thoroughly competent, not a braggart, yet willing to display the fruits of his efforts. With the exception of Rameses and his partisans, Moses enjoys the love of those near him and returns that love.

Above these, the two key elements of his personality are his compassion and his unswerving determination. His compassion shows in personal interactions, like his concern for his mother and interest in Memnet's death, as well as in his large projects. He pacifies Ethiopia by offering an alliance rather than conquering them. He builds the city by ensuring that the slaves have enough food and "one day in seven" to rest. And of course, he saves both Yochabel and Joshua from death.

Once Moses discovers he was born a Hebrew, his compassion extends even further into concern for the slaves. He goes out to experience slavery by participating in it, not just by watching it, as Scripture implies. Determination to act on that compassion becomes Moses' driving force.

He disappears from court life and his royal duties to be with the slaves. When later Rameses accuses him before Sethi of being the "deliverer," it is Moses' desire that the slaves should be free that causes Sethi to punish him, not just the murder he committed, as in Scripture.

Moses' determination to pursue his duties, whether those of a royal "son" or of slaves, is the second of his defining characteristics. His inter-actions with other characters show that once he sets his mind to a task, he does not swerve from it. Alone among the Egyptian royals, he is unmoved from his task by the persuasion or status of those who attempt to interfere, whether it is Nefretiri or his mother who tries to prevent his becoming involved with the slaves, or the sudden arrival of Sethi and Rameses at a critical moment in the erection of Sethi's obelisk.

All of this character development takes place in the first half of *The Ten Commandments* and must serve to sustain his character in the second act, for once Moses becomes God's messenger, personal, private interac-tion with individuals almost disappears. As God's prophet, he becomes a public figure representing God. His interactions with Pharaoh take the form of pronouncements of God's commands. Once the Hebrews leave Egypt, he speaks almost exclusively before the crowd as their leader. When he is not speaking God's orders, he acts to carry them out. His dis-cussions with Nefretiri and Bithia show that he is conscious of God's plan and intention and that consciousness shapes his words.

The film's portrayal of Moses becomes that of God's representative in this task to free the Hebrews, a task which consumes his personality. Indeed, Moses the person has vanished from view; not only has his person-ality vanished but so has his physical portrayal. After arriving in Midian, his body becomes completely covered with his Israelite robe, and after meeting God, his head and face become so obscured by hair and beard that the audience can barely see his smile. All that remains of Moses the man is occasional eruption of his compassion, which he shows on Passover night to Bithia and her bearers as well as to the frightened Eleazer.

# The Christianization of Moses and the Exodus

Making the biblical story relevant to *The Ten Commandments*'s view-ers' expectations of contemporary film entertainment, giving it a gripping plot and believable character development, and stirring their sense of moral justice are not the only tasks undertaken by the targumic method of story enhancement. This approach also helps render the story's message meaningful and relevant to the film's audience, an audience that should be understood as composed primarily of 1950s American Christians. This means that we need to investigate how the film aims to speak to its viewers as both Christians and Americans of the 1950s. Let us study each separately.

The Christianization of the Exodus story appears most prominently in *The Ten Commandments'* portrayal of Moses as a *type* of Jesus, as Alan Nadel first pointed out in his important essay. In keeping with both the method and the results of typology employed by Puritans, Moses presents a model for the coming Jesus. He is not Jesus himself but a Christ figure. To ensure that the audience understands this typological identity, the film brings in several incidents not found in the Old Testament that suggest an equivalence between Moses and Jesus. These incidents are all from the Gospels and are cast into the circumstances of the Moses story. The first such incident surrounds the birth of Moses. In Exodus 1, Pharaoh orders all the newborn Israelite sons to be cast into the river. *The Ten Commandments* enhances this story with a star that appears announcing the birth of a boy who will be a deliverer of the Hebrew slaves. The pharaoh, Rameses I, orders the killing of all newborn males by the sword. These additions parallel aspects of Jesus' birth found in the Gospels of Matthew and Luke. Second, following this event, there is constant talk of a "deliverer," in the same way as the Gospels have people talk of Jesus as the "messiah." Moses often denies that he is the deliverer, just as Jesus denies his messiahship and asks people not to talk about it. Third, both Yochabel and a dying old man who had been stomping in the mud talk about seeing the deliverer before they die. Both echo the Gospel incident of the pious Simeon seeing Jesus in the Temple (Luke 2:25-35). Fourth, Moses faces a trial before the Egyptian ruler Sethi, just as Jesus appeared in a trial before the Roman ruler Pilate. And just as Jesus' responses to Pilate force Pilate to condemn him (John 19:9-11), so too Moses' answer to Sethi compels Sethi to condemn him.

Finally, when Rameses sends Moses into the desert, Moses first appears with his arms and shoulders tied to a binding pole, mimicking the image of Jesus nailed to the cross. Rameses then mocks Moses and his "claim" of kingship, giving him the pole as a "scepter" and having a royal red robe put over his shoulders; this echoes the Roman soldiers mocking Jesus as king (John 19:2-3). The only thing missing is the crown of thorns.

The film's end puts the final touch on Moses as a Jesus-type. His last words are, "Go, proclaim liberty throughout all the lands, unto all the inhabitants thereof." While this quotation comes from Leviticus 25:10, Isaiah speaks of God's servant in the same terms, "The spirit of the Lord is upon me: because the Lord hath anointed me . . . to proclaim liberty to the captives" (Isa. 61:1). This is the passage that Luke indicates Jesus read in the Nazareth synagogue and applied to himself (Luke 4:16-22). Moses' proclamation implies the same claim and also echoes Jesus' so-called "Great Commission," with which he charges his disciples after his resurrection, "Go therefore and make disciples of all nations" (Matt. 28:19).

The notion that Moses functions as a type of Jesus was not new with DeMille. The Puritans made extensive use of it themselves, and it was later included in the *Scofield Reference Bible* (1909), which continues to be one of the most widely used reference Bibles in the English world. Let us be clear that this is typology, not identity. Moses is *not* Jesus; he is a foreshadowing of Jesus. Moses did not die or rise from the dead; he did not provide salvation from sin; he is not Paul's "Christ crucified" who was the "weakness of God" (1 Cor. 1:23, 25). Instead, Moses is a strong figure. He does not shy away from confrontation with the authorities or allow himself to die; Moses wields the power of God first to bring his enemies to agree to his demands, and then to crush them militarily. For the film, Moses is the messiah Jesus should have been.

Once the film begins this typological characterization, it must continue, for Christianity has a serious problem with the concept that the Law given to Moses can bring freedom. It must overcome this problem in the eyes of the audience if it is to make the film resonate. The problem is this. The church's earliest recorded theologian was Paul the Apostle. Most of the first eight chapters of his Letter to the Romans explains why the Law is not helpful. While the argument is long and complex, the key points are these: First, people who do not know the Law cannot know God. Hence they cannot be saved. Second, people who know the Law— that is, the Jews—know about God, but they cannot draw near to him because the law is incapable of being fulfilled by humans. Hence they cannot be saved. Since the Law is incapable of granting freedom to its followers, only the law of "the Spirit of Life in Christ Jesus" can set a person free from the "law of sin and death" (Rom. 8:2). To Christians who follow this belief closely, as many do, a film about the giving of the Law should not be particularly interesting.

DeMille overcomes this problem by Christianizing the Law. *The Ten Commandments* uses the targumic process to make the Law given to Moses a *type* for the "law of the Spirit," which resulted from Jesus' mission on earth. While the Law received by Moses is the Ten Commandments, it is treated as the type for the coming spiritual law of Christianity. Although the film's action is set in Egypt and the Sinai Desert, and the commandments are actually given on stone tablets, the language used to describe the giving of the law points to the Christian idea of the "Spirit of Life" in Jesus.

The key idea is that the law will be written on people's hearts and in their minds. Phrases based on this notion appear from the beginning to the end of the film. The opening narration describes Moses, for example, as "the seed of a man upon whose mind and heart would be written God's law and God's commandments." Another instance comes just before the Israelites begin walking out of Egypt. Moses says to Joshua, "Then let us go forth to the mountain of God, that he may write his commandments in our minds and upon our hearts forever."

Perhaps the most telling moment comes during Moses' talk with God at the burning bush. Here we have a scene in which all the dialogue comes from Exodus, except for four lines, two of which reiterate the intention to write the Law on people's hearts and in their minds. The table on the following page shows how close to Exodus this scene is. Two lines are placed into God's mouth to show God's intention: "I will put my laws into their hearts. And in their minds will I write them." The heavy and exacting use of scriptural dialogue in this scene helps ensure that these added lines are accepted by the audience as part of the scene, as part of God's "actual" comments to Moses.

The link between the notion that God will write on people's minds and hearts and Christianity is that this action is the key change for a "new covenant," which the later prophet Jeremiah says will come one day: "After those days, saith the Lord, I will put my law in their inward parts, and write it in their hearts" (Jer. 31:33, see 31:31-35). This is picked up in the Letter to the Hebrews, found in the New Testament, where the "new covenant" is identified as Christianity. In Hebrews 8:7–10:39, the writer's discussion of the Law is recast in terms of the old and new covenants, and the "Spirit of Christ" becomes the Holy Spirit. The passage cites Jeremiah at Hebrews 8:10-12, with the key phrase being translated into Greek as, "I will put my laws into their mind and write them in their hearts." This is the sign of the new covenant of

| | |
|---|---|
| God: [quietly] Moses. Moses. | Ex. 3:4 |
| Moses: I am here. | Ex. 3:4 |
| God: [louder] Put off thy shoes from off thy feet, for the place where are thou stands is holy ground. | Ex. 3:5 |
| I am the God of thy father. The god of Abraham, the God of Isaac, and the God of Jacob. | Ex. 3:6 |
| Moses: Lord. Lord. Why do you not hear the cries of their children in the bondage of Egypt? | — |
| God: I have surely seen the affliction of my people which are in Egypt. | Ex. 3:7 |
| And I have heard their cry by reason of their taskmasters. | Ex. 3:7 |
| For I know their sorrows. | Ex. 3:7 |
| Therefore, I will send thee, Moses, unto Pharaoh. | Ex. 3:10 |
| That thou mayest bring my people out of Egypt. | Ex. 3:10 |
| Moses: Who am I, my Lord, that you should send me? | Ex. 3:11 |
| How can I lead this people out of bondage? | Ex. 3:11 |
| What words can I speak that they will heed? | — |
| God: I will teach thee what thou wilt say. | Ex. 4:12 |
| When thou hast brought forth the people, they will serve me on this mountain. | Ex. 3:12 |
| I will put my laws into their hearts. | Heb. 8:10 |
| And in their minds will I write them. | Heb. 8:10 |
| Now therefore, Go! | Ex. 4:12 |
| And I will be with thee. | Ex. 4:12 |
| Moses: But if I say to your children that the God of their fathers has sent me. They will ask what is his name? How shall I answer them? | Ex. 3:13 |
| God: I am that I am. | Ex. 3:14 |
| Thou shalt say, I Am has sent me unto you. | Ex. 3:14 |

Christianity. Thus, the targumic insertion of this language into key moments of this film emphasizes the typological link between the Law of Moses and the "law of Christianity" as described in Hebrews.

If Moses is the type for Christ and his Law is the type for Christianity's spiritual law, then the Israelites are presented by the film as the type for Christians. Rather than seeing only God's Chosen People and their particular redemption in the Exodus from Egypt, the audience should see a representation of Christians. That this is DeMille's intention becomes clear from various remarks in the film that extend the specific events related toward all humanity. This universalizing tendency is a necessary aspect of Christianity, which claims that salvation is open to all. One example of this universal character comes during the night of terror when the firstborn are dying. Bithia says sadly to those around the table in Aaron's home, "They are my people." The equally sad reply comes, "All are God's people."

The strongest statement of the universal character of God comes from Moses in Midian. He says, "If this God is God, he would live on every mountain, in every valley. He would not be only the god of Israel, or of Ishmael alone, but of all men. It is said he created all men in his image. He would dwell in every heart, every mind, in every soul." The final sentence links universalization and the function of hearts and minds. The notion that God should dwell in hearts, minds, and souls should be seen as equivalent to the writing of the commandments on hearts and minds. The Christian character of this sentence's phrasing comes from Matthew 22:37, where the Israelite affirmation of faith, "You shall love the Lord your God with all your heart, and with all your soul and with all your might" (Deut. 6:4) is given as "You shall love the Lord your God with all your heart, and with all your soul and with all your mind." Thus, the film is faithful to its portrayal of the people Israel while still rendering them into a type for Christianity.

# The Americanization of Moses and the Exodus

*The Ten Commandments* not only transforms the foundational event of Judaism into one typifying Christian origins, but the film focuses that Christian character on 1950s America. Indeed, as we have seen, in the film's introduction DeMille describes the importance of the Moses story as directly relevant to the Cold War struggles of the midfifties. But his point is larger than this. In DeMille's epic, the struggle of Moses for the freedom of Israel from Egyptian tyranny reflects not just his belief that the Cold War antagonism between the United States and the Soviet Union reenacts the perennial contest between freedom and slavery, but that it serves as the *type* of the conflict. Thus, the struggles of the Israelites against the Egyptians prefigure a culminating and more historically significant set of difficulties taking place daily during the Cold War.

Puritan typological interpretation brought together entities from different moments in time, showing the movement of God's plan for history. Moses was a type for Jesus the antitype. The Puritan journey to America was the antitype of the Israelite Exodus from Egypt. Although based on Scripture, the typological pattern of history did not end with Jesus' incarnation and the New Testament but continued toward the foreordained culmination of God's plan for history. In this movement from type to antitype, the second term is always the more perfect, the more realized event, and even the Jesus of the incarnation functioned as a type prefiguring the antitype realized in the Jesus of the eschaton who will preside over the final days.

This typological view of American history underlies DeMille's use of the Moses narrative to indicate the religious and political implications of the American struggle against Soviet Communism. DeMille portrays the Moses narrative as the first example of "a battle that continues throughout the world today over whether men ought to be ruled by God's law, or whether they are to be ruled by the whims of a dictator." Moses initiates a typological sequence that moves through the Puritan view of the New World's role into the contemporary moment as the site of a culminating antitype: the struggle, as DeMille envisions it, between American democracy and Soviet tyranny.

DeMille's speech explicitly referring to America's current antagonism with the Soviet Union has caused many to look under every metaphorical rock and log to find Communism in the film. This limits DeMille's meaning. Rameses is a tyrant, and as such suggests not merely one instance but rather the history, as understood by many Americans, of America's continual struggle against tyranny. While DeMille may point to Russia in his speech, the film also adumbrates America's revolutionary conflict with Great Britain and the belief in America's historical mission first articulated by the Puritans and emphasized in the religious and political rhetoric of the American revolution. For many Americans, the revolutionary struggle against Britain signified America's role as promised land, the nation that would sweep away old world tyranny and move humankind toward a perfected future, namely, the millennial era of peace and enlightenment.

The Puritans left England for the New World because they were not allowed to worship as they believed God wished. In their typological understanding, England was the enemy of Israel (i.e., themselves), and their typologizing theology symbolized it as both Egypt and Babylon. Their interpretation cast the events of their actual and spiritual journey as guided by God as a sacred text that constituted the antitype of all that had gone before.

> [The Puritans] were not only spiritual Israelites. . . . They were also, uniquely, American Israelites, the sole reliable exegetes of a new, last book of scripture. Since they had migrated to another "holy Land," as Thomas Tillam hymned upon his first sight of Massachusetts—"The Antitype of what the Lord's people had of old"—they conferred upon the continent they left and the ocean they crossed the literal-spiritual contours of Egypt and Babylon. . . . They were a "second, far more glorious Israel." (Bercovitch, p. 113)

The parallel of the founding of Israel with the founding of America continued in force through the following centuries. In the early years of the United States, Thomas Jefferson even proposed that the Great Seal of the United States portray Moses leading Israel across the Red Sea.

*The Ten Commandments* brings the identification of America and Israel back into play. In Israel's exodus from Egypt, DeMille evokes a chain of typological occurrences that includes the Puritan emergence from Great Britain, the American Revolution, and the contemporary struggle against Soviet Communism.

The most obvious reference to Revolutionary War rhetoric lies in the film's opposition of freedom with tyranny. The law that Moses receives is the "Law of Freedom" as opposed to the tyranny of Egypt and its slavery. The language of liberty against tyranny and oppression was a staple of American writings encouraging rebellion against England, from Patrick Henry's "Give me liberty or give me death!" to the Declaration of Independence's claim that not only was liberty a human right endowed by the Creator but that any government that denied that right should be abolished:

> We hold these truths to be self-evident, that all men are created equal, that they are endowed by their Creator with certain unalienable Rights,

that among these are Life, Liberty, and the pursuit of Happiness. . . .
[W]henever any Form of Government becomes destructive of these
ends, it is the Right of the People to alter or to abolish it, and to institute new Government.

Not only does the Declaration identify freedom as one of the key rights
of humans, but it also states that governments that deny people freedom
should be changed. Of course, this is the very act that Moses accomplishes. The Israelites are enslaved, and God leads Moses to free them and
to set up a new government under God.

The Revolutionary work that fits *The Ten Commandments* better than
any other writing is Thomas Paine's *Common Sense.* Indeed, DeMille
could have designed his film on its key points. Paine identifies the political problems of the American colonies as stemming from the failings of
tyrants (DeMille's pharaohs). America is subject not only to "aristocrati-
cal tyranny in the persons of the peers" but also to "monarchical tyranny
in the person of the king," who suffers from "a thirst for absolute power
[which] is the natural disease of monarchy" (Paine, p. 9). Given this,
Paine calls out:

O ye that love mankind! Ye that dare oppose, not only the tyranny, but
the tyrant, stand forth! Every spot of the old world is overrun with
oppression. Freedom hath been hunted round the globe. (Paine, p. 33)

The solution according to Paine is for people to found a new nation and
base that nation on the rule of law rather than the whims of a dictator.

The present time, likewise, is that peculiar time, which never happens
to a nation but once, *viz.* the time of forming itself into a government.
Most nations have let slip the opportunity, and by that means have
been compelled to receive laws from their conquerors, instead of making laws for themselves. First, they had a king, and then a form of government; whereas, the articles or charter of government, should be
formed first, and men delegated to execute them afterward: but from the
errors of other nations, let us learn wisdom, and lay hold of the present
opportunity—*to begin government at the right end.* (Paine, p. 33)

The "right end" for Paine is at the beginning. He is arguing that the
American colonies should throw off the yoke of British rule and lay out
the laws, "the charter," for their own government. In other words, they
should follow the model of the Israelites who freed themselves from the
tyranny of Egypt and founded their own government.

DeMille's story of Moses follows Paine's claim that government should be founded upon the rule of law. Paine held that the law even replaced the king, saying, "in America THE LAW IS KING" (Paine, p. 31). The key difference between Paine and Moses is that Paine was a child of the Enlightenment and thought that human reason should guide the formation of the laws of a governmental charter, while for Moses, God was the founder and creator of the Law. As DeMille portrayed him, Moses made the point, "There is no freedom without the Law." And that law is the Law of God, which he made to ensure freedom.

So what the audience sees in *The Ten Commandments* is Israel as a symbol for America. Israel's release from slavery into freedom and its founding of a new nation upon law points, for DeMille, to the founding of America as the escape from British oppression and the formation of a new nation in the New World ruled by law rather than the whim of a monarchical dictator. By his use of these key ideas, which resonate deeply with American citizens, DeMille brought the foundational beliefs of the country's independence to the new battle against communist dictatorship. *The Ten Commandments* mustered the country's anti-British heritage for the new battle of ideas with Russia.

# The Bomb

From this perspective, the Moses narrative as a type of a later and more significant struggle allows DeMille to see God's actions against Ramses and the tyrannical Egyptians as the basis for the use of nuclear force in the cause of freedom from the Soviet threat. The plagues visited by God on Egypt because of that nation's enslavement of Israel suggest in *The Ten Commandments* the justifiable use of military force on behalf of the God-given right to freedom, a right threatened by Soviet Communism. In short, the transformation of the Nile into blood, the plague of locusts, the deaths of firstborn Egyptian sons, and the other plagues are to be understood as types whose antitypes are potential and justifiable actions in the Cold War between the United States and the Soviet Union.

This is especially significant for the international political context in which the film was released. In the late 1940s, the United States had developed a policy of containment of Communism, as discussed in chapter 2. There would be no attempt to reverse the Soviet expansion into eastern Europe following World War II or the Maoist takeover of the

Chinese government; however, the United States would resist strenuously any expansion of communist-dominated territory. As in the case of the Korean conflict, this policy of containment was carried out with the use of conventional weapons only. Before the release of *The Ten Commandments* in 1956 though, the Eisenhower administration had adopted a more aggressive policy on weapon use in the service of containment.

By the election of 1952, many Americans thought containment was not working. Not only had China fallen to communist forces, but the United States had become bogged down in Korea by fighting toward a truce that would leave a communist government in charge of the northern part of the peninsula. This seemed to validate communist control of the nations already under its sway, while failing to contain Communism and prevent its expansion into new arenas.

General Dwight Eisenhower, formerly the Supreme Commander of Allied Forces in Europe during World War II, was the 1952 Republican candidate for president. He articulated American disappointment and frustration at this situation in a campaign speech that August.

> Seven years ago this very month I left the army. . . . [S]even years ago today no one in our whole country would have dreamed that today we would be prey to fear.
>
> Who would have thought . . . that only seven years later America would have to be studying and analyzing the world in terms of fear and concern? We are threatened by a great tyranny—a tyranny that is brutal in its primitiveness. It is a tyranny that has brought thousands, millions of people into slave camps and is attempting to make all humankind its chattel.
>
> Now let America, saddened by the tragedy of lost opportunity, etch in its memory the roll of countries once independent now suffocating under this Russian pall.
>
> Latvia and her million people.
>
> Estonia and her million and a quarter, and Lithuania with more than twice that number.
>
> Poland and her twenty-five million, a country that for centuries has been the bulwark against Tartar savages.
>
> East Germany and her more than seventeen million.
>
> East Austria and her two million.
>
> Czechoslovakia and her twelve million—a nation that was born in the Czechoslovakian councils in America.
>
> Albania and her twelve hundred thousand.
>
> Bulgaria and Rumania and their twenty-three million.
>
> (Bernstein and Matusow, p. 294)

Eisenhower then turned the rest of his speech—and indeed his campaign—into a call for the United States to assist in enabling these, and other peoples threatened by communist aggression, to gain their freedom, to restore them "again to being masters of their own fate." "Dare we rest," cried Eisenhower, "while these millions of our kinsmen remain in slavery?" He ended the speech with his answer:

> We can never rest . . . until the enslaved nations of the world have in the fullness of freedom the right to choose their own path. . . .
>
> We must tell the Kremlin that never shall we desist in our aid to every man and woman of those shackled lands who seeks refuge with us, any man who keeps burning among his own people the flame of freedom or who is dedicated to the liberation of his fellows. (Bernstein and Matusow, p. 295)

The goal, Eisenhower proclaimed, was not merely containment, but "liberation" for those who seek freedom. Or, as Secretary of State Dulles would later explain, the United States intended to "roll back" communist gains and return freedom of political expression and rule to those now under communist sway.

To Eisenhower, Truman's handling of Korea showed the shortcomings of containment practiced only with the use of conventional weapons. It tied down the United States' military strength in a single location, thus leaving open the way for communist adventurism elsewhere. It allowed the communists to determine both the time and location of the battle. To a skilled military strategist like Eisenhower, this was an anathema.

In 1954, Secretary of State Foster Dulles announced President Eisenhower's new strategy. It quickly became known as Massive Retaliation. In a speech to the Council on Foreign Policy, Dulles argued that while a military response in the locality of the imminent danger should be undertaken, there was a more important second approach.

> Local defenses must be reinforced by the further deterrent of massive retaliatory power. A potential aggressor must know that he cannot always prescribe battle conditions that suit him. (Guhin, p. 229)

Although hidden in diplomatic jargon, the meaning of this statement was clear to Dulles's audience. The United States was threatening the use of nuclear weapons as a response to communist aggression. Moreover, it would not limit its targets to the area where the aggression was taking place. Instead, it might strike at strategic targets in the territory of the instigator of the aggression, for instance, Soviet Russia itself. Local conflict pursued by conventional armies and weapons, therefore, could be met with global nuclear conflict. By escalating the stakes in this manner, Eisenhower and Dulles hoped to discourage Soviet adventurism by making the potential negatives significantly more risky than the potential gain. However high the rhetoric soared, it was never carried out.

*The Ten Commandments* agrees with, and is even willing to intensify, the strategic view held by the Eisenhower White House. This is apparent in the climactic stages of the conflict between Moses and Rameses. When, after promising to allow the people of Israel to depart Egypt in peace, Rameses sends the Egyptian army to wipe them out, it is clear that faith in treaties with such an enemy is misguided. Rameses' attack is necessarily and justifiably met with an exercise of God's power called down by Moses that annihilates the Egyptian army in the closing waters of the Red Sea. Extending his forces beyond the limit to which he had agreed, Rameses' action serves, from the film's typological perspective, as a prophetic instance of the sort of expansionist communist aggression the Eisenhower administration had threatened to meet with a nuclear response.

It is important to note that in addition to this action against an army in the field, the film goes even further. After the failure of the initial plagues to win freedom for Israel, DeMille's epic makes an important addition to the biblical text. Here an angry Moses declares to Rameses that the next stage of the escalating confrontation will be determined by the pharaoh himself, "out of his own mouth." Thus when Rameses in the film decides to slaughter the firstborn of Israel, he condemns the firstborn of Egypt to the fate he had proposed for his slaves. This addition to the film provides the audience with a justification for its imagining of large-scale slaughter. The enemy intentions, like those of Rameses, are so devastatingly merciless that precisely the same overwhelming force that they threaten may justifiably be used against them. The wrath of God directed at an obdurate tyranny capable of planning the destruction of innocents serves the film as a type of the struggle enacted in the 1950s against an enemy the film characterizes, as Ronald Reagan will later put it, as an "evil empire."

# Suggested Readings

Bruce Babington and Peter W. Evans, *Biblical Epics: Sacred Narrative in the Hollywood Cinema* (Manchester: Manchester University Press, 1993).

Sacvan Bercovitch, *The Puritan Origins of the American Self* (New Haven: Yale University Press, 1975).

Barton J. Bernstein and Allen J. Matusow, *The Truman Administration: A Documentary History* (New York: Harper & Row, 1966).

Paul Boyer, *By the Bomb's Early Light: American Thought and Culture at the Dawn of the Atomic Age* (Chapel Hill: North Carolina University Press, 1985).

Michael A. Guhin, *John Foster Dulles: A Statesman and His Times* (New York: Columbia University Press, 1972).

Richard T. Hughes, *Myths America Lives By* (Urbana and Chicago: University of Illinois Press, 2003).

Josephus in Nine Volumes, vol. 4, *Jewish Antiquities, Books I-IV*, H. St. J. Thackeray, trans. (Cambridge: Harvard University Press, 1930).

Fred Kaplan, *The Wizards of Armageddon* (New York: Simon and Schuster, 1983).

Alan Nadel, *Containment Culture: American Narratives, Postmodernism, and the Atomic Age* (Durham: Duke University Press, 1995).

Thomas Paine, *Common Sense. Quotations from Common Sense and Other Writings*, Thomas Paine, ed. Gordon S. Wood (New York: The Modern Library, 2003).

Robert Torry, "The Wrath of God: Hollywood Religious Epics and American Cold War Policy," *Arizona Quarterly* 61:2 (2005): 67-86.

Melanie J. Wright, *Moses in America: Cultural Uses of Biblical Narrative* (Oxford: Oxford University Press, 2002).

# Filming Jesus

CHAPTER 5

# The Messiah of Peace

In 1956, even as *The Ten Commandments* was released, the world changed. The strident anticommunist rhetoric of the Truman and Eisenhower presidencies was put to the test and found wanting. In October, there was a revolution in Hungary. Rebels installed a new president who immediately proposed leaving the communist bloc of Eastern Europe and improving ties with the West. This was clearly done in the face of great pressure from the communist bloc. Shortly after, Russian tanks entered the country, put down the rebellion, and installed a new government.

The United States of America gave no assistance to the Hungarian rebels, despite its years of promises to help free nations subjugated by "communist slavery." The words of United States Secretary of State John Foster Dulles, repeated in diplomatic meetings around the world, were seen to be naught. As President Eisenhower realized at the time, they were impossible to back up. There was simply nothing the United States could do short of starting an atomic war that would have been able to assist the Hungarians and prevent the crushing of their rebellion. The limits of the power of nuclear weapons had been found.

This incident was followed over the next few years by several more indications that the Soviet Union was not the pushover that *The Ten Commandments* had implied. In fact, in a number of areas, the Soviet Union was superior to the United States. In 1957, the Soviets launched the world's first manmade satellite, Sputnik, a feat that the United States could not match. In the same year, the Soviets successfully tested the world's

---

* Read the Gospels of Matthew and Luke for this chapter.

first Intercontinental Ballistic Missile (ICBM), which could deliver nuclear warheads much faster than bomber planes.

Into this sobering new world, the first Jesus film since before World War II was released, *King of Kings*. Here was Jesus, the Son of God, providing the focus for an entire feature-length film. Here was—from the Christian viewpoint—a portrayal of a human with direct access to God's power, who had the ability "to call down angels." And the message this filmic Jesus brought to this new situation was peace. Peace even at the cost of losing one's life. Peace even at the cost of captivity, slavery, and the absence of political freedom. This Jesus simply did not countenance armed struggle or war.

The film's portrayal of Jesus comes straight out of the Gospels. With only a few exceptions, the words Jesus utters in this film come from Scripture and are rendered faithfully in the film. But of course this fidelity takes place within the film's targumic enhancement. Constructed around the scriptural portrayal of Jesus appear three additional and interlocking narratives: one centers on Barabbas, who provides Jesus a foil of violent rebellion against Rome; one focuses on the character Lucius, which casts this movie as a Roman conversion film; and one concentrates on John the Baptist to create a debate with *The Ten Commandments*. These additional narratives reshape the meaning of Jesus' words to emphasize the message of peace.

From the perspective of genre, *King of Kings* is a Roman conversion film. It fits the standard characteristics of this film type, with one key exception. That exception is the portrayal of Jesus. *King of Kings* adds into its mix a full portrayal of Jesus, rather than limiting his role primarily to off stage. While the Roman centurion Lucius goes through all the activities expected of his role, even conversion, he does it with Jesus on stage. Given Jesus' presence, the film must work out how to portray him and provide a valid yet engaging depiction, staying faithful to the Gospels while enhancing his role visually. Let us start with how that is done.

# Jesus the Peaceful Messiah

*King of Kings* portrays Jesus as a messiah who brings peace rather than rebellion, violence, and war. This depiction comes from the Gospels themselves. Most of the words Jesus utters originate in Scripture. Many of these follow the Bible exactly, providing a word-for-word restatement of one of the available translations of the New Testament (no longer just KJV). Often, the film provides its own translation or paraphrase of Jesus' remarks in the Gospels, shaping a sentence's exact wording to fit its staging of a scene. This careful adherence to the wording of Scripture characterizes perhaps 90 percent or more of Jesus' utterances. This, of course, leaves a few words and phrases that are added wholesale into the film. While most of these function to help a conversation sound more natural to a 1960s American audience, some derive from Christian theology or emphasize the purposes of the film.

The film's portrayal of Jesus' statements thus unfolds according to the rules of targum. It is not literal, in the notion that everything is always related exactly, but it is faithful in the sense of the two main targumic rules: first, when citing Scripture, do so straightforwardly. Second, when changes or additions are made, do so in a way that fits them into the literal renderings so that they appear to be authentic and go unnoticed. Of course, much of what Jesus says in the Gospels is left out. This secondary targumic rule applies not just in general—for many scenes in Scripture are entirely absent—but also in small details. Even for scenes enacted in the film, words or sentences are often left out. This enables the included scenes to be portrayed in a manner that remains cinematically coherent and consistent with the film's overall meaning.

Jesus' Sermon on the Mount provides a good example of how *King of Kings* stages Jesus in a targumic manner. The Sermon on the Mount takes up three chapters in the Gospel of Matthew (Matt. 5–7, see also the parallel material in Luke 6:17-49), making it the longest scene in that Gospel. It includes two well-known passages—the Beatitudes and the Lord's Prayer—and an assortment of sayings, parables, and observations about God. Jesus is the only speaker throughout these chapters.

From a cinematographic perspective, the sermon's length makes it difficult to stage so that it keeps a movie audience engaged. Its sudden changes from topic to topic make it difficult to follow. Yet it is also the one scene that provides a deep insight into the character of Jesus and his message. It is here, before a large crowd, that Jesus' understanding of himself, his mission, and his relationship to God appear. And, if his goal is to incite people against the Roman oppressors, here is where he would do it. Indeed, Pilate sends Lucius the Centurion to discover whether Jesus' speech encourages rebellion. Lucius later reports to Pilate that Jesus spoke only of "peace, love and the brotherhood of man."

*King of Kings's* staging of the Sermon on the Mount begins, as does Matthew 5, with the Beatitudes.

Blessed are you who are poor, for yours is the kingdom of heaven.
Blessed are the meek, for they shall inherit the earth.

All the Beatitudes are here, although they are slightly rearranged. But before Jesus utters the last one, a member of the crowd shouts a question and the last beatitude becomes a response to the question.

> **Crowd member:** Give us a sign from Heaven! Prove to us who you are.
> **Jesus:** Blessed are you when men shall curse you and separate you from their company, and reproach you and cast out your name as evil, for the Son of Man's sake.

Although it is unclear how Jesus' remark answers the question, this exchange provides the first indication of how the film makes use of Scripture in a targumic manner to overcome the challenge of staging this scene. From this moment, members of the crowd ask questions and Jesus responds. The sermon becomes a question-and-answer session—almost a press conference. Furthermore, although Jesus' response comes from Scripture, it is not from Matthew 5. Given the movement through the Beatitudes from Matthew 5:3 to Matthew 5:10, the audience would expect the last Beatitude to come from Matthew 5:11. Instead, it comes from the parallel passage at Luke 6:22. So the film targumically draws material from other places in the Gospels.

After the first, questions follow rapidly in succession, with Jesus answering each one. But the Sermon on the Mount is quickly left behind. Jesus' responses now come from all the Gospels, with no clear pattern. Some derive from the other synoptic Gospels, Mark and Luke, while others come back to Matthew's Sermon. Jesus' response to the fourth question cites the Gospel of John (John 10:11).

> **Crowd member:** Are you the messiah?
> **Jesus:** I am the Good Shepherd. The Good Shepherd lays down his life for his sheep.

Finally, the film's portrayal of the Sermon on the Mount concludes with perhaps its most well-known section, the Lord's Prayer, which it gives in Matthew's version rather than Luke's.

It is only Jesus' words that the film takes such great pains to render accurately. It does not show the same faithfulness with his actions or with the staging of the scenes in which he appears. The story of the woman caught in adultery—whom the film, following tradition, identifies as Mary Magdalene—comprises a case in point. Of the four Gospels, this scene appears only in John 8:3-11. John constructs the scene as a test set up by the Pharisees. They are trying to entrap Jesus, to make him choose between upholding Moses' Law (the law of the land) by condemning her and showing love and compassion (Jesus' own message) by pardoning her. In the Gospel, Jesus' statement that he who is without sin should cast the first stone constitutes an answer to their challenge that takes neither option of the trap. In *King of Kings*, by contrast, no Pharisees and no test appear. Instead, Mary is being chased by an excited mob intending to exact vigilante justice. Jesus' remark becomes a challenge to the crowd to prevent Mary's imminent stoning rather than an answer to a crafty questioner. While Jesus' point about sin is the same in both versions, the film's staging presents a tension-filled, emotion-laced confrontation, while John's Gospel depicts a calm, almost academic encounter.

*King of Kings*'s targumic portrayal of Jesus emphasizes his message of peace. Through its accurate presentation of Jesus' words, its choices about which words to include in the film, and its careful combining of passages from different Gospels, the film presents a picture of Jesus that is at once faithful to Scripture, yet portrays him only as a proponent of peace.

# What the Film Leaves Out

The choices are important for what they leave out as much as for what they include. The peaceful messiah portrayal requires the absence of certain Gospel sayings; missing are: "I have not come to bring peace, but a sword" (Matt. 10:34) and "A man's foes will be those in his own household" (Matt. 10:36). But this is not a roll-over-and-take-it approach to peace. *King of Kings* does not include Jesus' sayings about obeying and helping the authorities or oppressors. Also absent are Jesus' passivist comments like "Give therefore to the emperor the things that are the emperor's" (Matt. 22:21); "If anyone strikes you on the cheek, offer the other also; and from anyone who takes away your coat do not withhold even your shirt" (Luke 6:29); and "Love your enemies, do good to those who hate you" (Luke 6:27). Jesus' approach to peace in this film is a plan to be carried out, not simply a charge to be subservient to the oppressors.

It is important to note that Jesus is the only character for whom *King of Kings* follows the targumic approach to faithful rendering of Scripture.

For none of the other characters—from Mary and Peter to Pilate and Herod—does the film attempt anything more than a general adherence to their role in the story's plot. Peter actually denies Jesus four times rather than the biblical three, and Pilate flogs Jesus not as an intended prelude to releasing him (Luke 23:16), but because "he is different." Similarly, despite the enhanced role of Pilate's wife, the film never mentions her dream. And of course, the roles of the main players in the film—Lucius, Barabbas, Judas, and John—are largely invented, as are the scenes and lines of most lesser figures as well: Mary the Mother of Jesus, Mary Magdalene, Pilate, and Herod.

This observation reveals an important conclusion about *King of Kings*. As the first film since before World War II to explicitly portray Jesus as a central character, it faced a challenge as to how to do the portrayal. In the end, it produced a hybrid film. On the one hand, the role of Jesus was played according to the targumic rules found also in its predecessor film in the depiction of Scripture, *The Ten Commandments*. Indeed, as we shall see, John the Baptist explicitly parallels and challenges that film's portrayal of Moses. In this sense, *King of Kings* belongs to the genre of Scripture enactment films. On the other hand, we already mentioned the film also belongs to the genre of Roman conversion films. This is perhaps the dominant genre. Lucius and Pilate's wife find their lives impacted by Jesus throughout the film and finally are shown at the foot of the cross, gazing reverently at the crucified Jesus. Even Barabbas at the end is left considering the import of Jesus' sacrificial death in his place.

Given the extent to which *King of Kings* follows the conventions of the Roman conversion film rather than the Scripture enactment film, it should not be surprising that many of the techniques for conveying authenticity are missing in this film. Unlike *The Ten Commandments*, it does not appeal to historical sources like Josephus and Philo, or even to Scripture. While *King of Kings* shows architecture by necessity, it is not on display to add to the film's historical accuracy as it was in *The Ten Commandments*.

Clothing is in general appropriate for Palestine of the first century, but its role in authentication is not large. Perhaps only the blue and red worn by Mary, Jesus' mother, familiar from centuries of Christian artistic tradition, help make the film seem authentic to its audience.

In the end, not even narration plays an important authenticating role in *King of Kings*. Only occasionally does it take the task of moving the audience into scenes using Scripture. The most obvious of these occurs early in the film when Joseph and Mary go to Bethlehem. The narration there begins with a quotation from Scripture and then moves to Scripturelike language as the scene begins.

> And it came to pass in those days that a decree went out from Caesar Augustus that all the world should be taxed. And all went to be taxed, everyone into his own city.
>
> So it was that Joseph the carpenter went up from Galilee unto Bethlehem to be taxed with his espoused wife Mary who was with holy child.
>
> *He found his own city much corrupted by Rome. . . .*

The first three sentences are based on Luke 2:1-6, while the fourth and following have nothing to do with Scripture.

Most of the time, narration serves to tie together the story lines involving the film's five main characters, namely, Jesus, Lucius, Barabbas, Judas, and John. Most of these narrative transitions link Jesus to the other characters, interweaving the known Gospel story with the figures and stories introduced in the film. Given that the latter tales lack any basis in Scripture, the targumically faithful Jesus' story cannot serve to authenticate them in any important way. There is simply too much additional material. But the targumic method alerts us to the reverse effect. By tying the non-Scripture stories to that of Jesus, these stories give meaning to the faithful rendering of Jesus' tale. In the end, that meaning emphasizes the peaceful character of Jesus' message. Barabbas's pursuit of war against the Romans, John's violent prophecies about Herod and Rome, and even Lucius's role as a soldier who must commit violence at his superiors' orders, all cast into stark contrast Jesus' message of peace and love. To see how this process works, let us examine each of these characters in fuller detail.

# Superpower Struggles: Judas between Jesus and Barabbas

During the 1950s, the increasing stranglehold of Soviet Russia on the countries of eastern Europe was variously depicted as the enslavement of the people of those countries or as widespread, state-sponsored murder. The slavery imagery can be seen in Eisenhower's campaign remarks, as we saw earlier, when he observes:

[Communism is] . . . a tyranny that has brought thousands, millions of people into slave camps and is attempting to make all humankind its chattel. . . . We can never rest . . . until the enslaved nations of the world have in the fullness of freedom the right to choose their own path. (Bernstein and Matusow, pp. 294-95)

Such rhetoric is an index of the frustration of Eisenhower and his advisors over President Truman's policy of containment, which while opposing Soviet aggression was not concerned with the liberation of those countries that had fallen under Soviet domination at the end of World War II. Yet short of all-out confrontation with the Soviet Union, there was little, if anything, that could be done to effect a liberation of Soviet-controlled territory. Indeed, this idea of a "rollback" of Soviet control (favored especially by Eisenhower's secretary of state, John Foster Dulles), however much implied by Eisenhower's campaign speeches, was never acted upon through military means. The Eisenhower administration did not abandon containment, although as we have seen it added the threat of nuclear weapons to the policy. Despite Eisenhower's rhetoric, the United States was not prepared to risk war to aid Eastern bloc uprisings against Soviet rule, as was demonstrated in Hungary.

In this light, the subtext of the opening scenes of *King of Kings* in 1961 is evident. They portray the Roman conquest of Judea in 63 BC, followed by its "harvest": the people of the land. As the narrator describes the enslavement of the people of Judea, the Jews are a "crop," a "richness of people to be gathered." Enslavement is mixed with murder: "Like sheep from their own green fields, the Jews went to the slaughter," declares the speaker, and "forests of Roman crosses grew high on Jerusalem's hills." After years of Roman conversion films, there is no question that the Romans here are only thinly disguised Russians, and that *King of Kings* will once again wrestle with the problem of communist expansion.

Indeed, as the audience watches this opening sequence, the film's negative portrayal of Rome's subjugation of Judea encourages them to think of it in terms of current attitudes toward the Soviet subjugation of Eastern Europe. Coming in a film released after the eight years of the Eisenhower administration, these scenes recall the Eisenhower government's distaste for the Soviet domination of Eastern Europe, powerfully stated on February 23, 1953, by Secretary of State John Foster Dulles:

We, as a people, never have acquiesced, and never will acquiesce, in the enslavement of other peoples. Our nation, from its beginning, was and is inspired by the spirit of liberty. We do not accept or tolerate captivity as an irrevocable fact which can be finalized by force or by the lapse of time.

We do not accommodate ourselves to political settlements which are based upon contempt for the free will of peoples and which are imposed by the brutal occupation of alien armies or by revolutionary factions who serve alien masters. (Heller, pp. 166-67)

With the Roman armies chasing innocent Judeans across the screen and the illegitimate establishment first of Herod the Great and then of Herod Antipas, *King of Kings* invokes the American Cold War rhetoric about "alien armies," "alien masters," and the Soviet "contempt for the free will of peoples."

The film's solution to the Judean subjugation by Rome is anticipated by the final comment of the narrator in this opening sequence, "[T]he Jews survived by one promise: God would send the Messiah to deliver them forth." But while the film moves directly to the birth of Jesus, it will not (and of course cannot) depict Judea's deliverance as a military event. Indeed, the film's central tension lies in identifying the nature of that deliverance. *King of Kings* portrays a rival "messiah," Jesus Barabbas, who has a plan and an army of followers. It juxtaposes Barabbas's active attempts to drive out the Romans with Jesus of Nazareth's approach to the problem, which at first seems rather inadequate.

During our discussion of the film's portrayal of the Sermon on the Mount, we noted that although Jesus uttered several things that did not derive from Matthew's record of the sermon, nearly everything Jesus said came from one of the Gospels. One key exception to that observation was Jesus' remarks about Rome:

> **Crowd member:** If you can do miracles, call upon God to send hosts, to destroy the Romans and free our people from bondage.
> **Jesus:** Thou shalt not tempt the Lord, thy God. The Romans are conquerors. To conquer them would make you no different than they.

This brief comment conveys two points. First, by implication, it condemns the Romans for their character as conquerors. They are morally wrong. Second, it discourages rebellion by indicating that a direct attempt to conquer them, presumably by violence, is also wrong. While Jesus takes the moral high ground, he provides no hope of liberation from Roman oppression. Indeed, Lucius's report to Pilate after returning from spying on Jesus is, "He spoke of peace, love, and the brotherhood of man." *King of Kings* presents Jesus' refusal to engage Rome in attack or even condemning rhetoric as problematic for the disciples. Shortly after the Sermon on the Mount, Jesus withdraws from the crowds with his disciples, while the voiceover indicates:

> Jesus saw his own disciples doubt him. Awed by his miracles, faithful to him. Yet still they wondered why the Messiah could not raise up miraculous armies to strike Judea free. Could simple love and brotherhood be weapons against Rome?

Jesus' response to Roman tyranny here does not inspire the audience with confidence that he has a solution. This impression becomes even stronger when Jesus' approach is set beside that of Jesus Barabbas. Although the Gospels' Barabbas is merely a murderer who happens to be in prison at the time of Jesus' trial, *King of Kings* imagines him as the leader of an underground army who can bring armed and organized rebels out to attack Pilate's caravan to Jerusalem, even though it is guarded by an entire legion.

To ensure the film's audience appreciates the thematically central contrast between Jesus and Barabbas, the film makes Judas into a disciple of both. Judas is an advisor to Barabbas, part of his inner circle, who in *King of Kings* also becomes one of Jesus' disciples. Although he is sympathetic to Jesus' message of peace—understanding it as the peaceful overthrow of Rome—Judas's main priority is ridding Judea of Roman rule. In the end, we see that it does not matter to him whether that overthrow comes through peaceful or violent means.

Judas wants to bring Jesus and Barabbas together to work toward liberation hand-in-hand, and throughout the film he tries different means to bring the two together. Judas, in his desire to combine the forces of the two men he follows, cannot choose between what are diametrically opposed perspectives, as the narrator observes following Jesus' rescue of Mary Magdalene from stoning:

> And Barabbas so near to Jesus, now turned and fled from the Roman guards. Leaving behind a man seeking answers from one stone [the stone Jesus had held while challenging the crowd over Mary], whether to run with Barabbas the messiah of war, or walk with Jesus, the new Messiah of peace.

If the audience had missed earlier the intended parallels between Jesus and Barabbas, they are now clear. Both men are termed "messiah," and their differing approaches to Roman oppression are clear; one attempts war while the other follows peace. Judas, who is close to both, must choose one over the other, the narrator suggests. But he does not. Instead he continually tries to bring the two men together. Those attempts continue to juxtapose the two men's attitudes to the Romans. Indeed, each time Judas meets with Barabbas or the rebels, the topic is Jesus, and the debate is over war or peace.

In the film's first meeting between Judas and Barabbas, Judas relates that a new prophet has arisen, one greater than John the Baptist, as even John himself proclaims. Barabbas's first thought is to co-opt Jesus into his rebellion, but Judas says that Jesus speaks only of peace. In a later scene, Judas appears in Barabbas's sword factory to reveal that Jesus will shortly arrive in Jerusalem and speak in the temple. Judas proposes that Barabbas show his support of Jesus by having his rebels stand with him, keeping their swords hidden as a sign of controlled strength. Barabbas initially agrees, but once Judas leaves, Barabbas makes a different plan, one which Barabbas, not Jesus, will lead. It is a plan of violence and war, not a plan of peace.

After the failure of Barabbas's plan—with the death and injury of many of Barabbas's fighters and the innocent Jewish crowd, and Barabbas's capture by the Romans—Judas goes to the rebels once more. This time his plan is not one of peace, but one which will force Jesus to react with violence, to call upon the heavenly hosts to defend him and crush the Romans. In an exchange during which the rebels challenge Judas, Judas seemingly decides on the spot to betray Jesus into Roman hands. The result of this plan is, of course, the arrest, trial, and crucifixion of Jesus.

The test of whether the messiah of war or the messiah of peace has the better solution to Roman tyranny lies in the results of their actions. Barabbas's plans fail to make even a dent in Roman control. When the rebels and the crowd storm Herod's Antonia Fortress, the Romans unleash the ballista, their super weapon. The attackers are simply mowed down, with few remaining alive. When Judas later comes to the rebels' lair, they talk about running into the desert and hiding. When Judas says he will force Jesus' hand, they respond "Not with us!" With Barabbas's arrest and their defeat, the rebels have given up. For them, the rebellion is over. They will vanish into the countryside.

At first glance, it seems that Jesus' peaceful approach has fared no better. Jesus is arrested and crucified. Peter's denial of his association with Jesus symbolizes the disciples' demoralization and implies their dissolution. But Jesus' resurrection gives them new hope and direction. The film ends with the risen Jesus giving the disciples their marching orders:

> Do you know and love me?
> Feed my sheep, for my sheep are in all the nations.
> Go you into all the world and preach the gospel to every creature who hungers.
> I am with you always.
> Even until the end of the world.

Jesus' challenge to Roman rule does not end with his death, or even with his resurrection. He exercises his power through his followers and sends them out to make new followers, who will in turn make yet additional followers. The peaceful spread of the gospel will ultimately result in the conversion of the world. As the presence of Lucius and Pilate's wife (Caesar's daughter) at the foot of the cross indicates, it even points to the future conversion of the Roman Empire to Christianity. In this emphasis upon a slow but certain process of historical progress through the dissemination of Christian values, the film, like the earlier Roman conversion narratives, adapts a stance resonant with the postmillennialist beliefs we have seen to be so deeply entwined with the belief in America's redemptive historical mission.

With this refusal to advocate the use of violence to defeat tyranny, *King of Kings* turns away from the rhetoric of *The Ten Commandments*. If Rome is transparently a type of Soviet Russia, Barabbas and Jesus represent the two options available to the United States of America for confronting Soviet power. Barabbas advocated the use of unlimited force, the divine capacity of Jesus utterly to destroy the Romans should he will to do so. Jesus will not employ violence, no matter what the provocation. By emphasizing that Jesus has the correct answer—how could it do otherwise?—the film comes down solidly on the side of peace. Let us look at this more closely.

Like the United States, Jesus controls enormous power. The miracles he performs indicate for both Judas and the audience Jesus' access to divine, superhuman power. Recall Judas's discussion with the defeated rebels:

**Judas:** He has the power of miracles.
**A Follower:** He will not use his power except to heal the sick.
**Judas:** He can call down hosts to destroy the fortress of Pilate.
**Another Follower:** He preaches against violence.
**Judas:** He can, with a look, rock the foundations of Herod Antipas's palace and bring the walls down on the tyrant's head.

Referring first to the miracles themselves and then to the "look," the means by which the film identifies Jesus' use of his miraculous power, Judas indicates how Jesus can destroy the massive stone buildings of the two tyrants. By betraying Jesus to the Romans, Judas will force Jesus to use his power. Judas claims, "Once he feels the Roman sword at his throat, he will strike them down with the wave of one arm."

But after his arrest, Jesus does none of these things. Despite the mortal peril in which he finds himself, Jesus chooses the way of peace. He does not even consider the use of the destructive heavenly power available to him. Jesus is the messiah of peace because he wants to be, not because he has to be. As a commentary on how the United States should deal with the Soviet Union, the advice is clear. Do not use the nuclear weapons in the U.S. arsenal. Instead, deal with Russia's attempts to expand its hegemony by more peaceful means, such as diplomacy.

How are we to interpret this shift from the perspective of *The Ten Commandments*, released just five years earlier? In 1956, Moses' wielding of divine power advocated the will to use nuclear weapons to destroy the modern enemy, just as God destroyed the Egyptians. Now, in 1961, *King of Kings* advocates peace and emphasizes Jesus' refusal to perform the same unleashing of divine power celebrated in the earlier film. Things had clearly changed in five years.

The policy of Massive Retaliation that Eisenhower and Dulles had introduced in 1954 emphasized the strength of nuclear weapons and the willingness to use them, as we discussed in chapter 4. While this was a tough-guy policy, part of the reason for its formulation was to redress an apparent flaw in the logic of containment employing only conventional weapons. The addition of the nuclear threat derived from the fact that, given the ability of the communist nations to engage in a potential large number of small wars of "national liberation," the cost in men and money of a policy of containment restricted to conventional weapons would be immense. Fighting small war after small war would quickly drain the United States and its allies of resources. More significantly, perhaps, the administration hoped to balance the nation's budget and to decrease the size of the military that had maintained its high numbers from the end of World War II in 1945 through the Korean War of 1950–1953. Reliance on nuclear weapons would help accomplish these latter two goals. If the United States increased both the number of bombs and the number of planes to deliver them, then the nation could significantly draw down the number of soldiers in the army, thereby reducing the enormous costs of salary, maintenance, and conventional weapons.

This shift was successful in reducing the budget. It was also successful in weapons development and delivery. The United States developed the hydrogen bomb, a weapon significantly more powerful than the atom bomb it had dropped on Hiroshima and Nagasaki during the war. Production began immediately. The United States had introduced a new bomber, the B-52, to deliver these weapons to their targets.

But after 1956, the Soviet Union began to leapfrog the United States. In 1957, the Soviets launched the first Intercontinental Ballistic Missile (ICBM) for delivering nuclear warheads, nearly two years ahead of the United States' own development of such a weapon. In the same year, the Soviets launched Sputnik, the first human-made satellite to orbit the earth. Its ominous radio-beeping, heard whenever it was over the United States, became a symbol of the Soviet threat. Khrushchev's notorious warning to America, "we will bury you," rang in American ears. To top it off, the CIA told Eisenhower that Soviet manufacturing of these bombs and rockets was proceeding rapidly and that the United States suffered from a "missile gap"; they had more than we did. It was not until the Kennedy years that it was discovered how exaggerated those numbers were.

In this context, it became clear that a nuclear first strike would not wipe out the Soviet enemy. No matter how much destruction the United States could rain down upon that country, the Soviet Union would retain a significant capacity—in both bombs and missiles—to launch a counter-attack. The destruction of Moscow and Leningrad would most assuredly result in the destruction of New York and Washington. Furthermore, the consequences of a nuclear strike were being brought home to the American republic. The new civil defense program's emphasis on how to avoid fallout—from teaching students to "duck and cover" to the building of fallout shelters—made it clear that wherever the weapons went off, those who survived would not escape scot-free.

So it is not surprising that by 1961, *King of Kings* advocates following the way of the Messiah of Peace, rather than that of Barabbas, the messiah of war. If this sounds like the abandonment of the notion of liberation, it is not. Barabbas is not the only parallel to Jesus appearing in *King of Kings*. John the Baptist also serves as a foil to Jesus. The film uses that foil to expand on the details of how citizens of oppressed nations should react against their subjugation, and expounds upon the type of liberation they should seek in the dangerous world of the early 1960s.

# John the Baptist and the Stalemate of Eastern Europe

The inaction of the United States, unwilling to risk war with the Soviets over the Hungarian uprising in 1956, showed the emptiness of the Eisenhower administration's refusal to accept the "enslavement" of Eastern Europe. This is what happened. First, Hungarian students and workers, dissatisfied with the policies of the communist government, staged a nationwide strike. The government attempted to regain control of the situation by replacing the prime minister with Imre Nagy on October 24. He worked to gain control of the situation by attempting to implement many of the strikers' demands. Unfortunately, there was little time, for the Soviet government was deciding whether to intervene. Nagy announced Hungary's withdrawal from the Warsaw Pact—the military alliance of Soviet-dominated, Eastern European nations—declared neutrality, and appealed to the United Nations. But time ran out. Russian troops entered Budapest on November 4, eliminated the opposition, removed Mr. Nagy, and tightened its control over the country.

An Eastern European country made a bid for freedom and the United States had done nothing to assist. Even conventional military intervention was out of the question, for the United States had no contingency plans for such a situation, had no troops strategically located to intervene, and indeed, had never considered such intervention likely. The brutality with which the Soviets crushed the uprising, though, angered and appalled the Western world, and the United States' lack of action disturbed many. It is possible to see in *King of Kings* a retrospective, positive reevaluation of the failure to act by the United States during the Hungarian revolt.

It is in this context that John the Baptist's tirades against Herod and the Romans in *King of Kings* should be seen. Unlike Jesus, John is not a quiet, peaceful prophet. He proclaims God's anger and wrath at the sin of

King Herod and his wife, whom Herod had enticed away from his brother. While John is happy to shout out the dire punishments that God has in store for the Romans, his main target is the puppet king and his family—rulers who represent Rome rather than the people they govern, much as the rulers of Eastern European nations in the 1950s were seen as Moscow's tools. At Herod's banquet welcoming Pilate, John's imprecations can be heard shouted to the crowd outside the palace.

> Behold the sign of the pagan.
> As God overthrew Sodom and Gomorrah,
> So shall He send hosts to destroy the idol worshippers.
> The day is coming when the sword shall descend upon her legions,
> Her mighty kings and princes shall grow feeble,
> Her stolen treasures made worthless,
> Her cities shall crumble into dust.
> We shall raise our voice, and be heard.

John's words are not the peaceful admonitions about a heavenly kingdom that Jesus teaches. He talks about the destruction of the empire. It is not surprising that Barabbas wants John on his side, to excite the crowd on his behalf.

Just as John's message differs from that of Jesus, so does his ultimate fate. While his message excites crowds, it ultimately results in his death and in his failure to make any progress toward conquering the Romans. Like Barabbas, he moves Rome neither a jot nor a tittle. Unlike Barabbas, he dies because of his opposition to the ruling powers. But unlike the death of Jesus, John's execution brings no triumph. Once again, the film makes the point that violence will not achieve liberation. In fact, if we recall John's status in the Gospels as the predecessor of Jesus, whom he recognizes as far greater than himself, we see that the film has exploited this supercession of John by Jesus to represent the superiority of a policy opposed to violent confrontation to one of military aggressivity.

# *King of Kings* and *The Ten Commandments*

John constitutes a foil not just for Jesus and Barabbas but also for the figure of Moses in *The Ten Commandments*. This becomes clear after

Herod has John brought into the palace and then reluctantly has him arrested. When he arrives in the palace, John seems lethargic as Pilate tries to engage him, but then comes alive as unbidden he talks to Salome and Herodias. The images of John responding to Pilate's air of command and then to Salome's peculiar blandishments remind the viewer of another bearded, long-haired prophet, namely, *The Ten Commandments'* Moses being entertained by the mature Nefretiri. Despite John's more youthful look, his shaggy mane recalls that of Moses, and his rather awkward manner of speaking to Pilate echoes Moses' stilted addresses before Pharaoh, in line with Exodus 4:10's characterization of him as "slow of speech and slow of tongue." Molded and shaped by his experience in the desert, John, like Moses, uses his words to further his aim of bringing the leaders of a subjugated nation to act to free Israel from the yoke of their conquerors.

As if John's parallel with Moses was not clear enough, *King of Kings* expands Salome's role far beyond that found in Scripture to emphasize key similarities with Nefretiri, especially Nefretiri's reaction to Moses as a prophet. Each woman shows a sensual, unholy fascination with the prophet, and uses her sensual influence on the man in an attempt to disconcert him. When John and Moses reject these advances, the women then use their power over their lord and ruler—Herod and Rameses, respectively—to try to bring about the prophet's death. In each case, they incite the ruler—a family member—to take on the task of killing the prophet against that ruler's intentions.

In *The Ten Commandments*, Rameses' pursuit of Moses and the Israelites results in Moses' calling on God's heavenly power and the obliteration of the entire Egyptian army. In *King of Kings*, John's head is served on a platter. The radically different fates of John and Moses encapsulate the differences between the two films. Moses draws down massive retaliation upon his enemies and preserves the chosen people. John is destroyed and superseded by one far greater: Jesus as the advocate of peace. If in *The Ten Commandments* the power to obliterate a tyrannical enemy is the very token of divine favor, in *King of Kings* the refusal to do so fulfills the same purpose. In the face of Soviet nuclear capacities this later film revises the earlier one's view of what constitutes the performance of God's will and defines the favored nation. If the United States, to the disappointment of many, did nothing to aid the Hungarian uprising, *King of Kings* endeavors to show that such a refusal of violence, far from constituting a failure of righteous will, in fact, is a demonstration of righteousness.

So if the countries of Eastern Europe were not to gain their freedom through rebellion, do they have hope for any freedom at all? Are they destined to remain enslaved and oppressed under communist tyranny? *King of Kings* answers yes, although in a way that would not have likely been convincing to citizens of Eastern Europe, had they ever seen the film. The answer was that they could be free within their prisons.

While it is true, as we argued above, that Jesus' words in this film are predominantly from Scripture, there are some lines and even scenes where Jesus speaks words that originate solely within the film. The largest of these added sequences is when Jesus appears before the centurion Lucius and asks to visit John in prison. When asked why, Jesus responds that he wishes to "free him within his cell." Lucius scoffs, saying, "Freedom? Behind stone walls?" To which Jesus calmly replies, "You are free to come and go as you please, and yet you are still a prisoner because you place faith in nothing but your sword." He thus indicates that freedom of movement—won by violence, weapons, and war—falls short of real freedom. Lucius recognizes that Jesus is speaking of a spiritual freedom, not a physical freedom, brought about by divine means, and he lets Jesus visit John.

Jesus' visit to John's cell is played like the film's scenes of healing. It begins when Jesus' shadow appears over John's hunched body, as it did over the sick in the healing scenes. Jesus utters John's name and then stretches out his hand to John. As the music echoes that of the triumphal moments of healing, the narration of the first healing scene is enacted, "It was the time of miracles and Jesus put forth his hand. . . . For there went virtue out of him, and healed them all." John asks for Jesus' blessing and although Jesus remains silent, the looks that pass between them indicate the virtue that sets John free. Jesus uses his divine power neither to break John out of prison, nor to give him a physical freedom (John remains not only in prison but also in chains), but to give him a freedom of spirit, a peace, a liberation that does not depend on location, ability to move, or even speech. Thus, in this place of imprisonment, *King of Kings* shows Jesus using his divine power not for destruction, death, or to force liberation, but peacefully to enact spiritual liberation. The scenario of winning freedom by force portrayed in *The Ten Commandments* is a choice, and one that Jesus himself chooses not to pursue.

In the end, *King of Kings*' answer to the question of pursuing freedom through use of the incredible, divinelike power of the nuclear bomb is the opposite answer to that given by *The Ten Commandments* five years earlier. Whereas *The Ten Commandments* portrayed the successful liberation that use of such weapons by the United States would bring about, with no downside for the victors, *King of Kings* strongly argues against such use. Through the foils of both Barabbas and John the Baptist, the film indicates that the use of violence—even that of violent language—leads to the failure to liberate the people. Jesus' choice to use his divine power peacefully, instead of for violence and rebellion, sends the strong message that the United States should choose against using violence to achieve its goals with regard to the Soviet Union and Eastern Europe.

*King of Kings* was oddly prescient in its stance on these two points. At the time of *King of Kings'* release, the administration of the new President John Kennedy attempted to invade and liberate Cuba, completing a plan devised and set in motion by the Eisenhower administration. It was a disaster—as predicted by this film.

A few months later, Cuba used the incident to persuade Russia to send missiles to Cuba to protect it. While Kennedy faced down the Soviets and forced them to remove the threat, the downside of nuclear weapons, and the importance of peace, as symbolized in *King of Kings*, became even more important in reality. Violence begets violence.

# Vignette

## *The Greatest Story Ever Told* (1965)

In many ways, this film broke new ground in the post–World War II period for films dealing with Scripture. It followed neither their genres nor their interests. Unlike *The Ten Commandments*, it did not add a romance into the narrative, following the biblical romance films. Unlike *King of Kings*, it was not an expanded Roman conversion film, with an added Roman character who becomes a Christian. Furthermore, it ignored issues of freedom and slavery, of nuclear power, of the Cold War.

*The Greatest Story Ever Told* instead aims to present a Christian picture of Jesus, one that sees Jesus as the founder of Christianity, as the first Christian, rather than the carrier of a secular agenda or even a Jew of his time. Jesus is the Son of God and the fulfiller of prophecy in this film, with the disciples, John the Baptist, some Pharisees, and even the High Priest emphasizing the point. Rather than avoiding miracles like *King of Kings*, *Greatest Story* puts them on screen front and center. They are witnessed not only by the audience but also by soldiers, priests, and Pharisees who report back to Jerusalem. The blind Nazarene who Jesus heals even follows him to Jerusalem, where he bears witness to Jesus' power.

The film opens with Jesus' birth and the citation of John chapter 1. Most scenes are seasoned with liberal Scripture quotations. This is done in a targumic fashion, however, for the Scripture passages are often not from the scene being enacted. John the Baptist speaks a lot of Old Testament prophecy, for example.

The film also targumically diverges from Scripture, in a way that often emphasizes Christian theology. Jesus tells Pilate that God loves him, for example, and that Pilate should search harder to find the one, true God. Nicodemus berates Caiaphas for holding an illegal trial. And the entire film aims at authenticity by opening and closing within the art of a church sanctuary. Some of the more unusual moments added into the story are John the Baptist trying to "baptize" the soldiers who arrest him, Pilate commanding Jesus' flogging and it not being carried out, Judas killing himself (as a sacrifice?) in the Temple's altar fire.

The primary villains of the film are Herod the Great and his son Herod Antipas. The killing of Bethlehem's children reveals Herod's cruelty, while the poor state of the Israelite people is laid at his son's feet. Rome takes over the country only to restore order, if not peace and prosperity. They fear Jesus as king, a point repeatedly emphasized, while the priests fear Jesus the messiah.

# Suggested Readings

Barton J. Bernstein and Allen J. Matusow, *The Truman Administration: A Documentary History* (New York: Harper and Row, 1966).

J. L. Gaddis, P. H. Gordon, E. R. May, and J. Rosenberg, eds., *Cold War Statesmen Confront the Bomb: Nuclear Diplomacy since 1945* (Oxford: Oxford University Press, 1999).

Deane Heller and David Heller, *John Foster Dulles: Soldier for Peace* (New York: Holt, Rinehart and Winston, 1960).

Bill Lomax, *Hungary 1956* (New York: St. Martin's Press, 1976).

Thomas W. Simons, Jr., *Eastern Europe in the Postwar World*, 2nd ed. (New York: St. Martin's Press, 1991).

W. Barnes Tatum, *Jesus at the Movies: A Guide to the First Hundred Years* (Santa Rosa, Calif.: Polebridge Press, 1997).

Burton H. Throckmorton, *Gospel Parallels: NRSV Edition*, 5th ed. (Nashville: Thomas Nelson, 1992).

Robert Torry, "The Wrath of God: Hollywood Religious Epics and American Cold War Policy," *Arizona Quarterly* 61:2 (2005): 67-86.

# CHAPTER 6

# The Accidental Superstar

Like Moses in *The Ten Commandments*, Jesus in *King of Kings* provided a religious authority to support the film's vision of a properly conducted resistance to tyranny, and therefore helped define an ideal American political establishment. The film's imagery and its use of classical and liturgical music is derived from centuries of Christian artistic tradition. *Jesus Christ, Superstar*—issued first as a two-disk rock-and-roll album in 1970, later performed as a play, and then as a film in 1973—ended all that. Here was a Jesus film that cared not a whit for tradition or approval by the church. Jesus represented a growing movement among young Americans. No longer quiet and respectful of their elders as they had been in the 1950s, many American youth had become rebellious, creating a distinct youth culture in contentious conflict with their parents' vision of America.

*Jesus Christ, Superstar*'s adoption of Jesus as an antiestablishment hero showed that this new youth culture differed from the older generation in not only politics and musical taste but also in the very thing that lay at the heart of society, namely, religious belief. Young people were not afraid to reenvision Jesus as a countercultural icon who opposed the very pillars of American postwar society. Even though this rock opera had been composed by two Englishmen—Andrew Lloyd Webber and Tim Rice—it spoke to American Baby Boomers. Initially a flop in England, the album sold over 4 million copies in the United States. When Director Norman Jewison filmed the movie in Israel in 1972, he tapped into the energy and

---

* Read Mark 14–16 and John 12–13, 18–21.

the contrarian nature of America's youth movement—about which Webber and Rice knew little—capturing in his portrayal of Jesus and his followers key aspects of the growing conflict with the older generation. Jesus appears as the original rock-and-roll rebel, struggling against the fear and corruption of the establishment of his time. In the film, Jesus and his followers bear the strengths and weaknesses of the youth movement and its rock-and-roll heroes—its superstars—while the priestly council engage in the immoral and underhanded activities that the establishment had used in its attempts to silence the young American rebels.

# Creating the 1960s Youth Culture

Where did this divide between old and young come from? It was little evident in 1961, but its roots lay in the success of postwar American political and social response to the challenges of the Cold War and the nuclear threat. During World War II, Americans had united against the common Nazi enemy. Men had gone off to fight, and women had gone to the factories producing the goods necessary for victory. In the years after the battle against the Nazis, the Cold War began. Even though men came home from the front, America found itself engaged in a new global fight against expanding communist influence. This new threat required new sacrifices; Americans had to work together to achieve victory. The threat of Soviet nuclear power, of its ICBMs, and of fallout from nuclear radiation brought Americans behind the leadership of their government. Postwar American society continued practicing the lessons of conformity, duty, and sacrifice they had learned during World War II through the 1950s and into the start of the 1960s.

When John F. Kennedy took office in 1961, the social landscape was changing. The children born during and after World War II were reaching the age of awareness. They had not experienced the threat that Germany and Japan posed; their childhood had been during the 1950s, when they knew the duties and conformity expected of them, but understood little of the events that motivated their parents to follow these social norms. Whereas World War II had a huge influence on their parents, the Cold War and the threat of nuclear weapons had little real effect on their lives. It had few violent events, and what violence there was took place outside the United States. In many ways, many American youth came to see it as an imaginary threat—a boogie man the government conjured up to promote social conformity. The Cuban Missile Crisis under Kennedy perhaps represented the last event of the Cold War that could have persuaded them the threat was imminent or real. Instead, it merely delayed the crisis for a couple of years.

As the young became an increasingly large proportion of American society—50 percent of Americans were under 30 in the early 1960s, but 50 percent were under 25 by the late 1960s—the prominence of the voices of the rebels influenced American society and created new cultural debates (Manchester, p. 1100). At first, the older generation saw them as ungrateful; the decades of sacrifice that the older generation had undergone to preserve freedom and democracy had resulted in offspring who were disrespectful, unruly, and unmindful of the "truths" by which their elders lived. By the early 1970s, many members of the older generation saw the members of this youth movement as perhaps a greater threat to their way of life than communist expansion.

When President Nixon took office in 1968, he inaugurated a highly contentious period of generation conflict. Many young people returned the elder generation's dislike by seeing them as corrupt and fearful, as preaching social unity while hypocritically oppressing and excluding those who differed from the norm. Democracy and free speech may have been the watchwords of the postwar generation, but they were seemingly practiced more in their absence than in their presence. In other words, many youth saw themselves as promoting a true society of peace and brotherhood against the corrupt, win-at-all-costs philosophy of the establishment.

The split between the younger and older generations came about through many complex and complicated reasons. For our analysis of *Jesus Christ, Superstar*, let us focus on three key issues.

First, there was the rise of the youth culture. It may have begun with the enormous popularity of rock-and-roll music. It was loud and often raucous, and accompanied by new styles of dancing, which were often deemed lewd and lascivious by its adult critics. New styles of dress came into fashion, styles that displayed the body rather than covering it modestly. The introduction of the birth control pill in 1961 led to increased sexual activity both within marriage and outside of it. Sexual experimentation became a regular part of college life. Psychedelic drugs and other chemical means of stimulation were increasingly used among the youth; smoking marijuana seemingly became as common as drinking beer.

The essential image of these changes was known as the "hippie." Hippies not only listened to rock and roll, dressed in the new clothing styles, and carried on other practices, but they also experimented with new forms of social organization. Some hippies joined together in communes, where they governed themselves in an egalitarian fashion, theoretically treating men and women of all ethnic backgrounds equally. Peace and love were the watchwords of 1967's "Summer of Love" in San Francisco's Haight-Ashbury district, while the Woodstock music festival in August 1968 in upstate New York became a powerful symbol for the successful practice of brotherhood-sisterhood among the youth.

College-age youth increasingly identified themselves with this movement, listening to the music and selecting other aspects of dress, behavior, and belief as they wished. Many saw themselves as nonconformist, as rejecting the social norms of their elders. Their elders saw their calls for peace and love as naïve, and when some young people turned to social action, calling for honesty in political affairs and governance, the establishment began to see them as threatening. The widespread use of illegal drugs on campus brought about police attempts at enforcement. The hippies responded by seeing the police as the establishment's enforcers of conformity. They called the policemen "pigs." The link between rock and roll and illegal drugs reinforced the older generations' already negative views of the music. In the end, the youth began to view the older generation as corrupt and as attempting to enforce outmoded laws with force. These actions undermined the ruling class—the establishment—in the view of many young people, and made it morally bankrupt.

Second, the Vietnam War became increasingly contentious as it wore on. President Eisenhower, at first wary of involvement, began U.S. support of the South Vietnamese regime in the late 1950s. Kennedy continued it and Johnson expanded it, at the cost of his hopes for another term in office. After 1968, President Nixon began to withdraw U.S. troops and to encourage South Vietnamese troops to do the fighting. These presidents all saw Vietnam within the larger context of the U.S. Cold War strategy of containing communist expansion, a strategy that had begun after World War II. In the 1950s, China and North Korea had been lost to the communists, and they were determined that Vietnam would not suffer the same fate. The older generation understood that logic and largely agreed.

As more and more young men were drafted for service in Vietnam, the younger generation developed their own view of the matter. They saw the Vietnam War by itself, without its Cold War trappings. By 1968, Vietnam became the longest-running American war—a conflict in its own right.

They furthermore saw that it was the young men who were being sent to die there. Indeed, in the nine years prior to the United States' withdrawal in 1973, an average of nearly 100 American soldiers a week were being killed in Vietnam (Manchester, pp. 1125-26). Was the war worth it?

Increasingly, the young people's answer was no. The regime of South Vietnam was seen as corrupt. The strategy of the U.S. administration and its generals was not to win the war, but to fight to a stalemate. Hundreds of thousands of troops were tied up in Vietnam, and the students could not see it as a threat to the United States. The massacre of hundreds of women and children at the village of My Lai in 1968 merely gave solid evidence to the young people's belief that the war was accomplishing nothing except the death of innocent Vietnamese and young Americans.

America's youth, led by college students, did not take these developments quietly. Before the end of the Johnson administration, college campuses were being convulsed by antiwar riots. Students and other protesters marched on Washington calling for an end to the war. In 1969, a small antiwar demonstration at Kent State University in Ohio was fired upon by National Guardsmen. Four students were killed—including a ROTC cadet—and nine more were wounded. Many voices in the media said the students had brought it on themselves. Students across the United States saw the killings and the reaction as confirming their picture of the older generation and particularly its political representatives as using their control of law enforcement and the media to wage a corrupt battle against their opponents in the youth movement. Trials of radical antiwar protesters—such as the so-called Chicago Seven, the Seattle Seven, and the Kansas City Four—showed government prosecution to be inept and resulted in the acquittal of the defendants (Manchester, p. 1208).

Third, underlying and preceding both these developments was the civil rights movement, whose beginning is often identified with the 1955 Birmingham Bus Boycott. The struggle for equal rights under the law and for equal educational, employment, and residential rights is too complicated to go into in any detail here, but it pitted blacks against the white ruling establishment. The more the whites worked to keep down blacks—with mayors, police chiefs, and even governors acting demonstrably outside the law—the more the establishment was shown to be corrupt and self-serving. As the civil rights movement spawned the women's rights movement, this negative character was shown to be even more far-reaching in American society.

In response, the youth movement became increasingly egalitarian, welcoming members of all races, and treating men and women with equal rights—at least in theory. It also developed contempt for the established political order, seeing its moral pronouncements about conforming to social norms and fulfilling duties as indicating the bankruptcy of those very norms.

All three prongs—rock-and-roll culture, antiwar agitation, and civil rights expectations—came together to make up the youth movement of the 1960s and 1970s. It is in this light in 1973 that *Jesus Christ, Superstar* came to the screen. Its identification of Jesus and his followers with the youth movement gave a powerful new interpretation to Jesus' founding of Christianity, one that overcame the cooption of Christianity into the ruling establishment and laid out a foundation for seeing it as the underpinnings of the youth rebellion against the establishment of the time.

# Disciples and Priests

The first scene with Jesus and his followers, who apparently consist of the disciples and a group of women, shows them in a large, desert cave. Dressed in a variety of hippie clothes, they relax together, eating, chatting, flirting. They portray the comfortable feel of a hippie commune, living together with an egalitarian sharing of brotherly/sisterly love. Despite the film's immediate portrayal of disagreements between Judas and Jesus—which apparently arise from Judas's new clarity of mind—it appears that Judas has been an accepted and equal member of the group. The depiction of Jesus and his followers as representative of the current youth culture is clear.

*Superstar* portrays a cleaned-up version of the youth culture. Although clearly involved in group living and wearing hippie clothing—to say nothing of the rock-and-roll music—the elements of youth culture most offensive to outsiders are gone. There are no drugs and no sex. Although some of the odd clothing shows a great deal of skin, none of it is of a titillating nature—not even a glimpse or two of cleavage. Indeed, the most skin is shown by the bare-chested male soldiers, and by the decadent groupies of King Herod. Jesus and his followers could be characterized as "Jesus Freaks," the 1960s slang for hippies who "got high on Christ" rather than drugs.

The priests—High Priest Caiaphas, his assistant Annas, and the council— represent the corrupt establishment who oppose Jesus and his followers.

On the one hand, they are responsible for law and order, and provide political leadership under the Romans. Their largest concern is to enforce the social norms of their society, that is, to keep order. Those norms are part of a hierarchically organized society for which they serve as the top rung (under Rome). They find Jesus threatening because he and his disciples are straying from those norms in a rather public way. Caiaphas even thinks Jesus aims to set himself up as a king. On the other hand, their own actions reveal a corrupt, even immoral side. When Jesus visits the temple, he finds their hypocrisy. The temple market not only sells goats, vegetables, and clothing, but also is a haven for drug pushers and prostitutes. Most damning, their market does a roaring trade in arms sales to zealots and other rebels, despite the priests' concern about not provoking the Romans. Finally, they subject Jesus to unwarranted persecution, arrest him on trumped-up charges, and arrange for the Romans to kill him—an act of murder.

The key differences between the disciples and the priests point to the disciples' role as representing the current society's youth and establishment. The priests emphasize discipline, duty, and sacrifice. None of these seem important to Jesus and his followers. In their political role, the priests look beyond themselves to (fore)see larger threats to them and the nation, while the disciples seem to focus on themselves. When the disciples try to find out what's happening, Jesus tells them to focus on the present: "Save tomorrow for tomorrow. Think about today instead."

Indeed, the discussion among the priests shows them as rational thinkers—they think ahead and make plans to address the problems they see coming. By contrast, the disciples appear rather muddled. As they sing, "What's the buzz? Tell me what's a'happenin," their voices sound fuzzy, as if they don't really care. They come across as deadened and somewhat dull. Jesus responds to them by refusing to answer, and they give up, seemingly not interested. They do not plan ahead or anticipate problems, much like hippies.

Finally, the priests operate by fear, even among themselves. As Annas advised Caiaphas, "Frighten them [i.e., the council], or they won't see." In this they were much like the White House of the time. As Maine's Senator Edmund Muskie observed on election eve in 1970, Nixon practiced the "politics of fear" (Manchester, p. 1220). Jesus and his followers, by contrast, practiced love for each other, soothing one another, and trying to comfort each other when needed. This is of course the Woodstock ideal.

These identifications between groups in the film and in current society is so patently obvious that it seems unnecessary to argue. But the need to do so comes in part from the question of whether the film's presentation of the priesthood is anti-Semitic. The concern comes of course from the history of the Crucifixion story in inciting Christians of different centuries to persecute Jews. The main problem is that the Passion story—the narrative of Jesus' last week on earth—inherently puts the Jewish crowd and the priests in a bad light. This said, *Jesus Christ, Superstar* plays on that less than many tellings of the Passion, both before and since. This is because *Superstar*'s priests are so transparently a portrayal of the establishment enemies of the current youth culture. This impression is enhanced by their dress. The tall, black hats and the robes bear no resemblance to Jewish clothing in modern or even medieval times. The characters, physiques, and personalities of the figures fit no Jewish stereotypes of recent times. In short, they are generalized villains, with little to identify them specifically as Jews.

# Judas, the Great Betrayer

Out of the anonymous group of Jesus' disciples, one stands out. This is Judas, who appears from the start of the film as different from the other followers of Jesus. As he sings in the first line of the film's opening song, "My mind is clearer now. At last, all too well, I can see where we all soon will be." Judas exhibits none of the befuddlement found among the other disciples. They remain "blind, too much heaven on their minds." Judas can look into the future and anticipate coming events. He sees the coming threat. "We are occupied," he tries to remind Jesus, "Have you forgotten how put down we are. And they'll crush us if we go too far." And in a later song he criticizes Jesus and Mary, trying to convince them that it would take very little for their enemies to convict them.

The threat Judas sees is Jesus' increasing visibility. As Jesus gets more popular, he is noticed more and more. Some of that attention is what Jesus wants, but other attention will be less welcome. So Judas criticizes Jesus directly, trying to persuade him to be less flamboyant about his breaking of social norms, trying to persuade him not to go against his own teachings. He wants Jesus to follow the society's norms more closely. Judas sees Jesus' involvement with Mary Magdalene as the most threatening. Her occupation as a prostitute makes her a dangerous person to be around; Jesus' receiving of her attention suggests that he is violating the brotherly/sisterly love of the group. When Jesus rejects Judas's advice, Judas tries another approach, criticizing Mary for the waste of expensive perfume. It could have been sold, he suggests—in line with Jesus' teaching—and the money given to the poor. When Jesus rebuts this warning from Judas as well, Judas walks away from the group to be alone, pondering what to do to fix the situation.

Caiaphas the High Priest provides an important parallel to Judas. Among the priests, he is the one who sees the threat of Jesus most clearly. In his mind, it is Jesus' failure to follow social norms that endangers Israel, especially as Jesus becomes more and more popular and is watched by many more eyes. Caiaphas's talk with Annas early in the film helps him decide how to fix the situation, namely, by taking steps to ensure that "Jesus must die."

The parallel between Judas and Caiaphas reveals what has happened to Judas. His clear-sightedness makes him like the establishment. His new vision no longer allows him to be part of Jesus' followers—to be part of the youth movement. Instead, Judas thinks and acts like Caiaphas, like the leader of the establishment. As part of Jesus' band, Judas was accepted and welcomed as an equal. If we believe Judas's claim to have been Jesus' "right hand man all along," then he was a trusted advisor in Jesus' inner circle.

Even though Judas's new vision distances him from Jesus' other followers, it does not bring him closer to the establishment. When Judas goes to betray Jesus to the priests, they do not respect him. They treat him with arrogance and contempt, even as he agrees to deliver Jesus to them. After the civil rights and black power movements of the 1960s, the image of Judas—played by a black actor—kneeling before a group of mocking white men sends a strong message of continuing oppression. They toy with him. Persuading Judas to take money for his information, even though he does not wish to, they drop the money bag on the ground and he must grovel for it. It is in this position of submission that he utters the words that betray Jesus. The imagery indicates the complete contempt with which the priests hold Judas. The egalitarian character of the youth movement has not reached them. Despite the civil rights gains of black Americans, the establishment does not recognize them.

After the priests convict Jesus and send him to Pilate, Judas returns the money in remorse. The priests do not receive it and again treat him contemptuously. In his last set of lines, as he runs toward his suicide, Judas sings, "My mind is in darkness." Judas has lost his establishment-like clarity and instead has returned to the youth movement, become again one of Jesus' followers. In a reprise of Mary's song, Judas sings, "I don't know how to love him. I don't know why he moves me. . . . Does he love, does he love me too? Does he care for me?"

Ironically, Judas can now truly see what has happened, "God, I've been used. . . . I'll never know why you chose me for your crime, your foul, bloody crime." He sees that God has used him, and has made him betray Jesus' pure youth movement.

# Mary the Comforter

Mary Magdalene is a main character in *Jesus Christ, Superstar*, along with Jesus and Judas. Even though the canonical Gospels, true to the social circumstances of the time, never designate women as disciples, in the film, Mary portrays the ultimate disciple. She not only personifies the key values of the Jesus movement—love and devotion—but she also symbolizes what it means to join that movement and to leave one's former life behind. She represents the changes that conversion brings.

This increased visibility of Mary parallels the increasing roles of women in American society. Title VII of the 1964 Civil Rights Act prohibited employment discrimination on the basis of sex and enabled many women to move into jobs formerly barred to them, while Title IX of the 1972 Education Codes did the same for women's access to higher education, including access to training in Christian seminaries.

At the most fundamental level, Mary symbolizes the brotherly-sisterly love that constitutes the core value of Jesus and his movement. She is concerned about Jesus and the disciples, trying at different times to comfort Jesus, Judas, and Peter. Finding herself twice in the middle of disputes between Jesus and Judas, she tries to help settle them. As one of Jesus' key followers, she takes the initiative with Jesus and others to ensure the smooth interactions of the group. Unlike the disciples, who seem to be in a constant state of lethargy, she knows what to do and does it. Even Jesus notices this when she wipes his hot forehead with cool water. Jesus praises her actions, identifying her as the one person who is meeting his needs.

A closer look at Mary shows that she also symbolizes devotion—in particular, devotion to Jesus. All her main songs and most of her actions center on her relationship to Jesus. She is devoted to him, caring for him, feeding him, and comforting him. To make it clear that this is not just infatuation or man-woman love, she sings the song, "I don't know how to love him." Despite her expertise in "making love," what she feels for Jesus and her interaction with him is new to her. The song is part of her working through what this new relationship is and a step in defining who (and what, perhaps) Jesus is.

As a character in the film, then, Mary represents all new devotees to Jesus. Her alternating acts of devotion and wonderings about how to relate to Jesus symbolize for the film the process new converts go through as they become more involved in their worship of and devotion to Jesus.

Finally, Mary's character helps define what it means to be a convert. The two face-to-face arguments between Jesus and Judas actually center on Mary's standing within the movement. In the first argument, Judas says to Jesus, "It seems to me a strange thing, mystifying. That a man like you can waste his time with women of her kind. . . . It's not that I object to her profession, but she doesn't fit in well with what your teachings say." Judas does not see the change that her conversion has brought about; he sees only her "profession" of prostitute and does not understand that that profession no longer defines who she is. Jesus responds by saying, "She's with me now," indicating that as one of his followers, she—like Judas himself—should be defined by that category.

In the second argument, Judas objects to Mary anointing Jesus with expensive oil. The oil should have been sold and the money donated to the poor. Jesus' response is that his time with them is limited and Mary's act is a worthy use of that time. In other words, it is an act of devotion and worship. Anointing is also a way of recognizing the unique status of an individual. In ancient Israel, a man became a king by being anointed, and Jesus' possible kingship is one of the concerns of the film. Furthermore, the word "messiah" means "anointed one" and so Mary's act likewise indicates Jesus' place in God's grand scheme. At the same time, the Gospel's suggestion that this is preparation for burial, although unacknowledged, may be also in play (Mark 14:8).

A comparison with Mary reveals key aspects of Judas's actions. As Judas finds himself being distanced from Jesus because of his new ability "to see where we all soon will be," Mary is growing closer to Jesus. If Mary is replacing Judas at Jesus' right hand, then some of Judas's actions and words may be inspired by jealousy. Certainly both love Jesus. Mary loves Jesus with the spiritual love that characterizes his followers, and, by implication, that provides the symbolic foundation of the American youth movement. Judas also loves Jesus, but given his change at the start of the film, he now does it through the rational, thinking love of the establishment. Finally, both Mary and Judas want to go back to the beginning of the movement. Judas is uncomfortable with the god-talk that is being applied to Jesus. He does not like how the movement has changed. He is afraid it will end, and so, ironically, acts to bring about its end. Mary, when faced with the end as Jesus walks to his trial, sings, "Could we start again, please." She does not want it to stop.

Mary's embodiment of love, Jesus' core teaching, ultimately becomes a criticism of the modern, Christian church. The love and devotion that Mary gives to Jesus and by which the Jesus movement is symbolized is identified with the love that ideally guides the youth movement. If love is in the youth movement as its core value, then that means it no longer resides in the church, which is part of the corrupt establishment. According to the film, then, the existence of the youth movement shows the failure of the church to adhere to what is supposed to be its core value.

# The Accidental Jesus

What is it about Jesus that makes him a superstar? Is he God? Is it God's plan for him, or his own plans? Is it his important teachings? These possibilities comprise some of the usual answers given to the initial question, but none of them fit this film. There is no clear indication of Jesus' divinity. He does no miracles—other films' convention for showing divine power—not even when faced by a crowd of sick people who need healing. Jesus seems to have no plans and no goals—one of Judas's criticisms. And Jesus never seems to teach; he gives no important message. There is nothing about him that would give him an unusual standing, let alone that of a superstar.

The short answer is that people think he is a superstar, and therefore he is. The long answer is that Jesus is the target of other peoples' expectations, and it is those expectations that shape him. Jesus himself not only lacks goals, plans, and message, he lacks initiative. Jesus initiates few of the events or even verbal exchanges in the film, not even the ones he participates in. He reacts to people around him, rather than charting his own course among them and into his future. When he mentions "plans and forecasts," he does not seem to understand them. When his disciples ask, "When do we ride into Jerusalem?" Jesus seems unable to give an answer. The action in *Jesus Christ, Superstar* is rarely initiated by Jesus himself. Other people see Jesus and they place their expectations on him. And then they act on those expectations. It is their actions that move the plot forward.

But Jesus is not a blank slate on which people can project their thoughts willy-nilly. Their actions relating to him nearly always bring them to a point where what he is places a wall before their expectations and they can go no further. When Simon the Zealot, for instance, tries to persuade Jesus to act as an anti-Roman rebel and then become a great leader, Jesus quickly makes clear that he does not intend to go in that direction. Simon sings, "But add a touch of hate of Rome. . . . You'll get the power and the glory." Jesus answers him by saying, "Neither you Simon nor the fifty thousand . . . understand what power is. Understand what glory is." Similarly, the sick and wounded who crawl like spiders out of the rocks seeking healing from Jesus are refused.

But it is the expectations from more central characters that are the most telling. Mary gets closer to Jesus than anyone else in the film. As she holds him, comforts him, and tucks him into bed, she discovers he is not like any other man she has ever known. Her broad experience should have given her insight into all the ways men can be men, yet Jesus is something and someone she has not experienced. Indeed, he is so different that she cannot adapt her knowledge and skills to the situation. Her lack of understanding indicates that she has hit that wall where she realizes her expectations do not fit the reality of who Jesus is. Just what that reality is, however, remains unclear.

Judas opens the film with a song relating his disappointed expectations. Jesus is not who he was; he has become something that Judas dislikes and fears. Judas is afraid this new Jesus will cause their downfall. Judas then acts on that belief, at first trying to persuade Jesus to act differently—twice by criticizing Mary's caring treatment of Jesus. When his criticisms fail, he decides to go to the priests. Although what he intends is unclear, the handing over of Jesus to crucifixion is not his goal. In the end, Judas realizes that his perception of his role, based on his second set of mistaken expectations for Jesus, has been wrong as well.

Finally, the film's central plot centers around Caiaphas's expectation that Jesus will cause problems with Rome, perhaps "our elimination because of one man." After the arrest, Caiaphas tells Judas, "What you have done will be the saving of Israel." In Caiaphas's view, Jesus' rising popularity and visibility—particularly if they see Jesus as claiming the kingship—will cause the Romans to increase their oppression of the people Israel. So Caiaphas's expectations—and his expectations of Roman expectations of Jesus—cause him to act to eliminate Jesus, through arrest, trial before the council, and then transmitting him to Pilate for crucifixion. It is perhaps only Caiaphas's expectations that spawn actions that do not provoke a realization of the incorrectness of those expectations.

To all of these approaches, Jesus merely reacts. When Judas criticizes him, Jesus criticizes him back. When Mary comforts him, Jesus accepts comfort. When Caiaphas seeks his arrest, he allows it. When Pilate questions him, Jesus is either silent or complaining. With none of these characters does Jesus initiate action or speech. So the film's movement takes place through the actions of others with regard to Jesus and his reaction to those actions.

Jesus just goes with the flow. He does not attempt to set his own course or even to seek a clear understanding of the course he is on. He seems content to drift along, reacting to those around him. In the end, after he prays in the Garden of Gethsemane that the cup of his death be taken from him, he agrees to die. This is a grudging acceptance. He does not agree happily, but seems resigned to it. He has been boxed in by the actions of others, and at this point, when he finally tries to resist the path he is on, it is too late. He observes, "Everything is fixed, and [he] can't change it."

# The Accidental Teacher and Targumic Interpretation

Jesus' accidental character is borne out by the film's approach to his teachings, as indicated through targumic analysis. Since *Jesus Christ, Superstar* does not appeal to a faithful approach to Scripture as a means of gaining authority, there has been little need to invoke the targumic method for that purpose. Only occasionally does a statement of Jesus bear a literal relationship to its Gospel source. One of the few examples in this film takes place as Jesus begins to overturn the market tables in the temple. He sings, following Matthew 21:13, "My temple shall be a house of prayer, but you have made it a den of thieves."

A targumic analysis of the way the film's other sayings differ from those of the Gospels reveals a consistent shift. In places where the Gospels present Jesus' sayings as thoughtful teachings, *Jesus Christ, Superstar* changes them into offhand comments made on the spur of the moment. They are not inspired by a message that Jesus wishes to impart, but by other emotions. In the Sermon on the Mount, for instance, Jesus compares human needs to the beauty in which God clothes the lilies. This observation concludes with Matthew 6:34, "Therefore do not be anxious about tomorrow, for tomorrow will be anxious for itself. Let the day's own trouble be sufficient for the day." In *Superstar*, this teaching becomes part of Jesus' refusal to inform his disciples about their future activities. The disciples repetitively sing, "What's the buzz? Tell me what's a'happenin'." Jesus, plainly annoyed, tries to silence them by singing the following (Matthew 6:34): "Why should you want to know? Don't you mind about the future. Don't you try to think ahead. Save tomorrow for tomorrow. Think about today instead."

Similarly, the Gospels present the Last Supper as the time when Jesus teaches the disciples about communion. In the film, this is a moment when Jesus gives vent to his worry about his forthcoming death and his disciples' apparent insensitivity to him. Jesus sings, "For all you care, this wine could be my blood. For all you care, this bread could be my body." (Compare Matt. 26:26-28.)

The negative cast of Jesus' offhand remarks is evident well before the evening of his death. At one point, Mary Magdalene tries to calm Jesus for sleep by anointing him with oil. Judas criticizes her by saying she wasted the expensive ointment instead of using it to help the poor. He then wonders at what the 300 pieces of silver that it might have been sold for might have helped with, singing, "People who are starving, people who are hungry. They matter more than your feet and hair." Judas's words emphasize his concern for people who are poor, suggesting that Jesus has traded one night's comfort for many days of food for several people. *Superstar*'s scene draws upon the three Gospels containing the story: Matthew 26:6-13, Mark 14:3-9, and John 12:1-8. In the Gospels, Jesus' response is, "For you always will have the poor with you, and whenever you will, you can do good to them; but you will not always have me. She has done what she could; she has anointed my body beforehand for burying" (Mark 14:7-8). In this passage, Jesus calmly looks ahead to his death and sees the anointing as part of his preparation for his crucifixion and burial; it is appropriate to anoint him. Once he is gone, Jesus says, the poor will still be around to be helped. *Superstar* takes out the reference to death and instead enhances the contrast between the poor and Jesus, almost to the extent of denigrating the poor.

> Surely you're not saying we have the resources to save the poor from their lot. There will be poor always, pathetically struggling. Look at the good things you've got. Think while you still have me. Move while you still see me. You'll be lost, and you'll be sorry when I'm gone.

Jesus' comments have now become a disparagement of being able to help the poor, and an insult to them "pathetically struggling." In contrast, Jesus here sees no help for the disciples. When Jesus leaves they will not know what to do. Taken with the comments from the Last Supper and elsewhere in the film, Jesus here sees the failure of his movement when he is gone. The meaning of the anointing is missing.

## Jesus the Superstar

So how does Jesus become a superstar, according to *Jesus Christ, Superstar*? The answer is through acclamation. Jesus is not a superstar because of any divine status, choice by God, or even good planning on his part. Instead, it is a concatenation of circumstances. People flock to him for their own reasons. Simon is looking for a rebel leader, the sick and poor are looking for healing, the disciples are looking for fame. ("Then when we retire, we can write the Gospels, so they'll still talk about us when we've died.") The more people come to Jesus, the more popular he is.

The popularity results in his death when Caiaphas and Judas, but not Jesus himself, decide that Jesus' popularity is threatening. Jesus' triumphal entrance into Jerusalem, where the crowd carries him standing above them (not on a donkey), coupled with his rejection of Caiaphas's advice to calm the crowd, seals his fate.

Jesus' condemnation secures his superstar status. Before Jesus is even nailed to the cross, the sequence of the story is interrupted by a flashy, now-dead Judas descending from heaven (or at least the sky) on a cross. In a lively song-and-dance number, Judas proclaims Jesus a superstar, but then asks, "Who are you? What have you sacrificed?" Neither the song nor Jesus provides an answer. What is clear, however, is that his "death would be a record breaker" and ensure his permanent superstardom. Although the film gives no resurrection, this scene functions as a resurrection preview, with the transformation of filthy, wounded Jesus and his ruined clothes into a whole and healed body, clean skin, shining hair, and gleaming white robes. Certainly this constitutes an image of a heavenly, resurrected Jesus.

Jesus is a superstar not because of anything he does, but because of what is done to him. Others put their expectations on him and act in relationship to him because of those expectations. They cheer him, love him, condemn him, betray him, comfort him, show willingness to fight for him, and, ultimately, kill him. They do this not because the film shows something inherent in Jesus that causes this, but in reaction to each others' expectations and actions. If the crowd did not adulate him, then the priests would not have sought his death. If Judas had not started seeing Jesus with establishment eyes, then he would not have distanced himself from Jesus.

Ironically, Jesus' passive character in these circumstances reinforces his identification with the youth movement, and their legitimation. He is a Jesus who "goes with the flow," who moves with the crowd, who fits into the laid-back nature of the 1960s peace-and-love emphasis of the youth, or at least its mythology. The movement is, after all, without direction and decentralized. The goal is not to accomplish anything, but to enjoy life. By contrast, Jesus' seemingly directionless character undercuts the notion of Jesus as the pillar of the Christian church. The church has become part of the establishment, which has plans and goals. This Jesus does not, and thus cannot stand as the central foundation of the church. In this portrayal, then, the church's image of Jesus is illegitimate, as are they and their establishment allies. *Superstar* thus breaks the establishment's use of Jesus for legitimation; to follow Jesus does not require one to follow the establishment.

So in the end, who is this Jesus people follow? The film, having indicated its criticism of the church and its established positions, resists providing what it views as an inevitably restrictive vision—one that could ossify into precisely the kind of orthodoxy the film laments.

# Vignette

## *Godspell* (1973)

Like *Superstar*, *Godspell* moved from album to play to film, all the time reflecting the antiestablishment character of American youth culture of the sixties and early seventies. This is immediately obvious in the rock-and-roll music, and in the dress of characters, which blends hippie fashions, clown costumes, and, surprisingly, vaudeville styles. This last style is significant, for the film constitutes less a connected narrative than a vaudeville review, rotating from song-and-dance routines, to jokes, to story sketches—often with a vaudeville flavor. Furthermore, with the exception of Jesus and Judas/John the Baptist, there are no fixed roles; the actors seemingly play characters on an *ad hoc* basis.

John the Baptist opens the movie, calling the other characters out of their nine-to-five jobs in crowded New York City. As he baptizes them, the crowds disappear; until the film's closing seconds, the people are missing. The ten players dance, prance, and sing through an empty New York, including one dance routine on top of the World Trade Center; New York is a playground rather than a place of business. Each song, skit, or interaction relates to an event or parable in the Gospel of Matthew.

The most evident and continuous feature of the film is the exuberant joy that the players exhibit throughout; they have become like little children. The few moments when their smiles disappear are made more terrible by that sudden absence. Jesus' "death" on a fence at the film's end is the height of this. But as the players (disciples?) take him down and carry him away, the joy, the singing, and the dancing returns—a display in honor of Jesus suggesting resurrection, if not of the body then certainly of his spirit within them.

# Suggested Readings

Morris Dickstein, *Gates of Eden: American Culture in the Sixties* (Cambridge, Mass.: Harvard University Press, 1997).

William Manchester, *The Glory and the Dream: A Narrative History of America, 1932–1972* (New York: Bantam, 1984).

Michael Walsh, *Andrew Lloyd Webber* (New York: Harry N. Abrams, 1989).

# CHAPTER 7

# Tormenting Christ

In 325 CE at the Council of Nicea, the first churchwide convention to decide official Christian doctrine, one of the most hotly debated questions concerned the nature of Jesus. Was he human, God, or both? The Council decided he combined both natures, and church leaders spent the next few centuries formulating an orthodox definition of that divine/human interaction, while rejecting alternate descriptions.

That theological explanation of who Jesus was and how he combined the human and the divine has long been settled, but the film *The Last Temptation of Christ* (1988) raises again the question of Jesus' dual character. This time the focus is not on theology, but on psychology. The film seeks to investigate what kind of personality arises from someone who combines God and human within themselves. *The Last Temptation* answers this question by portraying a Jesus whose personality is divided and unstable. His human side experiences the divine as voices, as an eagle that digs its claws into his head, and as visions that make him scream at night. The film's plot follows how these two aspects of Jesus' character learn to exist in harmony and to work together.

Although the answers *Last Temptation* gives to the question of Jesus' personality belong primarily in the realm of psychology, they cannot avoid having theological implications. This is because the character of Jesus is inseparably linked to humanity's salvation. The early church struggled with the question of Jesus' nature because the answer determined the type of salvation Jesus brought to humankind, or even whether he could bring salvation at all. In the church's view, the success of salvation depended on who Jesus was.

One view of Christianity's mission of salvation is to rescue all human beings from the punishment that their sins deserve, and to give them the heavenly reward of which sin had deprived them. The punishment consists of eternal torment in hell, and the reward is eternal life in the paradise of heaven. According to the theology of Original Sin, all humans are born sinful and hence are condemned to hell. Their sinful nature comes from Adam's disobedience in the Garden of Eden. God placed the man he created, Adam, in the garden and allowed him to eat of any plant that grew there, with only one exception, the fruit of the Tree of the Knowledge of Good and Evil. Then a snake appeared and through temptation, persuaded Adam and Eve to eat that tree's fruit, usually symbolized as an apple. By this act, the doctrine of Original Sin states, the archetypal first couple brought sin into the world and condemned all their descendants to be born in sin. After death, humans were no longer eligible for heaven, but were destined for hell.

Medieval Christianity saw two tempters symbolized in this story. It viewed the snake as Satan, the Great Tempter, but also cast the Eve (representing all women) in that role, sometimes even equating her with Satan. On his famous fresco covering the ceiling of the Sistine Chapel, for instance, Michelangelo painted the snake with a woman's head and torso. Eve's tempting of Adam, reinforced by the effect the female body has on men, led some theologians to view her and her female descendants as sources of sin and evil.

To save humanity from its condemned situation, the doctrine of Original Sin presents Jesus as the Second Adam. He came into the world to free humanity from the sin that arose from the actions of the First Adam. Jesus' death and resurrection is understood as a sacrifice that atones for the sins of everyone, frees them from their sinful state, and makes them eligible to enter heaven.

The identification of Jesus as the Second Adam sets up a theological problem for understanding Jesus' character. Jesus' suffering and death redeems humanity from their sin, but just how does that work? While this question cannot be answered fully—it is, after all, a mystery of the church—the key lies in the combination of divine and human in Jesus. Because he is human, Jesus can take on humanity's sin, and, because he is divine, he can distribute redemption from that sin to all people. The problem is this: redemption comes from Jesus' death, but in a monotheistic religion like Christianity, God cannot die, for that would destroy God's eternal character. To address this difficulty, Christianity began to develop the concept of God as the Trinity, the so-called Three-in-One. In brief, this is the belief that God's one essence has three persons: God the Father, God the Son (Jesus), and God the Holy Spirit. So, the answer to the question of whether God could die is that God the Father did not die, but Jesus the God.

# Human and/or Divine

The doctrine of the Trinity did not arise full-fledged, but came about through decades of debate and the elimination of several alternatives. A brief examination of some of these theological attempts to balance Jesus' humanity and divinity, while preserving Christianity's monotheistic character and Jesus' salvific act, provides a comparative perspective on how *Last Temptation* performs its psychological inquiry.

Some approaches took the easy way out of this question; they simply decided that there was only one nature in Jesus. The Monarchian Modalists (ca. 200 CE) held that Jesus was part of a unified godhead. God the Father, God the Son, and God the Holy Spirit were not separate beings, but were aspects of a single being. This preserved monotheism at the cost of salvation. God could not die; he could only *appear* to die.

Arius (died 336) took the opposite position. Jesus was not God but rather one of his creations. Of course, Jesus was the first, most important and highest creation, but he was not divine in the same sense as God the Father. Monotheism is again preserved, but in the orthodox view the divine element necessary to spread salvation to humanity is gone.

Other positions combined the two elements. According to Bishop Nestorius (fifth century), the divine and human natures in Jesus remained separate within him. This gave rise to the charge not just of two gods, but of two Sons.

The Monophysite churches (fifth century onward) took a different tack. They argued that the divine and the human natures within Jesus were "commingled"—the two natures fused together into a single one. The problem was that this implied God could change, that he was not always and eternally the same.

Finally, the Adoptionists (ca. 200) thought Jesus changed over time. In his early life, he was merely a pious human. Then at baptism, Jesus' divine nature came into him. This interpretation derived from John 1:32, where the Holy Spirit descended upon Jesus like a dove. This solution again implied a changeable God, which was unacceptable.

The orthodox (=catholic) formulation arose in debate with these positions. It was initially formulated at the Council of Nicea (325 CE), but continuing debates required elaboration at the Council of Chalcedon in 451. The Nicene position held that Jesus was both fully human and fully God. The two natures were joined together and unified, but not commingled. Jesus was Man as God and God as Man at all times. He was begotten, not created, and made of the same substance as God the Father; that is, Jesus was divine.

The common aspect of these different theological formulations lies in their mechanistic character. They address the question of how Jesus can be both the God and the human necessary for humanity's salvation while still upholding the monotheistic character of Christianity. They do not address the question of what kind of personality this dual nature gave Jesus. Perhaps Jesus' divinity made him always serious, or perpetually "holier than thou." Or maybe, when he was off duty, he could let down his hair and kick back with his friends.

*The Last Temptation of Christ* is the last of the wave of Jesus films presenting an uncertain Christ, a wave which began with *Jesus Christ, Superstar* and was followed with films such as *Godspell* and *Jesus of Montreal. The Passion of the Christ*, which we will study in the next chapter, provides by contrast perhaps the most extreme example of the next stage, a Jesus who has no doubts about himself or his purpose. Coming just three years after the destruction of the World Trade Center towers in 2001, *The Passion* shows a Christ certain of his mission, who can bear tremendous, ongoing pain to accomplish his goal.

# The Incompatibility of God and Human

*The Last Temptation of Christ* opens with a shock for the viewer. Although in previous films we have heard Jesus pray, most notably in the Garden of Gethsemane, and thus we have had some access to his private thoughts, here the film's first gesture enables the audience to hear an interior monologue, to listen to Jesus' private thoughts. Such access is crucial to the psychological interests of Martin Scorsese's 1988 adaptation of the novel by Nikos Kazantzakis. Much of the film focuses upon the subjective torment of Jesus as a man who is, by theological definition, both human and divine. As we learn in this initial monologue, these aspects of Jesus' nature are by no means harmoniously integrated. This is what we hear, reinforced by a visual panning through a quiet grove of olive trees in the still, early morning: "The feeling begins. Very tender. Very loving. Then the pain starts. Claws slip underneath the skin and tear their way up. Just before they reach my eyes, they dig in. Then I remember." Here the dramatic movement from "loving" prelude to terrifying attack traces a movement from an initial sense of potential *rapture* to imagery suggestive of attack by a bird of prey, a *raptor*. Jesus experiences the unrelenting insistence of his divine nature as a besieging of his human character by an overwhelming otherness—a powerful *tremendum*, in Rudolf Otto's terminology, one that his weak human nature can barely endure. It comes as unwanted visions and dreams, as the cry and clawing of the raptor, as voices, and as an unseen but palpable presence. The result is a Jesus whose dual character is a torment, a site of recurring struggle between divine intention and human desire, one that can transform a walk along a lake into an episode of thrashing agony that leaves him lying helplessly on the ground.

The human aspect of Jesus resists and attempts to escape what it feels to be the terrifying, invasive force of an unintegrated divinity. Jesus wants merely to be a man, and, in the attempt to rid himself of God's presence, he devises a number of strategies of resistance. Hoping to offend God, he builds crosses for the Roman occupiers, then publicly assists in the crucifixion of condemned Jews, for which he receives the open contempt of the Jewish crowd, who see him as a traitor and collaborator.

He even visits the rooms of Mary Magdalene, the prostitute, where he watches others fornicate, although he dares not do so himself. This scene powerfully establishes the sexual side of Jesus' humanity. He has strong sexual desires focusing on a sensual, desirable woman. He wants to carry out those desires, yet he does not permit himself to do so. By continually holding himself in the presence of sin he seeks to torment God, to free himself from divine interference by bringing God into such an unholy circumstance.

In *Last Temptation*, Jesus' sexual feelings complicate the relationship between his human and divine natures. The film plays heavily on this issue because of its long history with Christianity. Sexual lust and its associated desires and activities have been problematic to the church from the beginning. The Catholic Church saw such an incompatibility between serving God and sexual thoughts and activity that it required celibacy of its priests, monks, and nuns. It raised marriage to a sacrament and hedged it around with strong sanctions against sexual activity outside those bounds. So when *Last Temptation* presents this aspect of Jesus' humanity, it drives to the heart of what the church has seen throughout its history as the key incompatibility between human and divine. Historically, humanity approached God by the rejection of sexuality.

So where does that leave us with regard to *The Last Temptation of Christ*? *Last Temptation* may be the most complex biblically themed film ever made. By itself, the psychological exploration of Jesus' two persons— that is, the interaction of his human and divine personalities—provides the grounds for an overwhelmingly complex exploration of possibilities. When the complications of an insistent human sexuality enters the arena, the film becomes almost impossible to interpret. Although to understand the film fully, both perspectives are required.

To achieve this goal, this chapter provides two sets of interpretations. The first approach explores how the film presents, and problematizes, the psychological relationship between Jesus' human and divine natures, looking at key techniques by which the film undermines its own story. The second will fold in Jesus' sexuality, a factor that shifts the interpretation of the film at certain moments by emphasizing the interference that human sexuality causes in relating to the divine.

The film's elements highlighted in this dual approach work to subvert, in a postmodern fashion, the idea of any notion of a unified, singular, and certain truth. Instead, the film reminds us of the primacy of interpretation and therefore the impossibility of access to an unmediated truth.

# Jesus and His Mission

Jesus' visit to a Jewish monastery at the top of an isolated cliff results in a purificatory vision that ends his internal struggles. Afterward he says to his rebel friend Judas, "I can't fight with God anymore." Jesus' two sides have worked out a way of cooperating. Jesus' human personality seems to be in control. God's communication with him comes through visions that appear externally; they seem to be outside of his body (as well as outside of his mind) in the world around him. Jesus' personality is now stable. But the intimate connection between the human and divine is gone. Jesus must now struggle to learn the mission that God has for him; it can no longer be readily communicated.

Jesus' relationship with his divine nature now becomes a discovery process, one in which he gradually learns how to recognize and use both aspects of his being. This can be readily seen in a rough overview of the key turning points of Jesus' development in the film—turning points that appear as visions revealing his mission. While this sounds somewhat like an elaborate version of the Adoptionist view, the difference is that it is not the divine or the human aspect that changes, but their relationship.

The first important change comes with the vision at the monastery. Snakes appear and speak to Jesus in the voice of Mary Magdalene. The voice says, "I forgive you"—something the real Mary had refused to do earlier in the film. After Jesus drives the snakes away, a young monk enters and tells Jesus that Jesus has been purified and that his mission is to go and speak God's message to others. This mission is that of "love."

Jesus' character also changes. He is no longer mentally tormented. He carries himself with confidence and seems of a single mind. He seems fully human, without the interference of a divine nature.

The second turning point occurs after a series of scenes in which Jesus begins to carry out this mission of love. Jesus goes out into the desert to seek God and reaffirm his mission. Here he has several visions, the first three of which he rejects as being from Satan. In the fourth, an ax appears, along with the figure of John the Baptist, who urges upon Jesus the mission of the ax. Jesus interprets this message as using the ax—that is, violent, armed resistance—to fight Satan where he appears in the world. Thus, before the mission of love is completed, Jesus has a new mission.

Along with this new mission, Jesus accesses the power of his divine character and begins to perform miracles. He performs healings and, in an odd scene, calls his disciples to the struggle by physically pulling his heart out of his chest and displaying it to them. This is obviously a reference to the Catholic symbol of the sacred heart—which indicates Jesus' love for humanity—but here with a meaning of destruction rather than love.

Once again, the mission changes before it is fulfilled. The third turning point comes when Jesus leads his disciples to Jerusalem in order to attack the Temple. He gathers them together in the Temple courts, readying them for the attack. Then, as they await his signal—and as he waits for God to give it—his hands begin bleeding with the stigmata. That is, blood starts dripping from a hole in each hand where the nails that will attach him to the cross will go. He fails to give the signal to attack and is instead helped away by Judas.

The mission now becomes that of crucifixion, to die for the sins of humanity. Jesus persuades Judas to deliver him to the priests. Judas does so, quite reluctantly. Jesus is arrested, put on trial, sent to Golgotha, and put on a cross.

But a fourth time the mission changes before it is finished. Suddenly, as Jesus is about to expire, an angel appears and persuades Jesus to come down from the cross. He does so, and then lives for many years. He marries, raises a family, and grows old.

Finally, when he is lying upon his deathbed, the disciples begin to appear. They argue that the mission is incomplete and that he needs to die on the cross. The angel is revealed as Satan, and Jesus' descent from the cross as against God's plan. Jesus then returns to the cross and is crucified. Humanity attains salvation.

This quick overview of the key plot shifts of *The Last Temptation* shows how the divine and human sides of Jesus work out a relationship. They begin in debilitating conflict and then, through purification, develop a working relationship. This relationship leaves Jesus' humanity in charge on a minute-to-minute, day-to-day basis, but seeking to do the will of Jesus' divine nature. Unfortunately, this working relationship has placed a psychological barrier between the two parts of Jesus' dual nature. Intimacy is exchanged for sanity. Whereas the communication between Jesus' two natures was too easy before the purification, afterwards it is too difficult. In fact, Jesus seems not reliably capable of testing his visions for veracity or origin. Sanity comes at the price of clear communication. Although Jesus does the right thing in the end, it is a close call.

Thus, *The Last Temptation* presents the psychological interaction of Jesus' two natures as either too much or not enough. They are either too close together or too far apart. There is not a compromise position where the human and the divine can readily coexist.

# What Is Really Going On?

This (over-)simplified plot overview of *The Last Temptation of Christ* raises important questions, for which the story provides some initially apparent answers. But as we look more closely at the details of the film, at how each key moment in the plot is developed and portrayed, the answers do not hold together. Indeed, the director, Martin Scorsese, created a film in which close examination raises new questions rather than settling the old ones. Take the purification scene in the monastery hut, for example. Jesus drives out two snakes. Did the snakes symbolize Satan,

as in the Adam and Eve story? Or, since Jesus no longer has psychological torment after the snakes leave, perhaps it was Satan and not God that
was causing his pain. Or, is God being represented with Satan's symbol?
Finally, why did the snake speak in Mary's voice? Is this intended to suggest that Mary is evil, that women are evil, that women are Satan, or
something else? So this apparently straightforward scene, upon closer
study, becomes a mass of questions rather than a definitive turning point.

*Last Temptation* creates this kind of subversion of meaning and interpretation throughout the film. Wherever the audience first thinks it sees
a clear portrayal, the meaning becomes subverted when considered further. There are three main techniques by which the film accomplishes
this effect: (1) it presents reality, visions, and symbolism with the same
verisimilitude; (2) it presents identity as unstable and changing; and
(3) it emphasizes the uncertainty of agents, both in determining the
origins of an act or vision, and in interpreting their meaning. Let us see
how each of these works.

"Verisimilitude" indicates the degree to which a film appears real to its
audience. *Last Temptation* does not allow the audience to distinguish
between the film's reality, Jesus' visions, and the symbolism of both.
There are no filmic conventions that assist viewers in distinguishing one
from another. For example, when Jesus goes to the Jewish monastery, he
is met and ushered into a hut by an old man. The next day Jesus discovers
that the old man was the community's leader and had been dead at the
time Jesus arrived. Both Jesus and the audience had perceived the old
man as real when he arrived; there was nothing indicating otherwise. In
hindsight, it clearly was a vision.

The scene where Jesus leaves the cross presents the same interpretive
difficulty. When the girl-angel appears, she seems real. Her statement
that he need not finish the mission fits with the pattern of the previous
two mission goals. The missions of love and the ax were both changed
before completion. After Jesus gets down from the cross, he leads a seemingly real life. He "marries" three women and raises a large family with
two of them, Mary and Martha. The children grow up, he grows old, and
then, when he is near death, his former associates, the disciples, come to
pay their last regards. It is only when Judas shows up and berates him that
Jesus decides that he made a mistake, the girl-angel is shown to be Satan,
and Jesus returns to the cross. He goes back in time to the moment when
he got down from the cross—to the same time, the same place, and the
same suffering and dying state that he was in when he left. This leaves the

audience wondering whether Jesus' married life actually happened or whether it was a vision of a dying man.

In other scenes, symbolic ambiguity intrudes upon the question of whether something really happened or whether it was a vision. In the desert temptations, when Satan's fire leaves, an apple tree appears in its place. While this is obviously part of the vision, it is also real, for Jesus can pluck an apple off the tree and eat it. But the tree also has a symbolic character, for it symbolizes the Tree of the Knowledge of Good and Evil from the Garden of Eden—the tree which Adam and Eve were not supposed to eat. Jesus eats from it. Is he repeating Adam's sin? But then the bite that Jesus takes from its fruit turns into blood in his mouth. Does this symbolize the punishment that Adam incurred, namely, death?

What about the ax that appears at Jesus' feet? It looks just as real (or as unreal) as all that has gone before, with one exception. The ax appears inside the circle rather than outside. Everything outside the circle has shown itself to be ephemeral. Suddenly John the Baptist appears at Jesus' side, giving a short speech that ends with, "Take this ax. Take this message to everyone." John then vanishes, but the ax stays. It is apparently real, for Jesus brings it with him when he rejoins the disciples. He displays it to them as a symbol of their mission.

The second way in which *The Last Temptation* undermines the audience's certainty of interpretation is by rendering people's identity unstable. For example, Satan appears as the girl-angel. Similarly, in Gethsemane, God the Father shows up to hand Jesus the cup. He does this in the guise of the disciple John (the Beloved). To make clear that this is not really John, the camera pans over to the three sleeping disciples, and there John lies.

The most problematic identity shift occurs with the snake's second appearance, during the desert temptation. Here the snake again speaks with Mary's voice. But this time the snake's identity is clearly Satan, because he talks about seeing Adam in Eden. But by the end of the speech, the snake's identity has shifted to Mary. She/it says, "Look . . . in my eyes. Look at my breasts. Do you recognize them? Just nod your head and we'll be in my bed together."

Again the question arises, does the snake represent Satan or Mary, or are they one and the same? But what has Mary done that would make her Satan? She is not a saint in this film, but there is no basis for making her into the devil. *The Last Temptation* treats her as a member of Jesus' band and even depicts her as partaking of the communion at the Last Supper.

But then there is that curious phrase the angel uses several times at the end of film, namely, "There is only one woman." Superficially, this sounds like a cheap way to persuade Jesus to bed the women Jesus desires. But if it is an interpretive clue, and the film follows this line, then Mary and all women are the same, including the "temptress" Eve in the Garden of Eden. Or perhaps this identity should be seen as symbolic, indicating that the lure of women and family is Satan's opposing plan.

To draw the film's meaning into even further doubt, a third strategy subverts the interpretation of the film. This strategy renders uncertain the visions by undermining their origins or their interpretation. It appears in both the monastery and the temptation visions.

The monastery vision could have been produced by three different sources. First, since Jesus drove the snakes away, the vision could have come from Satan, and Jesus' ridding himself of the snakes could be interpreted as his triumph over Satan. Second, since it was Jesus' purification, after which his human and divine natures settled into a working relationship, the vision could have come from God. Third, as we observed, since the snakes speak in Mary's voice, Jesus' human self could have produced the vision, especially since they say, "I forgive you." Jesus had earlier sought Mary's forgiveness, and she had refused to give it.

The meaning of the vision of the snakes becomes further problematized by the way it is interpreted within the film. Jesus does not give an interpretation; indeed, he seems not to understand its implications. Instead, the interpretation is given by a young monk who suddenly enters Jesus' hut. When Jesus says, "I have to stay." The monk responds by saying, "You have been purified. . . . Now you have to leave. You have to go back and speak to people." Is this interpretation correct? Jesus assumes so, but a brief consideration casts doubt. The monk did not see the vision, so where did his knowledge come from? When Judas challenges Jesus, Jesus parrots back the monk's remarks as his own. Furthermore, although Jesus acts on this interpretation, before the mission is completed, it is changed. Is this an indication that the interpretation was not what God intended? Or did God plan the mission in stages? Or did he simply change his mind?

The origin of the vision of John the Baptist in the temptation visions also is problematic. Perhaps its source is God, for John is the last in the series of four visions and the only one that manages to enter the protective circle Jesus drew around himself. But perhaps the source is Jesus' human side, for in the vision, John says the same thing that he said to Jesus over the campfire the evening following Jesus' baptism. Moreover, given Jesus' two conversations with John—the one at the campfire and the one in the vision—John functions as the dominant interpreter of the vision. Jesus' statement to his disciples when he returns to them is almost the same as what the Baptist told him before he went into the desert. John had spoken of challenging the world. Jesus adds simply that the world needs challenging because the devil is there. Once again, the vision is interpreted not by Jesus, but by another person, John. And again, while this vision launches the mission of the ax, in the end, the mission changes before completion. Perhaps it was another false direction.

So in the end, *Last Temptation* renders uncertain the interpretations of the key turning points in Jesus' ministry. While they are certainly points where Jesus changes the direction of his mission, whether he is going in the right direction is a matter of debate and interpretation.

# Channeling God's Message

If Jesus' human nature has problems understanding God's messages at the best of times, then his sexual desires short-circuit the communication process altogether. To function, then, Jesus must remove those desires so that the channels of communication can open. Again, the initial turning point comes during Jesus' vision at the monastery. Afterward, Jesus is open to having God speak through him.

Early in the film, in a desperate attempt to come to terms with the powerful divine presence within him, Jesus goes to a Jewish monastic community in the desert. There, he has a vision of entwined snakes, one of which speaks in the voice of Mary Magdalene. Jesus commands this powerfully sexual image to depart, and it does. A young monk interprets this vision as a purification. Although the monk does not explain his logic, he tells Jesus that the vision has come from "within you." The implication is that this exteriorizing and exorcising of sexual desire enables Jesus to control his merely human side more fully. He is no longer distracted by strong emotions that sex engenders.

The monk interprets this vision as a sign that Jesus is ready to speak for God, to begin his ministry. Jesus, however, is not fully convinced. He has no idea of what he will say. In a statement recalling God's response to Moses when he too complains that he is "slow of speech and slow of tongue"—"who gives speech to mortals? . . . Is it not I the Lord? Now go, and I will be with your mouth and teach you what you are to speak" (Exod. 4:10-12)—the interpreter says, "Open your mouth, and God will speak."

Indeed, Jesus does speak. Coming upon the stoning of Magdalene, Jesus shames and chastises the crowd with the famous invitation, "Let him who is without sin cast the first stone." Later, it becomes clear that Jesus saw a distinction between the words he spoke and his human response to the cruelty he witnessed. As he says to Judas, "I was filled with hate. I wanted to kill them." In this scene, the distinction between what Jesus feels as a human being enraged by cruelty and what he says suggests that in his unpremeditated speech—in the words divorced from his human personality—Jesus provides unmediated access to the will of God, who speaks through him as he did through Moses. Now that the early agonies he has experienced are gone and Jesus appears to allow his divine nature to speak, there remains the stark experiential distinction between Jesus' apparently divine and human aspects.

This distinction is made clear in the effects of his visit to John the Baptist. Recognizing Jesus as the Messiah, John finds a man uncertain about what his message is to be. Although Jesus had spoken forcefully of love to the crowd that had threatened Magdalene, he is now influenced by John's violent, apocalyptic fury. John argues that love is not enough to change a corrupt world, that the "tree is rotten and must be cut down." He reminds Jesus of the fate of Sodom and Gomorrah, and asserts that God's way is the way of violent punishment and destruction. In his uncertainty, Jesus goes alone to the desert, draws a circle in the rocky soil, and vows not to leave until God speaks to him. God does not, at least not directly. Instead, Jesus has a number of visions here. First, a snake speaks in the voice of Magdalene, tempting Jesus with the life of a normal man, with the joys of sex, home, and family. Second, a lion speaks in the voice of Judas, asserting that despite his apparent humility, Jesus desires power. Third, Satan himself appears as a pillar of fire, appealing to Jesus' vanity, reminding him that he is the Son of God, and offering to rule the world with him. All of these visitants Jesus dismisses. Then a vision of an apple tree filled with fruit appears; Jesus picks an apple, bites into it, and blood suddenly drips from it. (Is this a vision of John's rotten tree?) Finally comes a vision of John the Baptist, who hands Jesus an ax and tells him that God wants him to "stand up."

It is important to note that only the apple, the ax, and John pass beyond the barrier of the protective circle Jesus has drawn. The film's version of the temptation in the desert thus makes use of the opposition between inside and outside first articulated by the interpreter of Jesus' first snake vision. What lies outside the circle—the temptations of sex and family, of power and pride—are dismissed by Jesus. They represent the human passions and desires that he has gained power over, that have been, at least for the moment, expelled from his own psychological interiority. John and the rotten, bleeding apple that recalls John's description of the corrupt world requiring destruction, move into the circle. Jesus, embraced by John, picks up the ax John had previously given him and cuts down the apple tree.

Jesus then returns to his disciples and announces that he is inviting them to a war. If Jesus had earlier spoken spontaneously of love, he has now been convinced by John's rhetoric. Indeed, as he speaks with his disciples, he draws from his chest his bloody heart, and we watch as the blood falling into the water at his feet forms a scarlet mushroom shape, an audacious image depicting apocalyptic violence by means of the modern explosive icon. Jesus tells his disciples that he has a new mission; he now plans to "baptize with fire." Since this is a quotation from John the Baptist's own description of the nature of the Messiah, we see that Jesus has again opened his mouth to speak, but the voice that emerges does not speak as it had earlier, of love, but speaks in the "voice" of John. Judas the Zealot is of course pleased, kneeling before Jesus and addressing him as *Adonai* (Lord). If the violation of the circle by the vision of John suggests that he represents an error, a human passion running counter to the will of the divine, Jesus does not apprehend this meaning. He leads his disciples toward Jerusalem.

In Jerusalem, Jesus again speaks powerfully, in anger at the Temple practices he condemns. As in the scene with Magdalene, Jesus opens his mouth to speak as God; in fact, he says to the priest he confronts, "When I say 'I,' Rabbi, I'm saying God." Again, Jesus speaks not of love, but of war, "Don't make any mistakes, I didn't come to bring peace; I came to bring a sword." Here, in another example of Jesus opening his mouth to speak, the film complicates the question of Jesus' access to the divine. Are his words truly inspired by God? If so, how are we to account for the shifts between an advocacy of love and peace and the threat of the sword? Is Jesus here still under a mistaken acceptance of John's rhetoric, having given in to his human passion and anger, or, more radically, does the film suggest that the "divine" word is always an expression of human will and interpretation?

On the way to Jerusalem, Jesus performs a number of miracles, including the cleansing of lepers, the restoration of sight to a blind man, and most important, the resurrection of Lazarus. He also returns to his home of Nazareth, and in a version of Luke 4:16-30 is outraged at the skepticism with which he is met. He warns the Nazarenes of a coming destruction in which all that they have will burn.

Upon his arrival in Jerusalem, Jesus tells Judas of another dream, one in which Elijah came to him and showed him a prophecy that he understood to mean that he must be sacrificed on the cross. Judas is outraged and complains of Jesus' continual changing of plans, "Every day you have a different plan. First it's love, then it's the ax, and now you have to die." Jesus, however, is convinced of the correctness of his interpretation. On the next day he gathers his followers together in the Temple courts, apparently readying them for the attack. Then, as they await his signal (and as he asks God for a quick death), his hands begin bleeding with the stigmata. He fails to give the signal to attack and flees with Judas as Roman soldiers and Temple guards begin the slaughter. He overcomes his fear in the Garden of Gethsemane, and goes to his crucifixion. But again Jesus' understanding of his mission changes. Suddenly, as Jesus is about to expire, an angel appears and persuades him to come down from the cross. He does so, and then lives for many years. He marries, raises a family, and grows old. Many years later, during the destruction of the Temple by the Romans, Jesus is visited by several of his disciples, including Judas who will not forgive Jesus for betraying him by abandoning the cross. It is amidst the fire and slaughter that Jesus declares his willingness to die as he is now convinced that he had been meant to. Immediately he is returned to the cross. He speaks, "It is accomplished," and dies.

The film suggests that Jesus has finally made the correct choice, that he had belatedly understood the intentions of his divine aspect. Yet, the force of the film lies in Jesus' vacillations. He speaks first of love, then under the influence of John and his vision of the rotten fruit, he decides to adapt John's violent, apocalyptic desire to scourge a corrupt world. He then decides, on the authority of his dream of Elijah, that he is to be sacrificed, but is convinced by what he believes to be an angel that this extremity is not God's will. This is a Jesus for whom the questions, "Who am I, and what is my message?" are continually reactivated. In short, here Jesus asks of himself the very questions that theologians and laypersons have asked for centuries. How is it that the Jesus of the Gospels can speak of peace and forgiveness, and also of violence? Consider the following Gospel passages indicating love and violence: Matthew 5:44, "I say unto you, Love your enemies and pray for those who persecute you"; Matthew

10:34, "Do not think that I have come to bring peace to the earth: I have not come to bring peace, but a sword"; Luke 17:29-30, " . . . but on the day Lot left Sodom, it rained fire and sulfur from heaven and destroyed all of them—it will be like that on the day that the Son of Man is revealed"; Luke 12:49, "I came to bring fire to the world and how I wish it were already kindled"; Matthew 5:21-22, "You have heard that it was said in ancient times, 'You shall not murder.' . . . But I say unto you if you are angry with a brother or a sister, you will be liable to judgment."

One way the film suggests an answer to these apparent contradictions resides in its exploration of Jesus' subjectivity—the struggle, as we have seen, between his human and divine natures. If we accept this duality, we understand it as the cause of Jesus' vacillations. As a man, he is subject to mortal desires and limitations. He is influenced by sexual feeling, by anger, by pride, and most important, by his human limitation of understanding. He wishes to understand God's will, yet he fears that will—as well as an erasure of his human, individual reality.

# The Vacillation of (Mis)Interpretation

The divine in Jesus is rarely, if ever, understood clearly. Instead, the divine communicates in visions, in intuitions, and in materials that must be interpreted and which can be misunderstood. This ambiguity again indicates Jesus' dual nature, as viewed by the film. The divine communicates, but the human must interpret. This apparently leaves Jesus depending on others to give him the interpretation. In the first vision of snakes, for instance, a monk tells Jesus the meaning of his vision. When Jesus has a vision of John—who enters his protected circle as the snake, lion, and pillar of fire did not—Jesus interprets this event to mean that he is to follow John's lead, yet the later dream of Elijah causes him again to alter his mission. When an "angel" appears, Jesus accepts her restatement of his purpose and her assertion that he is not in fact the Messiah. In the case of the vision of John and the words of the angel, it seems clear that Jesus is led astray because his human passions—that is, anger and sexual desire—predispose him to error. In other words, when John's argument justifies anger and violence, Jesus willing accepts his words and abandons his own insistence that love can cure the ills of the world. Again, even though Jesus had been "purified," the vision of the entwined snakes symbolized by his dismissal of them from his presence—indicating the overcoming of his sexual desires—when the angel offers him a life in which the sex and companionship he still wants are available, he accepts her words as true. The ability infallibly to interpret, to avoid error and deceit, is not, the film suggests, a human characteristic. We often hear what we wish to hear; we interpret according to our desires and fears because of our imperfect human condition. In this context it is worth recalling that during the depiction of Jesus' dream of Elijah, we are shown in close-up the scroll Elijah has spread out and which, Jesus tells Judas, contained a prophecy, a "great secret from God." The scroll, as we see it, is empty. Could Jesus, given his status as son of God, the Messiah, see what mere human beings cannot?

Or does the image suggest that Jesus projects his meanings onto the text, and further, that all texts are "empty" until such an interpretive projection takes place? If Jesus, in his human aspect, vacillates, is uncertain of his identity and purpose, if he is given not the unmediated word of God but visions and dreams to interpret for guidance, he is a human like all humans. We have texts like the Gospels; some of us may even, like Jesus, have visions and dreams suggesting revelation. But as human beings, as this film presents Jesus is in his human aspect, we must interpret what we are given, and the act of interpretation cannot avoid the possibility of error. We cannot, however, completely escape the more radical suggestion, hinted at if not fully endorsed by the film, that Jesus may have been merely a man, caught in these interpretive complexities.

If, as we said, the film projects upon Jesus the interpretive difficulties faced by thinkers who in later centuries defined, questioned, and redefined who Jesus was and what his teachings "really" were, the film also places its viewers in other sorts of interpretive uncertainty and invites them to experience the claims of both reason and faith, both traditional belief and modern skepticism. Think for example of Jesus' first snake vision. Although it is interpreted for Jesus as a sign of his purification, it is notable that Jesus himself is apparently unable to perform the act of interpretation. Whether or not the interpretation is true, Jesus and the viewers are forced to rely upon the word of the interpreter for the vision's meaning. Again, the monk tells Jesus that the vision has come from "inside" him, but what exactly does that mean? We have suggested the primarily psychological reading that the vision shows that Jesus has exteriorized his sexual longing in the symbol of snakes and then expelled them, but the image of the snake also has a long biblical association, beginning in Genesis, with Satan. Could we not understand the event as depicting Jesus threatened by Satan and then exorcising that evil being from himself? Is this a supernatural or psychological event?

We are invited by the film to think of the debate over the meaning of the miracles Jesus performs in the Gospels. The traditional approach, of course, is to take miracles at face value, as genuine signs of Jesus' status as God. Others, however, have interpreted them from the perspective of modern medicine and psychology, suggesting that Jesus was a skilled healer of what we would today recognize as psychosomatic illnesses and symptoms of hysteria. In the scene depicting Jesus' experiences as he sits within his circle in the desert, we may again understand his visitors as hallucinatory projections by a man who has gone without food, water, and sleep for a number of days, or as genuine examples of supernatural agency. If we, like many modern skeptics, hold to the psychological interpretation of these events, what are we to do with the sequence in which Jesus physically reaches into his chest and removes his heart as he stands before his assembled disciples? What of the resurrection of Lazarus? As viewers we are kept off balance, invited to entertain the modern, psychological view of certain events, and then struck by the depiction of clearly miraculous occurrences. One way to understand what the film is doing is to see that it depicts, and involves its audience in, the complexities faced by modern consciousness confronted with the Gospels. How much are we to rely upon reason in this process? How much upon faith? Shall we, as Thomas Jefferson did, consider the miracles in the narrative to reflect an outdated and superstitious mode of thinking without value for the enlightened reader? Can we, should we, choose what to accept and what to abandon? Shall we abandon what we cannot explain rationally?

Although not drawn from the Gospels, the long sequence in which Jesus descends from the cross and goes off to live a long and normal human life ends the film with a model of precisely this conflict and uncertainty. We may understand all this to be a dramatic supernatural occurrence, the work, as we finally understand, of Satan, who nearly succeeds in misleading Jesus and destroying the work of redemption. When Jesus finally proclaims his willingness to die to redeem mankind, we understand that God, in his infinite mercy, returns Jesus to the cross to fulfill his purpose. Yet there is nothing to prevent our understanding these events psychologically, as an hallucination caused by the agony of Jesus' crucifixion, one that stages for him his desires to escape and live, but also reinforces in him his commitment to die to redeem the world. There is nothing in the film that allows us to be absolutely certain in choosing one interpretation over the other.

Ending in this way, the film depicts certainty and encourages uncertainty. Jesus is certain of who he is and what he has done; at his death, we hear him speak the famous words from the Gospel of John, "It is accomplished." On the one hand, even if we understand what Jesus has experienced to be a hallucination, we may still understand him as the Messiah who has finally fulfilled his purpose, whether or not his last temptation is supernatural or psychological. On the other hand, we may find in the psychological explanation of what occurs a denial altogether of the supernatural. Jesus has visions, and whatever he believes them to signify, they can be explained psychologically as representations of his deepest fears and desires. If this final "miracle" can be explained in this way, why not all miracles, no matter how powerfully attested to in the Gospels? Ending in this fashion, the film certainly allows, even encourages us to see Jesus as the Savior, as God and man combined, in whom the divine aspect ultimately subdues human hesitation, fear, and error to accomplish the task of redemption. Indeed, the interpretive and emotional struggle Jesus engages in to understand and fulfill God's purpose can be seen as a model for all human beings who, precisely as human beings, must undergo such an interpretive struggle—in reading the Gospels, in self-reflection, and in meditation—as they attempt to know the will of God. On the other hand, the ambiguity of the ending reminds us of the profound difficulty of that task.

# CHAPTER 8

---

# Violence and Redemption

The *Passion of the Christ* could not present a more different portrayal of Jesus from that in *The Last Temptation of Christ*. Whereas *Last Temptation* presented a Jesus whose personality and mission shifted throughout the film, *The Passion* presents a single, uniform portrayal of Jesus. Whereas the Jesus of *The Last Temptation* was uncertain, *The Passion*'s Jesus does not waiver an inch, despite the violence inflicted upon him and the hatred arrayed against him. *The Passion* presents a singular depiction of Jesus, one that reinforces the portrayal at every turn, rather than one that continually casts doubt upon itself.

As a film, *The Passion of the Christ* emphasizes its portrayal of Jesus as authentic and authoritative. It admits to no fictionalization but instead claims the authority of Scripture and Catholic tradition through extensive use of the targumic method and other modes of authentication. The film's financial success testifies to an American audience receptive to public affirmative of a "traditional," in essence antimodernist, depiction of religious "truth." If Protestant Evangelical Christianity has gained significant cultural influence in the United States recently, *The Passion* provides a Roman Catholic contribution to this conservative, antimodernist trend in religious discourse. Interestingly, despite the film's profoundly Catholic orientation, it found an enthusiastic audience among those same Protestants.

Yet, the two films share certain similarities that should not be overlooked. Like *The Last Temptation*, *The Passion* wants its audience to ponder the meaning of Jesus as both human and divine. Neither film is mere entertainment, but rather each gives a portrait of Jesus through which it

159

hopes to inspire the viewers to think deeply about him and his mission. The difference is that while *Last Temptation* expects an intellectual or meditative reaction, *The Passion* expects a spiritual reaction. It wants the members of the audience to follow Jesus, to become Christians.

*The Passion* thus provides an opportunity to explore the same three issues we examined in the *Last Temptation*, namely, the portrayal of Jesus as God and human, the film's link to the authority of Scripture, and the audience reaction it aims to achieve. Let us examine each of these in turn, beginning with the issue of authority.

# The Authority of Scripture

If the responses of early viewers of the film are any indication, many viewers saw *The Passion* as an authentic portrayal of the gospel story. In e-mails, online discussion lists, and "person on the street" interviews there was a repeated theme of "This is the most accurate rendition of Jesus I have seen." It is " . . . the truest . . . ," " . . . the most faithful . . . ," " . . . the most real . . . ," and so on. For many viewers, the film clearly was experienced as an accurate depiction of Jesus' last twelve hours. Their perception of it as a faithful reproduction of the Gospels gave it in their minds an authority equivalent to that of Scripture. In the media frenzy that surrounded the lead-up to its release and the first few weeks of its showing in theaters, many Christians—especially Catholics and evangelical Protestants—reacted to any criticism of the film as a criticism of Jesus himself. They rose to defend the film, its director Mel Gibson, and even conservative Catholic beliefs. Jewish groups recognized this religious investment in the film and sounded the alarm about what they saw as its anti-Semitic portrayal of Jews and Judaism. This criticism merely helped fan the flames of debate and heighten the stridently defensive statements about the film.

The general impression of *The Passion*'s accuracy was fed initially by the media hype prior to the film's opening. The media story began with Mel Gibson himself, who chose to promote the film through interviews and prescreenings before selected audiences. In his interviews, Gibson often emphasized the film's faithfulness to Scripture. In one interview (Corley and Webb, p. 2), he said, "I think that my first duty is to be as faithful as possible in telling the story so that it doesn't contradict the Scriptures." In another interview he equated Scripture with what actually happened, after all, John and Matthew, the Gospel writers, were eyewitnesses (Corley and Webb, p. 11). In a move that further authorized the film for Catholics, Gibson emphasized his use of what he considered another authoritative source, *The Dolorous Passion of Our Lord Jesus Christ*, a work that contained the visions of an early nineteenth-century nun, Anne Catherine Emmerich.

In another development, many of those who were invited to a prescreening were interviewed. Gary Hearon, executive director of the Dallas Baptist Association, said, "I didn't see anything I've not read in Scripture," while Southern Baptist Convention President Jack Graham stated, "The movie is biblical, powerful, and potentially life-changing." Scholar Darrell Bock, interviewed by Beliefnet.com, estimated that only about two minutes of dialogue was not scriptural. As these (pre-)views multiplied, the impression of the film's accuracy increased. When a statement attributed to Pope John Paul II appeared, even though it was later denied, the fix was in; the Pope's supposed words, "It is as it was," settled the matter for many people.

Gibson's decision to present the film's dialogue in ancient languages—Aramaic and Latin primarily—also provided an aura of authenticity to the film. Even though no primary sources about Jesus exist in those languages, Gibson's use of them gave a sense of verisimilitude. Few members of the audience could understand the spoken dialogue, of course; they followed the subtitles. So the actual words spoken were irrelevant. It was the impression of veracity and authentication that the ancient languages conveyed that was important, and lent the film an aura of historical exactitude.

While these general techniques promoting *The Passion*'s authenticity work well as far as they go, they would fail if not reinforced by details accessible to the audience. The specific impression of scriptural accuracy in the film's content was created by Gibson's use of the targumic method. By interweaving careful reenactments of scriptural scenes with additional elements—some familiar from Catholic tradition, many not—Gibson was able to create a film that gave an overall impression of faithful adherence to the Gospels. This use of the targumic method enhanced the film's authority, giving it a veneer of biblical authenticity. This authenticity extended to the nonbiblical scenes and lent them status as well. The viewers for whom Gibson's strategy was successful saw the film as a whole, rather than as discrete elements. Since the film *as a whole* was seen as authentic, the added elements were understood as authentic as well. Indeed, many viewers—especially those whose acquaintance with

Scripture was more impressionistic than immediate and detailed—failed to recognize that these scenes or details were not part of the original story.

The sequence of scenes called The Trial before Pilate provides a useful example of how the targumic method in *The Passion* worked. The film's added elements transformed a public trial into an arena for emphasizing God's truth, giving it new meaning, even while treating the original, scriptural aspects rather literally.

The film's structure and order of the different stages of the trial before Pilate come from John's Gospel (John 18–19). *The Passion* augments John's narrative with Jesus' visit to Herod, which appears only in Luke's Gospel (Luke 23:6-12), and Pilate's washing his hands, which appears only in Matthew (Matt. 27:24).

The trial itself is a series of conversations. Two conversations take place between Pilate and Jesus, and these follow John's Gospel quite closely (John 18:33-38, 19:10-11). Jesus' words are nearly exact, while Pilate's words are only slightly augmented. A third conversation takes place between Herod and Jesus. Given the paucity of information, this scene is almost entirely the creation of the film. It owes more to *Jesus Christ, Superstar* than any other source.

There are also four conversations between Pilate and Caiaphas the High Priest, who functions as the leader—the conductor, to use a musical metaphor—of the crowd. Indeed, the crowd's members in *The Passion*'s portrayal are essentially paid agitants following Caiaphas's direction. The conversations between Pilate and Caiaphas generally follow John's Gospel but are often augmented by material drawn from other Gospels or from Catholic traditions about the Passion. For Director Gibson, the authoritative source of these traditions is Anne Catherine Emmerich, a nineteenth-century Catholic nun and visionary. Her visions are recorded in a book known as *The Dolorous Passion of Our Lord Jesus Christ*. This book is a devotional guide, a favorite of Gibson, but largely unknown in most Catholic circles prior to the film.

# Truth and Targum Between Pilate and His Wife

The key to understanding *The Passion*'s targumization of Jesus' trial before Pilate comes from the role played by Pilate's wife, whom tradition names Claudia. In the Gospels, Pilate's wife appears in the narrative only in Matthew 27:19, where she sends a message to her husband telling him, "Have nothing to do with that righteous man, for I have suffered much over him today in a dream." *The Passion* expands that role and places two conversations between her and Pilate into the trial sequence. The addition of these scenes changes the drama of the trial and heightens the stakes of Pilate's decision beyond its importance in the Gospels.

The first talk between Claudia and Pilate comes just before the arrival of Jesus and the start of the trial. She meets him in the hallway as he walks to the courtyard and says to him, "Don't condemn this Galilean. He's holy. You will only bring trouble on yourself." Pilate responds to the word "trouble," ignoring the reference to the man. "Do you want to know my idea of trouble, Claudia? This stinking outpost, that filthy rabble out there." This brief exchange gives *The Passion*'s Pilate an advantage over Pilate as portrayed in the Gospels. In the Gospels, the priests work to define Jesus' character to Pilate during the trial. In the film, Claudia's warning prepares Pilate with knowledge about Jesus before the trial begins. The film's Pilate is much better informed than the Gospel's Pilate.

The second added scene between Pilate and Claudia comes after two exchanges between Pilate and Caiaphas, and a private conversation between Pilate and Jesus. It is Jesus' final words from that conversation that inspire Pilate's opening question to Claudia. Jesus' closing words were, "That is why I was born. To give testimony to the truth. All men who hear the truth hear my voice." Pilate's response had been, "Truth! What is truth?" The Gospel (John 18:37-8) leaves the matter there; it never defines truth. *The Passion* does not define it either, but Pilate and Claudia discuss how to identify it. Pilate asks, "What is truth, Claudia? Do you hear it, recognize it when it is spoken?" When she replies in the affirmative, he asks, "How? Can you tell me?" Her reply is key, and to Pilate, unsatisfactory: "If you will not hear the truth, no one can tell you." Claudia's reply points to the nature of the truth of which Jesus speaks. People can recognize it, but only if they choose to. If they "will not hear the truth," it cannot be explained or reported to them. This indicates that the truth of which Jesus—and Claudia—speak has a transcendent character; it is above all else. It is Truth with a capital "T." Jesus is thus a divine representative, a holy witness (if nothing else), to this Truth. It is not Jesus' truth—that is, it neither belongs to him nor did he make it up. The Truth, Claudia says, is obvious and apparent; it requires no special skill of insight. In comparison to *The Last Temptation*, it requires no extensive interpretation.

Given Claudia's inability to tell him how to recognize it, Pilate falls back on a truth he can recognize, his orders from Caesar. He juxtaposes the Truth of the highest power in the cosmos with the truth of the highest human power in the Roman Empire. He says,

> Do you want to know what my truth is, Claudia?
> I've been putting down rebellions in this rotten outpost for eleven years.
> If I don't condemn this man . . .
> I know Caiphas (*sic*) will start a rebellion.
> If I do condemn him, then his followers may.
> Either way, there will be bloodshed.
> Caesar has warned me, Claudia. Warned me twice.
> He swore that the next time the blood would be mine.
> That is my truth!

Pilate replaces the Truth to which Jesus witnesses with the truth given by Caesar. This is the truth that Pilate can recognize; as he says, it is "my truth." Pilate understands, however, that his wife sees something he does not. His respect for his wife encourages him to try to see that Truth, but he cannot. So Pilate is left with a choice between the reality of a clearly defined truth articulated by a powerful individual, Caesar, and a vague, unidentifiable truth represented by a man who is under arrest for sedition and beaten to a pulp—the opposite of a powerful ruler, indeed, a potential criminal.

The private exchange between Pilate and Claudia becomes objectified when he returns to the trial of Jesus before the crowd. Pilate's internal debate becomes represented by two people. The first is Caiaphas, who has already played upon Pilate's truth—the fear of unleashing a rebellion and Caesar's subsequent punishment. Caiaphas continues to keep on the pressure by stirring up the crowd, increasingly fomenting a riot with his words. The second is Claudia, whose presence now weighs on him as well. Gibson places her into the trial scenes, watching from a window. Cut-out shots show the audience that Pilate is aware of her presence. They exchange frequent glances, especially in moments of Pilate's decisions. Following his release of Barabbas and the crowd's calling for Jesus' crucifixion, the camera shows the couple exchanging a significant look. The look impels Pilate into a sudden decision, for he then calls out. "No! I will chastise him, but then I will set him free." Conversely, when Pilate washes his hands and condemns Jesus to death, he looks again to his wife. But she has now turned away and is walking into the building. Pilate followed his truth and not the Truth she understood. This brief added story element caps the targumic sequence by which Gibson's additions have recast the meaning of the trial scenes from the Gospels.

In general terms, Gibson took the idea of Claudia's involvement from Emmerich, but he did not follow the details of her visions. This is not Emmerich's story about "Pilate the weak man." Indeed, Emmerich's influence on Gibson has been overrated. Although he draws ideas and details from her visions, he shapes them to tell his own version of the story. Instead, this is Gibson's story about the Pilate who must choose between following his personal truth and the divine truth evidenced by Jesus. In the end, Pilate chooses human truth over a transcendent truth. The additional material involving Claudia, which Gibson has placed into his otherwise generally accurate portrayal of John's trial scenes, has thus recast them without changing them. While the Gospel's Pilate is little more than a judge at a religiously sensitive trial, *The Passion*'s Pilate is given the task of recognizing the Truth and then acting accordingly. The depiction of those scenes is by and large faithful to the Gospels and church tradition (as represented by Emmerich), but the addition of Pilate's interaction with Claudia has transformed the significance and meaning of Pilate's actions and his decision condemning Jesus. In *The Passion*, it is clear that Pilate condemns Jesus even though he knows Jesus' identity, which the Gospels did not portray him as knowing. In this light, Pilate's decisions condemn himself, for it is clear that he acted with full knowledge of the stakes before him.

# The Truth, the Audience, and Conversion

For *The Passion*, the addition of Claudia plays a further important role in the film. Although the Truth is never defined, the impact of hearing and recognizing the Truth becomes clear. Claudia is changed by her perception of the Truth. In a word, she converts. The outward manifestation of that change is compassion, the urge and action to relieve suffering. When Claudia sees Mary, Jesus' mother, and Mary Magdalene weeping at Jesus' whipping, Claudia brings them white cloths, which they later use to wipe up Jesus' blood.

Compassion becomes the key indicator for other characters in the film who see the Truth through Jesus. Veronica's conversion becomes clear when her compassion leads her to wipe the sweat and blood off Jesus' face. Simon's conversion becomes apparent when, after being forced to help carry Jesus' cross, he intervenes to stop the soldiers' beating of Jesus. The same holds true with the centurion, Abenader, whose personal change leads him to help the women take the deceased Jesus off the cross.

These figures all pass through the same steps as they move toward conversion and compassion. Each one begins by watching Jesus' suffering. Through that suffering Jesus testifies to the Truth, which they understand. This understanding changes them, that is, they convert. That conversion is then indicated by compassionate action.

Those who do not hear the Truth take a different path. Rather than showing compassion, they actually cause or add to suffering. This is particularly true for Pilate, as well as the priests Caiaphas and Annas, but also for the soldiers and for some members of the crowd.

The film's converts—such as Claudia and Simon—function as models for what Gibson hopes will be the response of his audience. He wants the film's audience to react to his Passion story by converting and showing compassion. This identification of the film's converts with the audience is straightforward. The converts on screen are people who are watching Jesus suffer. Indeed, Gibson emphasizes how his most prominent convert, Claudia, watches the entire trial from her window. The important verb here is "watching." The people who convert on screen are doing exactly what the members of the audience do as they view the film, namely, watching Jesus suffer. On screen and off screen, the viewers are sharing the same experience. They watch the cruelty against Jesus and his suffering for Truth. By presenting the conversion of these people in the film, *The Passion* encourages the audience to that step as well, to go from watching Jesus' suffering to their own conversion. It is not *imitatio Christi*, but *imitatio conversorum*.

# Jesus as God and Human

Jesus' personality in *The Passion* could not be more different from that found in *The Last Temptation*. In the earlier film, Jesus spent much of his life trying to work out the relationship between his two natures, God and human. These clearly separate entities did not coexist well. In *The*

*Passion*, by contrast, Jesus' personality is unified. It is impossible to distinguish between actions and statements guided by his human nature and those inspired by his divine nature. Both aspects seem to be operating in each moment and embracing the mission of suffering and death. The film thus portrays Jesus as unique; he is a God-human. Gibson's portrayal of this one-of-a-kind being is completely tied to his portrait of Jesus' suffering. From his first appearance in the Garden of Gethsemane, Jesus suffers. Any attempt to understand *The Passion*'s Jesus must understand him through his suffering.

Jesus' suffering brings out three key aspects of his character. First, Jesus' physical body receives extensive punishment and torture. The wounds cause him great pain, gradually weaken him, cause him difficulty in functioning, and drain him of large quantities of blood. Like any other human being, when he is injured, Jesus' body shows it. His body is the canvas on which the artistry of torture and suffering is portrayed. Second, Jesus' inner strength—which stems at least in part from his divine nature—enables him to endure the ongoing torment and pain and keep functioning. The film portrays the physical punishment of Jesus as excessive. Jesus receives injuries that far exceed what a normal human being could bear—to say nothing of exceeding what Scripture reports. Third, *The Passion* shows a Jesus whose commitment to the mission of suffering is unmovable. Even at the moments of his greatest pain, Jesus acts to ensure that the torture will continue—and sometimes even increase. In keeping with this portrayal, after the Gethsemane scene, the film never shows Jesus displaying any human emotions that we would expect in this circumstance. He never begs for mercy or even acts "on good behavior" to avoid further beatings; he does not cry; he does not try to escape or gain release. He does not try to overcome his adversaries through argument or force. This God-human Jesus is dedicated to his mission of suffering.

While the emphasis on Jesus' suffering is an important part of the church's theological interpretation of the Passion narrative, it does not form a significant part of the Gospels' telling of that story. There are only three, rather insignificant events in the Gospel tale in which Jesus is abused: (1) after Jesus is condemned in the trial at the High Priest's house, he is hit and slapped (Matt. 26:67-68, Mark 15:65, Luke 22:63-64); (2) he is flogged (based on a single phrase found in Mark 15:15, Luke 23:22, and John 19:1); and (3) a crown of thorns is put on Jesus' head and he is struck (Matt. 27:29-30, Mark 15:17-19, John 19:2-3). The Gospels tell of no abuse or mistreatment during his arrest, as he is brought from

Gethsemane to the High Priest's house, or on the way to his crucifixion. While these three acts of abuse certainly hurt Jesus, such physical harm was incurred by many people at the time and they bore the pain and survived. Jesus' sufferings in the Gospels are nothing any other strong, healthy man could not endure.

To make the suffering-focused theology of *The Passion* work, Gibson must therefore create new ways of inflicting pain and suffering on Jesus. Gibson extends the two scenes for which Scripture provides the most detail. In the slapping following Jesus' conviction of blasphemy at the High Priest's house, it begins with dramatic slaps administered by the chief priests and continues on to include soldiers, with crowd members surging forward to get their hand in. The film also elaborates the scene where soldiers place a crown of thorns on Jesus' head, emphasizing the thorns' sharpness when the soldiers use sticks to push the thorns onto Jesus' head to protect their own fingers from injury.

But the film goes even beyond these elaborations. The short comment "I will therefore have him flogged" (Luke 23:16) becomes an extended scene in which two soldiers vie with each other in their torment of Jesus. To this, Gibson adds two further extended scenes in which soldiers beat Jesus, scenes which have no basis in the biblical texts. The first of these is the ongoing torture that Jesus receives as the soldiers bring him from Gethsemane to the High Priest's house, and which includes being thrown off a bridge while wrapped in chains. The second is the ongoing abuse and beating while carrying the cross out to Golgotha. These three scenes thus provide the film's portrayal of Jesus being extensively and intensively beaten, even though only one has any link to Scripture, and that link contains no detail. These beatings, then, are Gibson's own creation (with some help from Emmerich), and they display Jesus' suffering as the focus of this film.

Both aspects of the targumic method stand out here. On the one hand, the portrayal of violence against Jesus in the slapping and crown of thorns scenes functions targumically to authorize the added scenes of violence. The violence in these known Gospel scenes implies the accuracy of violence elsewhere. On the other hand, the added scenes of beatings change the meaning of the Gospels' scenes. What the Gospels present as lapses in the proper treatment of criminals become for *The Passion* part of a pattern of abuse by the Roman and Jewish authorities.

Gibson's point is not only that Jesus the God-human can endure this suffering but also that Jesus actively encourages his punishment and guides events to ensure that he receives it. He wills and to a certain extent causes his own suffering. He is not merely a passive recipient of the torture the soldiers dish out, he challenges them to give him more. The flogging scene provides a good example. After extensive lashing with rods, Jesus collapses over the whipping post, physically spent—momentarily suggesting, perhaps, that he cannot take any more abuse. But then Jesus struggles to stand up, challenging the soldiers to give him more; they have not yet worn him down. And the soldiers react to the challenge, selecting a more damaging instrument of torture and lashing him again.

By the end of this whipping, Jesus has collapsed on the ground, apparently having had all he can take. A soldier unshackles one of his hands and Jesus flops onto his back, seemingly unconscious. But again, he struggles to rise, to indicate that his torturers have not yet beaten him down. They respond accordingly and begin beating him again, this time on the stomach. This determination to ensure his own suffering stems, for the film, from Jesus' divine nature.

This determination to ensure his suffering in the face of his physical weakness also characterizes Jesus' trip from Pilate's *praetorium* to Golgotha. Although Jesus falls several times due to his weakness, he always gets up. Unlike other film portrayals of this journey, Jesus never stops carrying his cross—again, unlike Scripture. When Simon of Cyrene is forced into service, he merely helps Jesus carry the cross; he does not do so alone. Simon does not take the cross from Jesus so that he can walk without it; instead Simon assists Jesus so that he can continue to carry the cross. Throughout the beatings and abuse he suffers as he walks, Jesus does not waver in his determination to pursue this course.

Finally, Jesus arrives at Golgotha and the Roman soldiers begin to attach him to the cross. The holes in the cross are pre-drilled, and the soldiers discover that Jesus' arms are too short. Once one hand is nailed to the cross, the other cannot reach the opposite hole. Here again Jesus' inner determination comes to the fore. Although it seemed no strength was left in him, he tries to pull his arm back from the soldier, resisting the attempt to stretch the arm. The soldier once again takes this as a challenge and pulls harder, wrenching Jesus' arm from its socket. Even at this stage of weakness, Jesus still chooses to challenge his torturers, to ensure that the abuse against him continues.

This same determination to ensure the path of suffering leading toward the cross appears in Jesus' manipulation of his trials. When Pilate asks Jesus to speak because he, Pilate, has the power to set Jesus free, Jesus rejects Pilate's implied offer of freedom. Following John 19:10-11, Jesus instead denies that Pilate has any such power. Within the context of Jesus' other acts to ensure his condemnation, this literal enactment of these verses reinforces that interpretation.

*The Passion* presents Jesus similarly acting to ensure his condemnation in his trial before the High Priest. The film has three witnesses testify to Jesus' wrongdoings. But their contradictions are so blatant that Caiaphas himself does not believe them. He shouts, "Either offer proof of his wrongdoing, or be quiet!" Two different priests then protest the proceedings, suggesting in specific ways that they are illegal. It begins to look as if Jesus might go free. Caiaphas then changes the trial's direction. He asks Jesus a direct question, based on Matthew 26:63, "Are you the Messiah? The son of the living God?" The Gospels have Jesus give three different answers to this question (John lacks this scene). In Matthew and Luke, Jesus' response avoids a direct answer; he does *not* say yes. In Mark, however, Jesus replies, "I am." Gibson chooses to use this line in the film. *The Passion* thus has Jesus ensure his condemnation here. Despite the possibility of a rigged trial, *The Passion* has Jesus make clear that he is guilty as charged. He is the Messiah, the Son of God. If that claim is blasphemy, then so be it.

# Jesus the Superhero, Not

What is Gibson trying to convey about Jesus? Gibson aims to portray a Jesus who appears as a God-human to audiences of the early twenty-first century, but without simply placing him into an already existing cinematic category, like that of superhero or action hero. Although these film types provide a way to indicate that a character has abilities beyond those of normal human beings, their specific approach to that task includes meanings that are inappropriate for *The Passion's* Jesus. And, in the end, Jesus would lose his unique character; he would simply become like Spiderman or the X-Men.

The problem is this. As a convention, a superhero does not suffer. Indeed, one of superheroes' main characteristics is the avoidance of not just suffering, but of injury and pain: Superman dodges bullets, Spiderman leaps out of the way of hurtling cars, and the *Fantastic Four's* Thing can stop a Mack truck in its tracks. The same is true of the related category of action heroes: Indiana Jones dodges crushing boulders, while Ripley in *Alien* escapes her self-destructing spaceship as it explodes. When these figures do get injured, it is either minor or readily reparable. When Darth Vader cuts off Luke Skywalker's hand in *The Empire Strikes Back*, Luke feels pain, but it is quickly repaired with a mechanical hand that ends the pain and returns it to full functionality. Indeed, the key to a good action film with such heroes is to put a seemingly unending series of obstacles in the hero's way that he or she must dodge to reach his or her goal.

Gibson's Jesus fulfills the opposite of this hero convention. Rather than avoiding or overcoming injury, Jesus continually works to ensure that he is beaten and punished. He uses his body and words to bring on suffering, not to avoid it. And, when he is injured, it is not quickly repaired or healed. He bears the marks on his body and the injuries interfere with his ability to function. In the end, Jesus even fails to overcome his enemies; he dies. True, he is resurrected. But that resurrection indicates his triumph over death, not a triumph against the people who caused his suffering and death.

So Jesus' divine nature cannot be portrayed through the standard film category of superheroes. Instead, that nature appears when he performs actions above or beyond those that mere human beings could do, such as the repeated interactions with his captors, guards, and judges to ensure his condemnation and to further the punishment he receives. Even when Jesus' suffering is at his limits, his inner determination to receive more takes his endurance to extreme lengths.

It is this excessive character of Jesus' torment and suffering that brings out another feature of Jesus' difference from normal humans. As we discussed in this chapter's introduction, it is important that Jesus is human as well as divine. Jesus' human aspects show the suffering through his damaged human body, and as a human being, Jesus endures the pain and suffering, as would any other person. But it is his ability to endure excessive amounts of suffering that distinguishes him from ordinary humans and shows hints of his divine character. This is a difference of degree, rather than a difference of category, as it is with superheroes. But this is as it should be, for otherwise Jesus is not human, but only a divine being. If that is the case, then he cannot take on humanity's sins and effect salvation.

# Why Does Jesus Need to Suffer?

*The Passion* unites Jesus' human and divine natures into a seamless whole, and that union enables him to bear and to pursue suffering.

Gibson's film goes to great lengths to show the solidity of that union in the suffering Jesus undergoes during his last hours, even expanding and inventing tortures and torments beyond both the Gospel story and Christian tradition. The final question, then, is why? Why does Jesus need to suffer at all? The answer lies in the realm of theology.

The first major alteration—addition if you will—in the film's version of the Passion story is the presence of Satan in the Garden of Gethsemane. *The Passion* opens with Jesus in the Garden of Gethsemane, already undergoing what is traditionally referred to as the "Agony in the Garden." In the Gospel story, this is an emotional scene where Jesus tries to get out of going to his death. He prays, asking "My Father, if it be possible, let this cup pass from me" (Matt. 26:39). God refuses, yet gives Jesus the inner strength to carry out his will. As the audience of *The Passion* sees Jesus shaking and sweating with emotion, suddenly Satan appears and begins talking to Jesus. Anyone familiar with the Gospel narrative will wonder where he comes from, for Satan is not part of the Gethsemane story. There are two answers.

The first answer is that Gibson borrows the idea of Satan's presence from Emmerich, but creates his own dramatization. Her vision is much more extensive, for she describes page after page of images depicting the sinfulness of humanity, which Satan puts before Jesus (Emmerich, pp. 100–117).

The second answer becomes clear as Satan speaks. Satan tempts Jesus, trying to persuade him not to go through with the sacrifice. At the moment of Jesus' greatest doubt and hesitancy, Satan tells Jesus, "Do you really believe that one man can bear the full burden of sin? . . . No one man can carry this burden I tell you." Then a snake, a Christian symbol of Satan (see Rev. 12:9), comes out from under his robes and crawls over to Jesus.

What is this? Both Satan and the snake refer back to the Garden of Eden where the snake, usually understood in Christianity as Satan, tempts Adam and Eve to disobey God by eating the fruit of the Tree of the Knowledge of Good and Evil (Gen. 2–3). The snake is successful, and Adam eats the fruit and brings sin into the world. Indeed, according to the doctrine of Original Sin, all of Adam and Eve's descendants—that is, all humanity—become cursed with sin. It states that a Second Adam— Jesus the Christ—can fix this problem only by taking on the sins of all humanity and paying the price of a sacrificial death.

So *The Passion* creates a typological scene, again following some ideas found in Emmerich. It presents the "Temptation in the Garden of

Gethsemane" to match the "Temptation in the Garden of Eden." Whereas the Satan tempted the First Adam to eat the fruit, here the Satan tempts the Second Adam *not* to drink the cup. Whereas the First Adam failed and brought sin into the world, Jesus the Second Adam will not fail, but will free the world from that sin. Jesus' crushing of the snake is a sign of his determination to succeed, and suggests the theological completion of God's cursing of the snake in Genesis 3:15. This added scene indicates that *The Passion* relates how Jesus took on humanity's sins and provided salvation, thus triumphing over Satan. Jesus the Second Adam fixes what the First Adam broke.

Gibson goes on to depict the mechanism by which Jesus "takes on" human sin. This mechanism is suffering. If Jesus' death is the sacrifice by which Jesus atones for the sins of humanity, then the suffering prior to his death is the means by which Jesus and those sins are linked. Through the experience of suffering, the depraved sins of humanity are transferred to Jesus. Given the enormous number of people and their sins, Jesus must be seen to suffer an extraordinary amount. Otherwise, the impression is left that humanity was not really all that bad and did not need Jesus to atone for them. So in the end, *The Passion* has Jesus as the unique God-human go through the key elements of the traditional Christian theology of Original Sin, the explanation of how Jesus brought salvation to humans. The film is not an enactment of the Gospel story, but a dramatization of the Passion's place in the theology of Original Sin.

# Suggested Readings

Anne Catherine Emmerich, *The Dolorous Passion of Our Lord Jesus Christ* (Rockford, Ill.: Tan Books and Publishers, 1928, 1983).

Kathleen E. Corley and Robert L. Webb, *Jesus and Mel Gibson's* The Passion of the Christ: *The Film, The Gospels and the Claims of History* (London: Continuum, 2004).

S. Brent Plate, *Re-Viewing the Passion: Mel Gibson's Film and Its Critics* (New York: Palgrave-Macmillan, 2004).

# Varieties of Religion in American Film

# CHAPTER 9

# The Devil: Screening Humanity's Enemy

The horror film has often been described as the most conservative of Hollywood genres. The reason for this is obvious. The horror film deals with the violent disruption of the status quo by some monstrous figure or force, and the energies of the narrative are devoted to effecting a return to normality. Change thus functions as dangerous and disruptive. In the most important variety of the horror film, supernatural horror, the conservative interests are even more clearly marked. Simply by virtue of such films' reliance on ghosts, demons, vampires, werewolves, and other such creatures, these films depend upon our willingness to accept a prescientific world in which supernatural forces are encountered and in which the only reliable way to deal with them is combat with methods, religious and magical, that prove more powerful than the tools employed by modern, rational culture.

The very existence of supernatural evil in horror films requires the existence of its opposite, namely, supernatural good—the power of God ultimately to defeat the monstrous. Thus prayer, crucifixes, and religious ritual are often combined with such folkloric tools as garlic, silver bullets, and stakes through the heart in the struggle against supernatural beings. Supernatural horror films thus ironically constitute one of the few film genres that take seriously belief in God; movies about the devil view God and his power as real and undoubted. In fact, God is the only one who can defeat the devil.

The danger is that while the devil can accomplish his plans on his own, God's ability to defeat the devil requires belief. God can overcome a demon or the devil only if people believe. Thus personified evil's greatest help is lack of belief. In these films, lack of belief comes from science and the secular worldview that accompanies it. If the modern world is deprived of a belief in the supernatural, it becomes endangered from attack by precisely those forces it denies. Such a world requires a return to faith—not as mere belief, but as a method of deliverance from evil. The issue faced by these films thus centers on the possibility that the desacralization that modernity has brought about—the removal of the spiritual from the natural—may comprise a delusion rather than a recognition of the true character of the world. More specifically, each calls into question the exceptionalist vision of America we have discussed in other chapters. Since this belief had its roots in the religious vision of America as a nation whose millennial potential derived from God's particular favor, the films criticize a modern America they see as having replaced religion with a sterile, materialist ideology, as having abandoned the very source of its special promise. It is worth contrasting these films with *Close Encounters of the Third Kind* discussed in chapter 10. As we will see, this film from the same period attempts to reinvigorate a sense of American millennial promise in the midst of cultural doubt and trauma.

# Drowning Out the Word in *The Exorcist*

One of the best American films to make use of the conservative discourse of horror is *The Exorcist* (1973). While the film has been widely discussed, quite often from a psychoanalytic perspective, our interests instead center on the religious and cultural implications of its use of sound and speech. These stress the clarity of the Word and all that term implies about truth and the necessity of a culture united against the threatening and disorganizing powers of noise, otherness, and falsehood. Despite the powerfully disquieting nature of its imagery—the wounding of Regan's body, the famous image of her head twisted 180 degrees, her disturbing use of the crucifix, the explosions of green vomit—*The Exorcist* is equally concerned with auditory effects that form a crucial aspect of its portrayal of the threatening and demonic. The film introduces us to sound as the index of a threatening foreignness prior to its initial shot. It opens with a black screen and the sound of the Moslem Call to Prayer.

Although the Call comprises a benign invitation to Muslims to come and worship God, in the film its strangeness to Western audiences functions to emphasize the foreign character of the situation. The screen then brightens to disclose a shot of Baghdad and the subtitle, "Iraq." An aerial tracking shot brings us into the archaeological dig overseen by Father Merrin, one of the most dramatic aspects of which is the insistent din made by the laborers. We hear the sounds of the multitude of picks and shovels employed by the Iraqi work teams intermingled with commands and conversations in Arabic. In fact, there is no English whatever spoken in this initial sequence that ends with a cut to another aerial shot, this time of Washington, D.C.

For the average American viewer, this absence of spoken English (emphasized by the English subtitles throughout the sequence) is a precipitation into the "noise" of an exotic foreign language, one exacerbated by the din of actual noise that repeatedly arises on the soundtrack. In addition to the sound of picks and shovels, there is the din of the triple hammers pounding away in the blacksmith's shop into which Merrin gazes as he moves through the streets of Baghdad; there is the clatter of the carriage carrying a desiccated old woman who grimaces at Merrin from her toothless mouth as he is almost run over in a narrow alley; there is the sound of dogs snarling as they fight in the rubble of Merrin's archaeological dig in the final shot of the film's opening sequence. It is also in this sequence that the film depicts Iraq as an intensely foreign site filled with threatening, inundating noise through the use of a sound effect that will be repeated throughout: the almost subliminal buzzing noise that Director Friedkin's sound technicians created by recording the buzz of bees enclosed in a bottle.

In fact, the very "noisiness" of the film's opening is underscored when the clock ticking in the background as Merrin examines the demonic clay head statuette suddenly stops. This evokes not only Merrin's eventual heart attack in his confrontation with the demon inhabiting Regan but also, perhaps, in a film so dedicated to the disturbing sounds of Regan's possession, the silence that will return to the house when the demon has finally been defeated. The shift from Iraq to America for the remainder of the film again evokes noise prior to any visual representation of demonic threat. As in the shot of Baghdad, a high angle shot of Washington establishes the location. As we look down upon the rush-hour traffic, we hear the cacophony made by the hundreds of cars below—the roaring of engines, the honking of horns that register the ceaseless noise of the modern American city. The initial shot showing the interior of the MacNeil house takes the form of a subtle match cut in that it focuses on the open window in Regan's room, through which a cold wind enters like the sound of the city noises outside. The permeability of the house to noise as an invasive force is emphasized immediately, for Chris MacNeil hears a disturbing sound in the attic that she initially attributes to rats, but which signals the infestation of the house with a much worse presence.

Permeability to external forces constitutes the theme of the film. Sound, much more than the other senses, is capable of exhibiting this threat. Unlike sight, for example, which can be controlled by the mere turning of the head or the closing of the eyes, sound is particularly invasive, finding its way through windows and doors, through hands held over the ears. The Gospel of John's opening sentence declares, "In the beginning was the Word," and *The Exorcist* reminds us that the Word is constantly threatened by noise. We are certainly disturbed by the visual horrors the films presents. We watch as Regan's body is slashed by unseen claws, as she turns her head completely around, as she masturbates with a crucifix, and as her face becomes a swollen, mottled, oozing mask. At the same time we are equally disturbed by the sounds that Regan emits. She moans, curses, blasphemes, screams obscenities, channels or mimics the voices of the dead, speaks in foreign languages and backwards in English. Indeed, in the famous scene in which Regan spews vomit at Father Karras, the disgusting green liquid issuing from her mouth can be seen as a metaphoric equivalent of her disturbing vocalizations. In the final sequence dealing with the exorcism performed by Merrin and Karras, the demon inhabiting Regan deploys all its verbal weapons in an attempt to resist the ritual spoken by Karras and Merrin, who struggle against the infernal din.

The film's final, dramatic contest of voices reminds us of the technical definition of noise as an interference with a signal or message, something that invades a transmission and corrupts or obliterates information. Noise, too, is not merely restricted to nonlinguistic interference like static. Language itself can function as a noise if it interferes with another message. Think, for example, of the confusion and loss of information resulting from picking up two adjacent radio stations at the same time. *The Exorcist* is concerned precisely with the dramatizing of such interference, with the threat posed to the Word and a religious worldview by competing discourses, languages whose dangers to a sustainable Truth are symbolized in the demonic cacophony that overtakes Regan and sub-merges her identity beneath a tide of corrupt and corrupting noise.

A good example of this theme of other "languages" as disruptive noise can be found in the film's medical sequences. The scene in which Regan is given a painful medical examination is redolent with noise and terror as the X-ray apparatus circles her tightly strapped body while the machinery emits a series of explosive banging sounds. Furthermore, if the motif of possession is that of a violent intrusion into the body of a helpless victim, this medical procedure, beginning with the graphic spurting of Regan's blood as a tube is inserted into her jugular vein, enacts precisely such an horrific physical intrusion. Regan's screams and the violent curses she directs at the technicians during the procedure make quite apparent the film's equation of this violent bodily intrusion with that performed by the demon inhabiting her. This sequence, depicting Regan's physical violation and with its emphasis on horrific noise, is worth considering in some detail. Regan's "possession" by the apparatus of medical technology as a physical event is perhaps less significant than the more subtle implications here. The absence in the X-rays and other tests of any sign of physical damage or malignancy reveals the deficiencies of medical science (and by extension of science in general).

Regan's problem cannot be located or understood by medical means, and the attempt to do so, like Regan's screams and curses during her exorcism, serves as noise. The discourse of science thus prevents an accurate understanding of Regan's condition and delays the use of the religious procedures that can conceptualize and deal with the supernatural.

If medical science thus operates as conceptual noise disguising or disrupting the truth of Regan's condition, the discourse of the law in the form of the criminal investigation undertaken by Detective Kinderman serves a similar purpose. In his efforts to discover the murderer of Bert Demmings, Kinderman represents the discourse and procedure of secular law, the power of the paternal state to discern truth and guilt. However, as the procedures of medical science cannot properly identify the cause of Regan's suffering, so Kinderman, who seeks a human criminal in his investigation of the murder, is incapable of perceiving the true facts of the case he investigates: the demonic is a category to which his investigative procedures remain utterly blind. The physicians attending Regan will never fully know what has in fact transpired, and Kinderman will not solve his case; the criminal he seeks is beyond the epistemological capacities of his powers of detection.

Several commentators have noted that the film allows the audience to speculate on nonparanormal explanations for Regan's bizarre and violent behavior. Yet, it does so merely to rebuke our own discursive limitations. That Regan may be motivated by an unconscious rage at her parents' divorce exacerbated by the jealousy engendered by a belief that her mother is in love with Demmings is hinted at as an explanation for her "possession" and the murder of the man she imagines to be her mother's lover. On the other hand, Demmings's continual drunken declarations that Karl, the butler, is a former Nazi invite the audience to speculate that Karl may be Demmings's killer. To speculate in this manner, though, is finally to participate in the blindness of the conceptually inadequate and therefore spurious authority represented by the discourses of law and science.

The failure of the physicians to cure Regan and the failure of Kinderman to understand the nature of the crime he investigates indicate the film's indictment of a modern, secularized world suffering from a lack of genuine authority. The film's purpose is to reestablish authority in the form of revitalized religious belief and action. Regan's possession is ultimately a metaphor for the contamination of modern American society by secularism and scientific materialism—forces, the film implies, that have had a corrosive effect upon all aspects of American life. This point is dramatically made late in the film when, in preparation for the rite of exorcism, Karras attempts to provide Merrin with the details of the case. He says, "I think it would be helpful if I gave you some background on the different personalities Regan has manifested. So far, there seem to be three." Merrin dismisses the suggestion, replying, "There is only one." Both Regan's possessed body and the evil-contaminated house she resides in become images of an America whose troubles can be located in a single cause, the "one" to be expelled by the religious forces brought to bear by Merrin and Karras. The demon inhabiting Regan concentrates within a single figure all that the film sees as polluting the body/house of America. In Regan's possessed body are collected the filth, poverty, crime, alienation, and despair infecting the American social body. Regan speaks in the voice of the drunken subway transient; she speaks in the voice of Karras's lonely and impoverished mother; and she enacts the slurred, obscene speech of the alcoholic Bert Demmings. She speaks in foreign tongues and babbles in reversed English. In her, as in an America condemned by the film's religious conservatism, resides an unsettling noise both drowning out the authority of the genuine and saving Word and exhibiting the despair arising from its absence. This absence, the cause of all the film deplores, is the meaning of the "one," the demon that represents the failures of a modern society unmindful of religious truth.

Such a terrifying evocation of loss of order and definition takes place, as has been commonly noted, in the context of a host of missing fathers. Regan's father (divorced from mother, Chris) is, for example, in France. His absence is underscored when Chris, with increasing rage and frustration, attempts to reach him by telephone on Regan's birthday. "He doesn't even call his own daughter on her birthday," Chris complains. In the context of the film's thematic emphasis upon the absence of God's paternal authority in the secular world inhabited by the characters, this unavailability of the father's voice gains significance as the film develops. It prefigures the dramatic need for the Word represented as the need for Christian faith in general, and for the words of the rite of exorcism spoken eventually by Merrin and Karras, the two Catholic fathers who come to Regan's aid. Indeed, the theme of the missing father occurs again and again in the film in various literal and symbolic forms. For example, Chris complains during the shooting of a scene in the film she stars in that she doesn't understand the dramatic situation and asks to speak to the writer. She is told that he is in France. "Hiding?" she asks. Like Regan's father, this author, the "father" of the script, is unreachable in a foreign location. Father Merrin, of course, has been absent from America in Iraq, and he will be associated with other foreign locales when his involvement in an exorcism in Africa is discussed later in the film.

The most significant example, though, of the motif of the absent father is Karras himself. Karras (whose own father is dead) is, as the film makes clear, suffering from a crisis of faith. He complains to one of his colleagues that he is "unfit" to serve as a psychiatric counselor to other priests because he fears he has lost the religious beliefs that have thus far sustained him. Having in this way become absent to those who need him, Karras asks to be reassigned. Indeed, his initial discussion with Chris emphasizes the degree of his estrangement from what the film will stress as the necessary, illuminating, and ordering discourse of religion. As he counsels Chris against employing an exorcism to help her daughter, he tells her that science now has a contemporary language to define the condition plaguing Regan: "Terms like mental illness, paranoia, schizophrenia." He has been educated, he explains to her, in "places like Harvard, Johns Hopkins, and Bellevue," places that as centers of scientific enlightenment prove to be the dispensers of a discourse woefully inadequate to the circumstances with which Karras will have to deal in grappling with a real demon, an actual possession. If Regan has been possessed by a demonic foreign entity expressing itself through a cacophony of voices, languages, and sounds that submerge her identity ("She is in here. With us," the demon says when Karras asks where Regan is), Karras is equally possessed by the foreign discourses of science and psychiatry, the conceptual noise that has invaded him and threatens his capacity to make use of the discourse of religion.

Karras's doubts have come at least in part from the secular education he has received. When we recall that a priest's *vocation* refers literally to his *call* to God's service, we see again the film's emphasis upon communication and the forces that disrupt it. God called Karras to his vocation, but his education for that service drowned the voice of the call with secular learning. The prolonged exorcism with which the film ends takes the form of Karras's resubmission to the powerful and authoritative message of Catholic Christianity as, guided by Father Merrin, he repeats the ritual of exorcism and pronounces the responses to Merrin's invocations.

The dramatic apex of the film is, of course, the ritual of exorcism, and in addition to the disturbing visual effects for which the sequence is famous, the exorcism is emphatically an auditory event. Karras and Merrin fight a battle of voices in which the cries, moans, threats, lies, and blasphemies made by the possessed Regan are countered by the repeated words of the ritual spoken by the priests. As Karras and Merrin repeat the formulae of the Rite of Exorcism, their voices rising to drown out the demons, we witness a struggle between the paternal Word and demonic noise. The exact (and exacting) repetition of the words of the rite performed in tandem by the older and younger priest underscores Karras's renewed commitment to his vocation. As the younger priest, he is heir to the transmission of the authority of a ritual handed down from "father" to "son," a ritual whose power lies in its unchanging exactitude. In the repetition of the words of the ritual as the priests perform it and begin again and again as the struggle continues, we experience the sacred words in a powerful demonstration of their solid, authoritative, unchanging repeatability. This is the action of the coherent, masterful Word of religious faith arrayed against the diabolical cacophony raging against it.

The ultimate defeat of the demon, however, requires another form of repetition: the radical *Imitatio Christi* (imitation of Christ) performed by Father Karras after Merrin's death. Karras, enraged, at first strikes Regan in a misguided attempt to combat the evil residing within her. It is following this error that Karras knows in an instant what to do. He invites the demon to possess him and is immediately inhabited. Like the Jesus who exorcises demons and, even more significantly, like the Jesus who voluntarily assumes the sins of mankind in a self-sacrificial act of redemption, Karras lifts the evil burden from Regan and takes it upon himself. He struggles for control as the demon within him attempts to choke Regan, and manages to leap from the window to the sidewalk below. That Karras, dying on the pavement, participates in the ritual of extreme unction performed by Father Dyer reveals that he has defeated the possessing demon. This scene is not, however, without a degree of suspense. We wonder as Father Dyer begins the ritual whether Karras or the demon will respond to its questions. It is worth noting that as Dyer asks these questions of Karras and Karras responds by squeezing Dyer's hand, we have a model of clear, unambiguous communication between the two, uncontaminated by any intervening noise of demonic speech or sound. This perfect communicative clarity of ritual questions and answers ends the exorcism sequence with a final emphasis on the redemptive power of adherence to religious dogma, on the necessity of the uncorrupted transmission of religious truth. When, in the final moments of the film, Regan, although having forgotten every detail of her possession, sees Father Dyer's crucifix and stands on her toes to kiss it, we are to understand that at a deep and permanent level, Regan has herself received the message.

# Thinking the Unthinkable: *The Omen*

A few years after the commercial success of *The Exorcist*, another Hollywood film, *The Omen*, returned to the theme of demonic evil inhabiting a child. Damian, the problem child in this film, is not, however, an innocent possessed, but is rather the literal son of Satan. Damian is not, as his diplomat father comes to learn, to undergo exorcism, but is rather to be slaughtered on a Christian altar if the world is to be saved from satanic conquest. This unthinkable act, the necessity of which tortures ambassador Robert Thorn until he makes a final decision in the last minutes of the film, is in a number of ways the thematic focal point of the narrative. *The Omen* is a film about the unthinkable, not merely in terms of the bloody butchering of a child it presents as the only means to defeat supernatural evil, but, more important, in its frantic diagnosis of modern Western society as become so debilitated by rationality and materialist beliefs that the supernatural truths of religion have become for many precisely unthinkable, incapable of informing thought and action.

Religion in *The Omen*, as in *The Exorcist*, is simply and reductively defined as concerning a struggle between supernatural forces of good and evil and the necessity of human belief and engagement in that struggle. Indeed, the film emphasizes the importance of human action because, although the power of supernatural evil is represented by Damian and his growing powers, God seems utterly to have abandoned the fight. Satan's plot is challenged only by the actions of a small band of persons, dwindling finally to Thorn alone. The meaning of God's immediate presence is clear. The secular world stands essentially defenseless because it has abandoned belief in God and the supernatural. If God is absent, the film implies, it is because humanity has ejected him through lack of belief. God's absence thus empowers an evil whose strength depends upon a lack of belief in its very existence.

Like *The Exorcist*, *The Omen* focuses upon the contamination of American domesticity. If in the former film the possessing evil enters and contaminates an American home and child, Damian, the child of Satan, functions in the same fashion. In fact, the home and family he invades— that of Robert Thorn, American ambassador first to Italy and then to Great Britain, and lifelong friend of the President of the United States— registers even more emphatically than does *The Exorcist* that the invaded home symbolizes American culture in general. Thorn's residence and the embassy he heads are circumscribed islands of American culture and authority, surrounded by foreign territory and culture. As in *The Exorcist*, this domestic American space is contaminated by a foreign otherness. Thorn, awaiting the birth of his child in a Roman hospital, is told that the child has died and is convinced by a priest to substitute without his wife's knowledge another child born that very evening. It is the secret adoption of this mysterious infant that introduces the foreign into the heart of the American microcosm of Ambassador Thorn's home and family.

This theme of contamination, as in *The Exorcist*, imagines religion as a violent, radically therapeutic means of purification. Thorn must be convinced in the course of the narrative to engage in a series of actions abhorrent to his rational secularism. When the repentant priest travels to London to warn Thorn of the threat posed by Damian, the priest tells the outraged ambassador that he must daily trust in Christ and daily "drink his blood." The very phrasing of the priest's insistence that Thorn take communion each day takes on a disturbingly violent resonance. That is, the common ritual of communion foreshadows here the sense of unthinkability central to the film's thematic interests. Thorn, of course, must not only "drink blood" if he is to defeat Satan; he learns that to end the threat to the world posed by his adopted son, he must sacrifice the boy on an altar in a church. Thorn's initial and understandable reluctance is gradually worn down by his experience of the violence undertaken by his satanic opponents: the deaths of his nanny; his wife; his real child; Father Spiletto, the repentant priest; and Keith Jennings, the photographer who joins him in his gradual discernment of the truth of Damian's disturbing parentage and potential.

Thorn's outrage at the instructions he receives in Jerusalem concerning the ritual he is to perform—"I refuse to murder a child," he shouts at Jennings—lies at the center of the film's disturbing narrative intentions. We realize, hearing Thorn, that he is of course right. It is unimaginable, unthinkable that a mainstream American film depicts so outrageous an event. From the moment that we realize the film's villain is a small child and that only ritual slaughter will stop him, we know as culturally aware viewers that such an action is profoundly unlikely to take place. If the plot had not prevented such a solution, Damian could have been killed by some sort of accident without risking any excessive audience discomfort. To have him stabbed repeatedly in a church by his adoptive father would dramatically cross the line. This, as we have suggested above, is the point. *The Omen*, in its restrictive definition of religion as consisting solely in the techniques of violent ritual resistance to supernatural evil, stacks the conceptual deck against us. Religion, demanding the unthinkable, becomes in what the film depicts as its essential content, unthinkable. Religion is portrayed through this narrative strategy as lying far outside the conceptual habits and intellectual dogma of secular Western, and especially American, culture. If in a notable sequence Damian refuses, to his parents' significant embarrassment, to enter a church where a wedding to which the Thorns have been invited is to take place, it is clear, since this is obviously the first time Damian has been to church, that the Thorns are not in the habit of religious observance. Robert Thorn, finally disturbed enough by the violence taking place around Damian, and at least partially open to the arguments of Jennings—the photographer who is convinced of supernatural forces at work in Thorn's life—begins his education in religion. This education significantly deals with little but the apocalyptic contents of the book of Revelation and other works allegedly prophetic of the end time and the advent of the Antichrist, usually associated with the Great Beast of Revelation. In his growing conviction that Damian may in fact be allied with dark forces, Thorn joins Jennings in a quest to discover the truth of Damian's origins. In the course of the pair's travel to Italy and Israel they discover, of course, the terrible truth that Damian was born of a jackal and that his adoption by Thorn has been made possible by the murder at birth of Thorn's infant son.

What is particularly significant about the investigation undertaken by Thorn and Jennings is the way it further and further alienates them from the rational mainstream culture of which Thorn is the product and model representative. Following the photographically predicted death of Jennings in Jerusalem, Thorn is prepared to do what is necessary to rid the world of Damian and the threat he represents. In his killing of Damian's satanic nanny guardian and attempt to perform the bloody ritual on a church altar to destroy the child he now fully believes to be nonhuman, Thorn joins the other characters in the film whose beliefs and behavior have placed them well outside the cultural norms of their world.

Like Father Brennan whose walls are covered with pages torn from the Bible to keep evil from entering his room, and like the now terribly burned and silent Father Spiletto, who five years before had convinced Thorn to substitute Damian for his dead infant, Thorn has, from the perspective of the rational modern world, become hopelessly insane. From that normative perspective his actions, the killing of a middle-aged woman and the attempt to kill his son, are clearly monstrous. The film's most dramatic sequence in which Thorn drags the kicking, screaming Damian up the aisle of a church and prepares to stab the boy as he pleads, "Daddy, don't," is profoundly disturbing. We are both horrified by Thorn's pitiless intensity and, having shared Thorn's discoveries, hopeful that he will succeed in his monstrous task. Like a modern Abraham, Thorn is prepared to sacrifice a "son" (who is, admittedly, not an innocent Isaac). There is, of course, no divine intervention. The logic of the film is that God wills the violent death, but God's will is defeated by the policeman's bullet that kills Thorn before he can complete the act. In the final scene we see Damian standing with the President of the United States and the First Lady at Thorn's funeral. It is implied that Damian will again be adopted, this time into the most powerful family on earth. He turns and smiles disturbingly at the camera.

As does *The Exorcist, The Omen* depicts the contamination of American society by a dangerous force that is finally less the foreign, demonic presence against which the properly informed characters struggle than it is the secular, rationalist cultural perspective that hampers that struggle. Father Karras, in his self-sacrifice manages to defeat the demon in the earlier film. Thorn does not. He has doubtless been judged insane by the world he leaves behind, and in that judgment dies the hope of evil's defeat.

# Vignette

## *Rosemary's Baby* (1968)

In both *The Exorcist* and *The Omen*, confrontation with supernatural evil is hindered and even disabled by the rational, materialistic biases of contemporary society. This is also the case in the film that began the "satanic child" spate of films, *Rosemary's Baby*. Here Rosemary is exploited, with the assistance of her husband, Guy, by a coven of Satanists living in her apartment building. This group has chosen Rosemary to bear the son of Satan, the Antichrist. Hutch, an elderly friend of Rosemary's and an author of adventure stories for boys, is the only character to realize the nature of the threat to Rosemary and to attempt to help her. For his efforts, he is murdered by the coven. Hutch's profession is of course significant: as a writer for children, he is, from the perspective of the "adult" world, given to naïve fantasy. Rosemary's dealings with her obstetrician—which represent the scientific worldview in general—constitute a criticism of the medical community for its blindness to the supernatural (as in this chapter's two main films). Indeed, at one point in the film there is a shot of the famous *Time* magazine cover from 1968 that asks the question, "Is God Dead?" When Rosemary comes to the obstetrician for help and tells him her story about Satanists, he returns her to the clutches of her regular doctor, who belongs to the coven.

This dangerously limiting rationalism is added to a materialistic desire for success, fame, and wealth in the film's critique of a society spiritually unprepared to confront evil. Guy, an actor, goes along with the coven's plot because he receives its black magical aid. With the coven's assistance, he is given a role that will make his career.

In a strategy aimed at involving the audience in a clash between the religious, supernatural view of the world and the rational, scientific view, *Rosemary's Baby* invites viewers at first to suspect that Rosemary's problems may in fact be psychological, a paranoia brought about for purely medical reasons. In the end, though, when Rosemary discovers that her child is in fact the spawn of Satan, the audience is forced to accept the reality of the supernatural evil that has ensnared her.

# Suggested Reading

Noël Carroll, *The Philosophy of Horror or Paradoxes of the Heart* (New York: Routledge, 1990).

CHAPTER 10

# God as Alien: Humanity's Helper

The nature of the divine has been a focus of human speculation as far back as written records go. Ideas of god—or gods, or goddesses—have differed from religion to religion, from culture to culture. Even within a single religion, there have been various ways of envisioning god. In Christianity, for example, Jesus spoke about God both as a father who loved his children and would see that they were clothed and fed, and as a terrifying authority whose presence would fill the earth on the day of judgment. Beginning with the recording of Jesus' words, descriptions of Christianity's God appear in literary form. In America, such writings are found in a wide range of literature from sermons and other theological writings of early eighteenth-century New England to contemporary speculation about God's nature in short stories, novels, and best-selling thrillers such as the *Left Behind* series.

Speculation about God is not restricted to writing. The genre of science-fiction films lends itself easily to such imaginings; in one form, it even requires it. When science fiction imagines aliens as greater than human beings—as opposed to exploring the fear that creatures lower than humans in the animal kingdom might acquire greater power (as do the ants in *Them* and the chimpanzees in *Planet of the Apes*), it often codes their technological, moral, and spiritual superiority as divine power, making them like "God." *The Day the Earth Stood Still* is a good example of gods from space. If World War II showed that humans could acquire godlike powers of destruction in the atomic bomb, then a superior alien race could be advanced enough to control that weapon. Klaatu's intergalactic civilization not only controlled weapons of even greater destructive power but they also had the superior moral development that put such weapons under strict control and ensured interplanetary peace. When Klaatu rises from the dead, in imitation of Christ, he further demonstrates the godlike superiority of his civilization.

Once science-fiction films begin depicting aliens with godlike powers, they become a genre for informal and unofficial theological speculation, a medium for experimenting with different divine features. Since explicit discussions of God run the danger of sacrilege if too fanciful, imagining aliens with divine powers became a safe way to explore how assigning different powers to god(s) (i.e., superior intelligent beings), or giving them different ways of relating to humans on earth, could work out. This chapter explores two different portrayals of aliens as gods.

*Close Encounters of the Third Kind* depicts the first contact humanity has with aliens from outer space. Before the arrival of the giant mothership at the end of the film, the aliens communicate with humans in much the same way that Christianity's God has communicated with his followers. They send visions, issue people a "call" for service, and put a compulsion on certain humans to meet them. These people respond in a religious fashion: they forsake all, undertake a pilgrimage, and are challenged by various temptations and weaknesses along the way (to which many succumb). Despite the science fiction scenario of *Close Encounters*, its use of religion and imaginings of God fit easily into Protestant conceptions.

*2001: A Space Odyssey*, which we will examine first, concerns itself with the question of evolutionary change. A film especially interesting in the midst of the contemporary struggle between Darwinian evolutionists and the defenders of "intelligent design," the film clearly takes the side of the latter, at least in the case of human beings. While it does not directly specify a creator of the universe as a whole, it does imagine human evolution as precipitated and supervised by an alien culture of godlike power.

# The Spiritual Emptiness of Technological Evolution

The most complex and sophisticated example of the theme of the godlike alien is Stanley Kubrick's *2001: A Space Odyssey* (1968). Here several questions traditionally addressed by religion concerning humanity's place in the universe and the possibility of a "divinely" mandated design to history are centered in a mysterious monolith that appears at—or perhaps even creates—pivotal moments in human development. In its initial appearance to the apelike protohumans in the film's opening sequence, the monolith communicates to those who come into contact with it the insight leading to the development of tools. The famous match cut from the bone club hurled into the air to the image of a space craft floating in space eloquently traces in image the technological path of development resulting from the initial intervention of an alien intelligence. As the mission to Jupiter in the film's longest section makes clear, humans' second encounter with a monolith has been designed to occur when human technological abilities have developed sufficiently to enable space travel. The monolith, which was "intentionally buried" on the moon, directs spaceship *Discovery's* journey to orbit around Jupiter where Bowman will encounter the third monolith and be launched upon his transcendent interstellar journey. Indeed, progress as a dramatic self-transcendence initiated by contact with the monolith constitutes the thematic center of the film. Like the hand of divine providence or the spark of religious intuition, the experience initiated by this extraterrestrial artifact brings about sudden, revelatory change and dramatic human transformation.

The middle section of the film emphasizes powerfully the need for such radical change. The human civilization that has built a space station and bases on the moon has, despite these achievements, fallen into an intellectual and spiritual exhaustion. Kubrick set up this section's ironic imagery with great deliberateness. In what was the finest achievement of cinematic special effects in film as of 1968, he propels humanity from prehistory into a near future in which a spacecraft dances a beautiful duet with a space station as it approaches for landing while the *Blue Danube Waltz* plays on the soundtrack. If for the audience this is an immersion in imagery of profound and moving beauty, the film's characters do not appreciate it. In a shot pattern significantly repeated throughout the film, Kubrick matches the universe's beauty and grandeur with human banality and boredom, for in the following shot the audience sees the astronaut Heywood Floyd aboard the shuttle on his way to the moon to supervise the investigation of the recently discovered monolith. Floyd ignores the magnificence of space outside his window, instead sleeping in his seat with a television program on the screen before him. Slightly later we see the shuttle stewardesses watching a sumo wrestling match on a television broadcast and Floyd, asleep again, as another stewardess brings him his in-flight meal. This contrast between cosmic magnificence and human insensitivity is repeated when, shortly after Floyd has landed on the space station, he engages in a banal phone conversation with his young daughter as the brilliantly lit earth swings in space outside the portal behind him.

The aesthetic and spiritual vacuity of the civilization Kubrick presents is again communicated imagistically in his visual emphasis on repetition and redundancy. As in subsequent films, Kubrick delights in the use of settings that emphasize a dispiriting visual repetition. The space station, whose accommodations are operated by the Hilton hotel chain, provides a good example of this device. As Floyd walks along a corridor we see arranged along his path duplicate examples of "modern" furniture, chairs of a particularly tasteless reddish pink and small tables at which people gather to drink and talk. At one of these duplicate sites, Floyd stops momentarily to exchange banal pleasantries with a group of Russian scientists from whom he insists on withholding any information about the discovery he has come to investigate.

Once Floyd boards the spaceship *Discovery*, the film intensifies this emphasis on deadening repetition. The opening sequence moves from a shot depicting the magnificence of interplanetary space to an interior in which Frank Poole, one of the two astronauts, runs in circles along the floor of the spinning drum that provides artificial gravity to the living quarters on the ship. The image is precisely that of a hamster running on a wheel. As he runs, he passes the cryogenic containers in which the remainder of the crew lay in suspension until the ship reaches Jupiter. Again, the image of these containers is instructive in that it implies an erasure of individual identity. We see merely three identical boxes holding, as Poole will later say, persons who sleep but do not dream. In the same fashion, the marked resemblance between Poole and Bowman, emphasized especially when they face each other inside the pod as one would face a mirror image, stresses a profound lack of difference, a monotonous sameness in the world of the *Discovery* as a microcosm of the civilization that created it.

The "god" of this world is HAL the supercomputer. He is, within the limits of the ship, essentially omniscient, omnipotent, and omnipresent. The film's story, however, works to expose HAL as a false god, one that represents man's technological achievements as having reached a limit that now needs to be transcended.

We first "see" HAL as we first see Bowman when, entering the central area of the spacecraft, Bowman appears reflected in one of HAL's red camera eyes. This image, in which Bowman appears distorted within the circular frame of HAL's vision as he climbs down a ladder, is another of the film's subtle and important images. Bowman's distorted image suggests that he is cramped within the technological world HAL personifies. His image is twisted to fit into the enclosure that represents the world of the *Discovery* and by extension the enclosure of the technological world containing human reality.

The repeated image of Bowman's face reflected in HAL's eye provides another important example of the imagery of mirrors, repetition, and doubling that signifies the malaise and emptiness of the film portrayal of humankind. This repeated reflecting imagery reveals the environment as entirely manmade. Since the world of the *Discovery* symbolizes technological society, everything upon which man gazes is, as an artifact created by the human mind, a reflection of that human mind. HAL, an artificial intelligence designed by humans on the model of human intelligence, is only the most extreme example of this reflection. To look into HAL's eye is, as the image of Bowman suggests, to look upon oneself. To see nothing but oneself, the film implies, is to be trapped within a solipsistic enclosure; humanity is all that matters. Poole and Bowman represent a humanity sealed off from a vast exterior, a wider reality whose symbol is the infinity of space. This is manifest in the exterior shots in which we see the ship floating in the immensity of the universe before a cut inserts us into the interior of *Discovery* to see Poole circling and circling his rigidly bounded space and Bowman distorted in the constricting circle of HAL's gaze. Their job may be space exploration, but they see only the human creations they brought with them.

The godlike HAL is a false god who claims an omniscience belied by his incorrect prediction that the AE35 will fail. When Poole and Bowman are forced to accept HAL's failure, they begin their escape from the entrapment he represents—an escape fatal for Poole but that produces Bowman's transcendence. After HAL kills Poole and abandons Bowman outside the ship in the pod he hurriedly entered without his spacesuit, Bowman reenters *Discovery*. This sequence uses one of the film's central metaphors, activated by the double meaning of the word "pod." Several times in the dialogue the characters refer to these vehicles—the A, B, and C pods—used for extravehicular work. For the last of these, the C pod, Kubrick invites the audience to hear "seed pod," which signals the symbolism of Bowman's actions when sealed outside the ship by HAL. When Bowman uses the explosive bolts to blow the door of the pod and flies into space unprotected by a helmet, his bursting from the seed pod becomes a metaphor for his passage into another stage of existence, one that will be completed in his metamorphosis into the star child at the film's end. After Bowman reenters *Discovery* and shuts down HAL, he learns the mission's purpose: to locate the monolith orbiting in Jupiter space. Bowman's abandonment of the technological enclosure represented by HAL marks the evolutionary mandate revealed by the third monolith. Bowman will pass into another stage of being, one infinitely superior to that of technological man.

The monoliths are artifacts of absolute otherness, the products of an alien intelligence completely different from humanity. Most important, the surface of each monument is a deep and *nonreflective* black. Each contrasts powerfully with the world of reflections that is the *Discovery*, where to look upon anything is to see the self. The utter otherness of the monoliths—as well as the profound effect the monolith in Jupiter orbit has upon Bowman as he undertakes his voyage "Beyond the Infinite"—links Kubrick's depiction of the alien intelligence behind these artifacts with what Rudolf Otto, the influential theologian and theorist of religious experience, terms the *mysterium tremendum*. By *tremendum* Otto seeks to identify the powerful awe-fulness—fascinatingly attractive, yet inherently fear-inspiring quality— of an encounter with the *mysterium*. By *mysterium*, Otto means that which is "wholly other." The *mysterium tremendum* is beyond rational comprehension; it is an experience of radical difference and absolute otherness so powerful as to cause a "stupor"—"an astonishment that strikes us dumb"—in the face of "that which is quite beyond the sphere of the usual, the intelligible, and the familiar, which therefore falls quite outside the limit of the 'canny,' and is contrasted with it, filling the mind with blank wonder and astonishment" (Otto, p. 26). The absolute nonreflective otherness of the monoliths, in which one sees no sign of oneself, draws Bowman into the transcendent journey depicted in the famous "light show," the film's powerful display of light, sound, and image that resists translation into merely rational terms, and whose stupefying, overwhelming effect is registered in the shots of Bowman's contorted face as he plunges further and further into dramatic otherness.

Here Kubrick provides Bowman (and, of course, the audience) with the antithesis of the repetition and redundancy characterizing life inside

*Discovery*. Bowman is thrust into an experience of absolute newness and complete unpredictability suggestive of the new form he will assume at the end of the film. In the mysterious final sequence Bowman, over what may be years or mere minutes, witnesses his aging to the point of extreme old age and imminent death. The fourth appearance of a monolith brings about his rebirth and transforms him into the new form of the star child that floats above the earth and turns, with a faint smile, to face the audience in the film's final shot. It is worth noting the final gesture of the old Bowman as he raises his hand, one finger extended, toward the monolith standing at the foot of his bed. By thus quoting the gesture of the newly formed Adam reaching up toward God in Michelangelo's depiction of the creation on the ceiling of the Sistine Chapel, the film insists upon the godlike status of the alien intelligence who have newly created Bowman as, it is implied, the first of a new form of human being.

*2001: A Space Odyssey* remains the most complex and sophisticated example of the science fiction theme of substituting for a traditional deity alien beings whose powers and purposes are godlike. The alien powers that contact humankind in the film provide a sense of design and intention in the universe and especially in the life of humanity. If science has made problematic the traditional, supernatural idea of God, scientific speculation can be used to recover a sense of the numinous, a faith in the possibility of intentional, meaningful design as opposed to mere random event.

# Restoring America's Chosen Standing

Steven Spielberg's 1977 *Close Encounters of the Third Kind*, an immensely popular film at the time of its release, makes use of the "divine" alien for quite overt therapeutic and political purposes. In this film, the cultural malaise deriving from the Vietnam conflict and the political scandals surrounding Watergate and the resignation of President Richard Nixon forms the context for Spielberg's updated version of what we have discussed as a central American myth: that of American exceptionalism. Here the events predicting an alien landing and the spectacular realization of those predictions updates American millennialism through the advent of benign aliens on American soil. In the face of depressing historical events and a loss of American confidence in its role as a "city on a hill" this film seeks to reinvigorate the myth of America's special historical role through a subtle reversal of the meaning of current events. In its depiction of what initially seem to be threatening events and portents, the film guides its viewers toward an interpretive revision of history, one that recalls the puritan notion of understanding guided by and informed by faith.

It is important first to see how the extended final sequence of the film, in which the alien mothership eventually lands at Devils Tower National Monument in Wyoming, offers us a science fiction version of the events traditionally associated with the second coming of Christ predicted in the Gospels, known theologically as the *parousia*. If the dead are to rise at the coming of Christ, here we see the return of the unaged abductees, some of whom have been missing for years, as they exit one by one from the mothership. Paul's promise in 1 Thessalonians 4:16 that the redeemed will "meet the Lord in the air," a passage that led in the nineteenth century to the now-popular evangelical doctrine of the rapture, finds its science fiction equivalent in the ascent into the ship by Neary and the other Americans chosen to join the aliens, followed by the ascent of the craft as it lifts off with these privileged travelers.

The film makes use of other examples of Christian imagery and ideas. For example, Neary is converted to a belief in UFOs when he sees a blinding light on the road. We are doubtless invited to think of Paul's experience on the road to Damascus as recorded in Acts 9. We have, too, the examples of those "called" to faith in all the other persons, like Neary's friend Jillian and the others who travel to Wyoming, whose experience with a UFO leads them into a devoted, obsessive pursuit of a fuller communion with the visitors. Of course, most of these who have been called are not chosen. Only Neary and Jillian make it to the landing site. Indeed, when Neary, Jillian, and another man drawn to Devils Tower escape and attempt to reach the site prepared for the landing, this third pilgrim succumbs to the sleeping agent dispensed by the army, an event that recalls Paul's injunction in 1 Thessalonians 5:6 that those expecting salvation at the advent of the parousia must remain "awake."

In fact, if 1 Thessalonians is an epistle written specifically to encourage the members of the church at Thessalonica who had grown discouraged awaiting the second coming, *Close Encounters of the Third Kind* attempts a similar act of encouragement in its rehabilitation of the millennial national myth first constructed by the Puritans. The American withdrawal from Vietnam in 1973, the fall of Saigon in 1975, and the scandals of the Nixon White House, we should recall, took place just prior to a national event of great significance: the 1976 American Bicentennial. This event, taking place a year before the release of the film, is subtly woven into the narrative through its repeated reference to wonders in the sky—emphasized by imagery recalling the aerial fireworks of the typical American Fourth of July celebration.

Consider, for example, the scene in which Neary joins a number of people on a hillside at sunset awaiting the return of the UFOs that have been seen for several nights. We see people sitting in lawn chairs expectantly watching the sky, eating Kentucky Fried Chicken, and passing the time playing cards. By thus evoking a situation familiar to any American, that of a crowd awaiting the beginning of the traditional Fourth of July fireworks display, Spielberg manages to evoke both the celebrative mood of the national anniversary and to suggest the historical reasons for a sense of anxiety and foreboding surrounding the event. As the watchers await the arrival of the glorious light show of the UFOs, suddenly lights appear in the distance and the crowd rises to its feet in anticipation. Their enthusiasm, though, changes to fear and confusion as the "UFOs" are revealed to be government helicopters swooping over the crowd. This sudden appearance of helicopters introduces into the film one of the most prevalent and emotionally loaded images of the Vietnam War: that of American gunships riding shotgun in the skies of Vietnam and delivering troops to combat in that problematic and nationally traumatic conflict. That the helicopters "attack" Americans as they await the symbolic Fourth of July celebration gives the film a powerful and eloquent symbol of the film's core concerns. The horrors of the war and the political conflict it caused at home prevent a wholehearted celebration of what had been a belief in the special identity of America, its role as a redemptive and progressive historical force for good.

Yet the film's structure aims precisely to counter the dark implications of this scene. In the midst of what it depicts as a period of national loss of confidence and belief, the film argues, the signs of renewed hope and purpose appear everywhere. In fact, such signs are precisely those that seem at first to indicate the opposite. The opening sequence, for example, takes place in the Mexican desert as a group of American researchers are astounded to discover the navy aircraft (without their pilots) that had disappeared in the Bermuda Triangle in the 1940s. This evocation of lost young servicemen is, of course, an image of significant import and emotional power in the period just after the years of combat in Vietnam, which saw the death of over forty-five thousand American soldiers. Here, too, the group speaks to an old Mexican peasant who has witnessed the arrival of the UFOs that apparently returned the planes. His face, deeply reddened as if by a severe sunburn, also in context suggests the imagery of napalm and its terrible effects implanted in the American consciousness during the Vietnam years. We move from this scene to that of a near collision between an airliner and a UFO as air control operators fearfully watch the screen. Following this there is the scene suggestive of a horror film in which Jillian, terrified by the arrival of a UFO at her rural home, witnesses the kidnapping of her son, Barry, by the aliens.

It is, though, the difference between Barry's and Jillian's response to the appearance of the aliens that gives us our first indication of the film's redemptive and therapeutic intentions. Barry is awakened to wonder at the sudden animation of his battery-powered toys and responds joyfully to the events that so terrify his mother, inviting the unseen aliens to "come in." Barry's innocent wonder welcomes what so disturbs his mother. In his privileged "reading" of the advent of the aliens we are given a model for a rejuvenated perception, are invited to become, as the Gospels invite us to be, like "little children," capable of unobstructed faith, belief, and wonder (see Mark 10:15). Neary, though, whose enthusiasm for UFOs after his initial encounter matches Barry's, is increasingly troubled by his obsession. He is unable to convince his family to share his enthusiasm, and he begins to sculpt a mysterious shape in any material that comes to hand—in shaving cream and in mashed potatoes. Neary's loss of his family who become certain that he is insane, and the loss of his job, though traumatic, conform ultimately to the transformative logic of the film's narrative and thematic pattern. Late in the film, when Neary and Jillian have been picked up in Wyoming by the army, he is interrogated by Lacombe, the French UFO expert. Neary is asked whether he exhibits a number of distressing symptoms including ringing of the ears, migraine headaches, and irritation of the skin. When Neary admits to several of these, Lacombe nods sagely. What Lacombe knows, of course, is that these symptoms, however distressing, are in fact the signs of Neary's "election." He is one of those chosen by the aliens, invited to the landing about to take place at Devils Tower. These physical symptoms, like the disturbing events we discussed earlier, are to be understood not as signs of impending disaster, but rather as those of an imminent miraculous event. This reversal of implication lies at the heart of the film and recalls one of the central tenets of puritan belief: the central role of the American New World in a divinely ordained historical pattern.

As Sacvan Bercovitch explains, the Puritans extended the scope of scriptural interpretation beyond the text of the Bible. For them, the events of history after Jesus' lifetime were equally imbued with divine significance. History was a book to be read for signs of God's intentions in the world. Central to these intentions was America as a text to be read for its divine significance. It is worth recalling the following passage from Bercovitch:

> When [the puritans] announced that "America" was a figural sign . . . they broke free of the restrictions of exegesis. . . . [They] enlisted hermeneutics in what amounted to a private typology of current affairs. They were not only spiritual Israelites. . . . They were also, uniquely, American Israelites, the sole, reliable exegetes of a new, last book of scripture. (Bercovitch, pp.112-13)

As this "new book of scripture," America could be properly interpreted only by Americans guided by their faith in the New World's historical and spiritual destiny: "The perceiver had to identify with the divine meaning of the New World if he was to understand his environment correctly. He had to 'cast his account' as an American" (Bercovitch, p. 114).

In the same way, *Close Encounters*'s viewer is invited to "cast his account" as an American by engaging in a process in which initially troubling signs are revealed in the course of the film to be the compelling indicators of the inevitable justification of the American enterprise. When the audience first sees Devils Tower, for example, it is surrounded by barbed wire and armed soldiers and protected by official lies concocted by the government to prevent public knowledge of the alien landing about to take place. It is devilish indeed. Yet the tower, dedicated by Teddy Roosevelt as the first American Monument, is the site of a symbolic parousia resonant with the wonder forecast by the Puritans in their initial vision of American glory. As a symbol of America, the tower's meaning changes as the film achieves its visionary climax. Or, more precisely, the true meaning of the tower is revealed and experienced by a common American whose "faith" has led him there.

The film's viewer is invited to identify with Neary and to share his experiences of wonder, anxiety, and ultimate enlightenment. It is important to note, though, that there are two perspectives in the film. One is that of Neary and the other typical Americans called to the site. The other is that of the government officials who realize quite early in the film the significance of Devils Tower and who work in secret to prepare for the landing. The viewer thus shares both perspectives and experiences their ultimate confluence as Neary comes to know what the officials know and to share in the event for which they have been preparing. In their passion for secrecy, the government officials fail to appreciate what Lacombe, the only foreigner among them, appreciates—that common Americans like Neary have been specifically invited to the landing. This secrecy is the major fault of those in authority. The film addresses the distrust of government caused by the official lies of the Vietnam and Watergate era by another use of the strategy of reversal we have discussed. Government lies and secrecy, the film declares, are wrong, but the secret they protect is not a guilty knowledge but rather the reality of the imminent alien contact. Such secrecy is ill informed because the truth is not disastrous but wonderful, and the purpose of the government has been to do all that it can to prepare for and facilitate a marvelous event. Secrecy only promotes uninformed anxiety, and everything is better—much, much better—than the uninformed realize. In lamenting the withholding of information by the government, the film promotes a populist vision of American triumph, one available to common persons who have been invited to the alien arrival. This landing—filled with lights in the sky as UFOs swoop and glide over the landing site, and which culminates in the appearance of the huge, brightly lit mothership as hundreds look upward in awe—redeems the spoiled "Fourth of July" celebration earlier in the film. As Neary joins the government personnel at the landing site and is in fact chosen to be one of those to board the ship for a journey to the stars, the distinction between those on the "inside" and common Americans collapses.

# Redeeming American Culture

There is another removal of difference operating in the film, common to Spielberg's films of this period. This feature of the film concerns what we might call the redemption of American mass culture. Here are some examples of what we mean. When Neary manages to awaken his family to take them to the site where he watched several UFOs speeding along the roadway, he tells his wife that they looked like ice cream cones or shells. She responds, "You mean like a taco? Like one of those Sara Lee moon-shaped cookies?" In another scene, the searchlight from one of the ships falls briefly in close-up on a McDonald's sign, bathing it in an unearthly radiance, suggesting a heightened, mysterious significance. Neary's fascination with UFOs is momentarily undermined, then suddenly renewed as he awakens from sleep to see a comic Martian in a Saturday morning TV cartoon.

It is in fact television that finally reveals to Neary the identity of the image of the tower that has for weeks haunted him. Just prior to this televised revelation, Neary, having built a huge model of the tower in his recreation room, now abandoned by his family, and fearing for his sanity, stares dejectedly from his window. It is at this point that an advertising jingle delivers from his television a message of millennial hope: "The king is coming,/ let's hear the call./ When you've said Bud, you've said it all!" It is directly following this commercial that Neary sees on the evening news the image of the tower that has been his obsession. As Lacombe later explains to the commanding officer at the Devils Tower compound, "For every one of these anxious, anguished people who have come here . . . there must be hundreds of others also touched by the implanted vision who never made it this far—simply because they don't watch television." It is also at the Devils Tower that we see the trucks that have been disguised by the government bringing supplies: they bear the logos of Piggly-Wiggly, Coca Cola, and Baskin Robbins. If Puritan exegetes read the New World landscape for signs of grace, emblems of impending glory, in *Close Encounters* the landscape of American consumer culture radiates a millennial significance. In another example of the technique of reversal we have examined earlier, the critical view of American consumerism and the apparently "degraded" level of American mass culture is countered by the film's revelatory enthusiasm. Fast food, television programs, ice cream, and cookies—all the apparently meaningless junk of modern American culture—is presented as imbued with a powerful redemptive meaning.

*Close Encounters* ultimately suggests that the most powerful redemptive force in American mass culture is film itself. It is film that invites us to become "as little children," sharing the hopeful, visionary perspective Spielberg wishes to restore to a nation battered by the onslaughts of history and doubt. The area prepared for the promised arrival of the benevolent aliens lies, as we have noted, at the foot of the first American Monument. It is also, importantly, like nothing else so much as a film set: a place of movie cameras, lights, and sound recording devices where the marvelous makes its awe-inspiring appearance. It may be more accurate to say that the landing site serves as a metaphor for not only the production, but also the viewing of film. Think of one of Spielberg's favorite shots, that of viewers gazing in wonder at the scene before them, into the light containing marvels. This is Spielberg's most compelling point, that film has the power to restore in a troubled time a sense of the mythic power of America first powerfully articulated in the religious vision of puritan New England.

# Vignettes

## E. T. (1982)

E. T. is also concerned with redemptive meaning. Many commentators on the film have noted E. T.'s Christlike attributes: he can heal and perform other miracles, he descends from above, and he returns to his celestial realm. He dies and is resurrected, and he appears to his "disciples" following his resurrection in his white shroud, displaying a red beating heart visible in his chest.

It is important to connect E. T.'s "divine" status with his repeatedly emphasized connections to American mass culture. First, and most obviously, he looks like a stuffed toy creature (E. T. dolls were very popular for several years after the release of the film). In fact, he lives in a closet filled with such toys, and he hides among these, unrecognized in the welter of dolls, teddy bears, and other stuffed animals when Marian, the mother, looks into Elliot's room. He delights in television and gets his idea for a device to broadcast a signal to his alien companions from a *Flash Gordon* comic strip in the newspaper. This device, too, is constructed out of everyday items found in Elliot's house. Just as Jesus' coming, for Christians, organizes the Bible into a meaningful whole, so the figure of E. T. draws together and illuminates with significance the commonplace elements of Elliot's suburban world.

## The Fifth Element (1997)

If *2001* presents aliens as the divinelike agents of intelligent design and *Close Encounters* presents them as the gods who choose their followers and call the faithful to them, then *The Fifth Element* presents its main alien protagonist as a Christ who is opposed by an alien figure of pure evil at the ordained time of the apocalyptic end. This Christ figure is deemed perfect, as she is reconstructed from her DNA after the "descent" of her spacecraft is violently prevented by the approaching evil.

The film symbolizes the evil as a dark, burning asteroid that is either intelligent or contains unseen intelligent beings. Its approach with the intent to destroy earth was predicted millennia earlier by an alien race who built a temple in Egypt to function as a weapon against it. This temple has been guarded since then by a tiny priesthood, waiting for the return of the evil and the alien/divine savior.

The savior arrives despite the attempts to prevent her and astounds everyone, including the priests, because in her perfection she combines femininity, beauty, strength, agility, and high intelligence. Yet she remains innocent and vulnerable, despite her commitment to her salvific mission. In the end, with destruction rapidly approaching, she takes the world's evils upon herself—in the knowledge of all humanity's wars—and then sacrifices herself on the temple's altar to become the channel for the light that triumphs over the darkness. Her "resurrection" from that experience once again confounds the authorities, for it crosses the line by which Christianity has separated sexuality from the divine.

# Suggested Readings

Sacvan Bercovitch, *The Puritan Origins of the American Self* (New Haven: Yale University Press, 1975).

Brenda Denzler, *The Lure of the Edge: Scientific Passions, Religious Beliefs, and the Pursuit of UFOs* (Berkeley: University of California Press, 2001).

James R. Lewis, *The Gods Have Landed: New Religions from Other Worlds* (Albany, N.Y.: SUNY Press, 1995).

Thomas Allen Nelson, *Kubrick: Inside a Film Artist's Maze* (Bloomington & Indianapolis: Indiana University Press, 2000).

Rudolf Otto, *The Idea of the Holy*, translated by John W. Harvey, 2nd ed. (London: Oxford University Press, 1950).

Christopher Partridge, *UFO Religions* (London: Routledge, 2003).

# CHAPTER 11

# Religion and Scandal, Crime and Innocence

Jesus was a criminal. He was tried before the highest judge of the land, condemned as a criminal, and punished by crucifixion. This fact, as the Apostle Paul later wrote, is "the scandal of the cross" (Gal. 5:11). In this context, the Greek word *skandalon* is often translated as "stumbling block"; Paul uses it to indicate that Jesus' execution is a stumbling block that prevents people from taking the Christian message seriously (1 Cor. 1:23).

According to Christianity, the circumstances of Jesus' execution were more complex. Jesus may have been condemned, but he was innocent. After all, as Mark 14:55-59 indicates, those who testified against him lied, and they did this so badly that they contradicted each other and could not convict him. It was not until Jesus himself spoke blasphemy before the High Priest (Mark 14:60-64) that he was condemned. So Jesus was guilty.

Yet, he spoke the truth. So he was innocent. So what is the scandal of which Paul writes, that Jesus was crucified as a criminal, or that he was crucified even though he was innocent?

There is one sense in which Jesus clearly was not innocent. He was not ignorant of the events in which he was involved, nor did he fail to understand their meaning. His prayerful trauma in the Garden of Gethsemane before his arrest makes this clear (Mark 14:32-36). Jesus knew what he was doing and what the consequences would be.

So Jesus himself was a scandal, even though he stands as the central pillar of Christianity. But what of Christians themselves? Can they be both pious believers and scandalous at the same time? Can they be both innocent and criminal? The two films of this chapter explore different ways in which a Christian could be all these at once. We say "could be" because the films themselves set out the circumstances in which this may be true, but leave the audience to judge.

# The Mystery of Innocence

*Agnes of God* (1985) constitutes, in several important ways, a mystery narrative. At the simplest level, it deals with an investigation into the killing of a newborn infant in a Canadian convent, a closed world cut off from the outside by walls and guarded gates. The baby, born to Agnes, is found dead in a wastepaper basket in Agnes's cell. The court appoints a psychiatrist, Dr. Martha Livingston, to investigate the mental state of this unusual, perhaps mentally ill, novice to ascertain if she should stand trial for manslaughter. Livingston, however, becomes more involved in the case than expected. Rather than simply determining whether or not Agnes is sane, Dr. Livingston ultimately becomes a detective attempting to work out exactly what has occurred in the convent.

It does not take Livingston long to discover that Agnes is profoundly naïve—innocent, even—as the result of being raised by an alcoholic, abusive mother who kept her from any schooling. Agnes claims not even to have known she was pregnant, and she cannot provide any answer to Livingston's questions concerning the father of the child. Indeed, she can reveal nothing whatever about its conception. Faced with the extreme difficulty of gaining entrance into the walled and gated convent—especially for any man other than the nuns' confessor, the very aged Pere Martineau—Livingston approaches the problem with the usual detective's questions: who is the father? How did he gain access to the convent? Or did Agnes somehow escape to meet him on the outside? Was Agnes raped or seduced? Livingston's questions aim at identifying a man—a human man—who was able to impregnate Agnes.

Within the religious world of the convent, however, other possibilities arise. Perhaps Agnes's conception occurred through supernatural means. Not only is this supported by Agnes's innocence, but a supernatural entity is identified as a possible partner, namely, the Archangel Michael. This possibility is complicated by Agnes's special character, as Livingston learns while interviewing the novice. She is a visionary. As a young girl, she began to see the "beautiful lady" who has continued to visit her throughout her life. Indeed, Agnes claims that the beautiful voice in which she sings her moving canticles comes from the Lady.

Dr. Livingston at first finds the notion that the Angel Michael is the father preposterous and dismisses it disdainfully. This reaction indicates Livingston's assumption of the superiority of science and reason. This brings her into conflict with the convent's Mother Superior, who fears that Dr. Livingston's investigation will not only erode Agnes's religious faith, but her own faith, now revitalized by Agnes. Agnes represents for Mother Superior an innocent and profoundly joyous faith, something to be protected from the skeptical scientific modernity represented by Dr. Livingston.

Although Livingston's assigned task centers on the newborn's death, the film focuses on the infant's conception—a mysterious, possibly supernatural event. As in *The Exorcist* in chapter 9, *Agnes of God* brings together the approaches of law, medicine, and religion in an attempt to solve the mystery. Each approach defines the problem in a different manner; each approach allows certain evidence to be included and other evidence to be excluded; each approach enables certain kinds of explanations and invalidates others. Crucially, each approach defines the key question differently: Is Agnes guilty? Is Agnes sane? Is Agnes a saint impregnated by the Archangel Michael? The film keeps these questions in play, to allow within the realm of possibility even that last—for most viewers—most challenging and unlikely of explanations.

In an attempt to disturb the predictable attitudes of many viewers to the events it represents, to call into question a sense of basic and unshakable certainties, the film adopts a fascinating strategy. Dr. Livingston, in attempting to discern what took place and to judge the degree of Agnes's innocence, asks her on several occasions if she understands the "facts of life." Does she know "where babies come from"? Although Dr. Livingston repeats this question in a number of ways throughout the film, she never receives the expected answer from Agnes. A simple reading of this pattern might suggest that Agnes is either truly uninformed or so traumatized by her mother's molestation that she represses all sexual knowledge, but instead this repeatedly unsuccessful line of questioning confronts Dr. Livingston and the film's viewers with what the film implies is the unanswerability of that simple question and thus with a sense of the essential mysteriousness of reality. When she is first asked where the baby came from, Agnes says, "They say it came from the wastepaper basket," referring to the basket in which the body of the infant was found. Dr.

Livingston, attempting of course to determine the degree of Agnes's sexual knowledge, asks, "Where did it come from before that?" Agnes responds, "From God." Frustrated, Dr. Livingston tries again: "Do you know where babies come from?" Agnes asks, "Don't you?" In a following scene, Agnes asks Livingston, "Where do you think babies come from?" and the psychiatrist says, "From their mothers and fathers, of course." Agnes then explains to the doctor her idea that good and bad babies are in fact good and fallen angels, respectively, with quite different methods of taking up residence in the mother's body. The repetition of the question and Agnes's refusal to give the expected answer return the viewers again and again to the problematic nature of a question to which the film's viewers have an immediate and unquestioned answer.

Agnes's silence and myth-making in response to the question divert us from the realm of simple, automatic responses based upon a scientific worldview. They remind us that, although the biological answer Dr. Livingston attempts to extract from Agnes provides an undoubted explanation of the mechanism of human reproduction, the question of origins implies a larger context than the psychiatrist intends to invoke, the one with which Agnes is primarily concerned. It implies, ultimately, the question of all origins, moving from the source of life to the source of all that exists. Why, to cite a famous philosophical and theological question, is there anything rather than nothing? For Agnes the answer is simple: because God exists. Agnes's myth of good and bad babies and her assertion that God is the origin of life reminds us of her discussion with Mother Superior, who reprimands Agnes for not eating. Agnes says that she intends only to eat communion wafers, to which Mother Superior responds, "I don't believe the host contains the recommended daily allowance of anything." Agnes, shocked, responds, "Of God!" Again the film stages a sudden contextual shift, from the realm of science to that of religion and faith. Agnes in her innocence lives only in that second world. Her visions and her beautiful, haunting songs, which she claims to come from the "Lady" singing within her, are, like art and myth, means of admitting and celebrating the mystery of life.

# Clues to the Loss of Innocence

In the end, the film's narrative takes the form of a mystery for which no answer can ultimately be found. This in turn evokes the viewer's expectations only to subvert them. As Dr. Livingston begins to act less as a psychiatrist and more like a detective investigating a crime, the film engages the traditional apparatus of the mystery story. Indeed, the fact that Agnes—sequestered within the walls of the convent and thus presumably beyond the reach of any men—has become pregnant aligns the narrative with a common mystery subgenre: the locked room problem, in which the detective must reason out an explanation for a murder that has taken place in a room locked from the inside. In emphasizing investigation, the film seeks to remind the audience that if crime is a violation of human law, then miracles are also a violation of law—of the physical laws it is the function of science to discover.

Livingston in the course of her investigation follows clues and tips, interviews suspects, searches the convent and studies its architectural plans. She discovers a secret tunnel leading from the laundry to the barn, where she suspects Agnes was raped or seduced. One of the nuns whispers to her that she ought to research Agnes's records stored in the convent basement, and she finds that Mother Superior is in fact Agnes's aunt. Livingston learns that one of the nuns, the now-deceased Sister Paul, had a curious relationship with the young novice. Sister Paul would tell Agnes that she was beautiful and that "all God's angels would like to sleep beside her." Has Sister Paul, who revealed the secret passage to Agnes, and who seems to have told Agnes that she was to have an assignation with the Archangel Michael, preyed upon the novice's faith and innocence, for unknown reasons, to facilitate a seduction? Mother Superior's story of a nun (perhaps Sister Paul?) depressed at the onset of menopause, suggests perhaps a motive for arranging such an event, a misguided attempt to "save" Agnes from enforced childlessness. Through a tip from a friend on the police force Livingston discovers that none of the other cells in the convent contained a wastepaper basket, and she later finds out that Mother Superior, despite her earlier assertions, knew of the pregnancy and placed the basket in the room. For a time Livingston suspects that Mother Superior was the one who killed the infant in an attempt to avoid scandal and to protect her niece.

Unlike the traditional detective story, though, the mysteries in the film are not resolved in the course of the investigation. Under hypnotism, Agnes does describe a trip to the barn through the tunnel shown her by Sister Paul, but she describes not an ordinary rape or seduction, but rather a visionary event in which an unspecified "he" comes to her:

**Agnes:** Yes. Yes, I do.
Why me?
Wait. I want to see you.
**Livingston:** What do you see?
**Agnes:** Halos. Dividing and dividing.
Feathers are stars falling.
Falling into the iris of God's eye.
Oh, oh. It's so lovely. It's so blue.
Yellow, black wings, brown, blood!
No. Red! His blood!

Throughout Agnes's account the viewer sees only the empty barn—empty, that is, except for the rays of light through the roof and the scores of doves in flight. Presumably, this is Agnes's recollection under hypnosis of what she has experienced. If this is so, then why do we not see all that she sees? Where is the "he" that she describes? Or does the film suggest that Agnes only intuited the presence of a visitor who may or may not be the Archangel Michael? By contrast, perhaps the audience should interpret the sequence as revealing that there was in fact nobody there at all—precisely what appears on the screen. The detective's approach through descriptive fact answers nothing.

But seen within the religious discourse, Agnes's experience takes on fuller significance. The event happened the night Sister Paul died. When Sister Paul whispered the name "Michael" to Agnes, Agnes left the room to follow the tunnel to the barn. Once in the barn, a powerful light from outside shines through the roof and windows, more light than we would expect to see in the middle of the night. This illumination from above, accompanied by the doves in flight, supplies the scene with traditional images of the appearance of the sacred. The doves symbolize the descent of the paraclete, the Holy Spirit, and the heavenly rays of light have a long artistic tradition of portraying the immaculate conception. Additionally, they suggest, as in the case of Paul on the road to Damascus, the sudden revelation of divine presence, a theophany. Understood in this manner, these references to iconographic tradition suggest an appearance of the sacred that must be represented symbolically, in a form the limited human mind can grasp.

Perhaps the psychological approach explains this better. Agnes responds to the light and the doves through the lens of her religious training and fervent belief. Does this suggest that, having been prepared by Sister Paul for the arrival of Michael, Agnes has interpreted the rape or seduction by a human as a supernatural experience? If the film makes use of the concept of the locked room mystery, then both the discovered tunnel and the hypnotic trance provide ways of access into the "locked room," the site of the mysterious event at the time of its occurrence.

In the end, having become witnesses to the mysterious event, we are left not with solutions but with interpretive cues. We are not given the clarity of a resolution to the mystery the film stages. The film provides neither a human and rational explanation of Agnes's experience nor proof of a supernatural event.

Rather we are faced with the resoluteness of that mystery, with the fact that all we can ever do is interpret what we are given. In a sense the film suggests that our attempts fully to resolve the mysteries of the world and of faith are doomed to failure, that reality in a sense remains a "locked room," the contents of which can never fully be known with an absolute knowledge. The film ultimately sustains not a solution, but rather the recognition of mystery. Dr. Livingston, the lapsed Catholic who felt a need to rescue Agnes from superstitious delusion and to discover rational explanation for the events at the convent, ends with a renewed faith. Her faith adheres not to any particular doctrine, but to the enduring questions for which there may be no final answers.

# Can the Guilty Be Faithful?

Sonny, or The Apostle E. F., as he renames himself as the protagonist of *The Apostle* (1998), is a Pentecostal preacher and a deeply flawed man. There is no sense in which he can be declared "innocent." Coming in the wake of the various scandals that rocked the Pentecostal, televangelist community at that time—such as those of Jim Bakker and Jimmy Swaggert—the film presents a character whose story traces a redemptive progress that emphasizes the fallibility of the merely human even as it recognizes the complex sources of beatitude and violence and testifies to the archetypal power of biblical narrative. If the question about Agnes is how she can be innocent and pure before God yet commit a crime, then the question about Sonny is how a wrongdoer can serve God faithfully.

Sonny, the successful, charismatic minister of a Texas Pentecostal church is precipitated into a crisis when he discovers that his wife, Jessie, has been having an affair with Horace, the youth minister at the church. In the tense conversation with his wife following his discovery of her infidelity, we learn several things about Sonny. Jessie's obvious physical fear as the two talk suggests that Sonny can be a violent man, something that his attack upon Horace will shortly confirm. This capacity for violence is further emphasized by the fact that Jessie unloads the pistol lying on the coffee table, the weapon we have seen Sonny take with him to Horace's house the night his suspicions about his wife are validated. In that scene we see Sonny overcome his anger and place the gun on the dashboard of his car, saying to himself, "Thou shalt not kill." When Sonny is driven by his friend, Joe, to confront his wife at their home, he tells Joe to come running if he feels that Sonny is about to attack his wife. It is during this tense discussion between Sonny and Jessie that we are given an important insight into Sonny's character. Suggesting that Sonny not make too much of a public issue about her infidelity, Jessie warns, "I certainly know as much about what you have done as you think I know." Sonny admits to his "roving eye" and his "wicked, wicked ways," but explains that he has been unfaithful because he "loves to evangelize." This apparent *non sequitur*, given by Sonny as an obvious and uncontestable explanation for his behavior provides us with an important clue to Sonny's subsequent behavior, both his violent crime and his obsessive need to start anew with the founding of another church.

When, despite his earlier self-control when he was armed with his pistol, Sonny becomes enraged over the loss of his wife, children, and church, and strikes Horace with a baseball bat, we are shocked by his violence. Yet however terrible the act, which does in fact lead to Horace's death, we note that Sonny has acted out of outraged love for his family and his despair at suddenly, like Job, having been dispossessed of all that is dear to him. The Job parallel has in fact been made explicit earlier in the film as Sonny, alone in his boyhood room in his mother's house, shouts out to God his questions and complaints. "I know that I am a sinner, but I am your servant, Lord," Sonny insists, and he asks to be given peace and to be shown a sign. There is no response from above. If Sonny, like Job, refuses to "curse God," he does not hesitate to argue. "I'm mad at you," he shouts toward the ceiling while his mother in her room below explains to a neighbor upset about the noise that "ever since he was a little bitty boy, sometimes he talks to the Lord, and sometimes he yells at the Lord." If Sonny, God's servant who suffers a terrible loss, is like Job, his fleeing Dallas after delivering the blow that will lead to Horace's death aligns him with Moses who, in Exodus chapter 2, flees Egypt after the killing of an Egyptian he sees beating a Hebrew. Job's encounter with

God in the whirlwind and Moses' meeting with God in the desert of Midian and return to Egypt to free the enslaved find subtle parallels in Sonny's experiences of exile and return.

After his hurried flight from Dallas, Sonny's first act is to perform the first of two symbolic deaths that, taken together, form the whole of an attempt to enact Paul's insistence upon the crucifying of the "old self . . . so that the body of sin may be destroyed" (Romans 6:6). Sonny sinks his car in a pond, destroys his driver's license and other forms of identification, and sets off on foot. The second half of the ritual occurs when Sonny is staying a few days with the one-legged man on the bayou, who offers him a tent to sleep in. After fasting, Sonny baptizes himself anew and adopts the name The Apostle E. F. Again the film invites us to discern the biblical parallels. When his benefactor asks Sonny if he has anywhere to stay, Sonny responds "Not yet, but the Lord leads me." We may well recall Luke 9:58: "And Jesus said . . . 'Foxes have holes, and birds of the air have nests; but the Son of Man has nowhere to lay his head.'" Given that Sonny has named himself an apostle, we may also see in his travels after unburdening himself of his car and identity Jesus' injunction to his apostles in Luke 9:3, "Take nothing for your journey, no staff, nor bag, nor bread, nor money—not even an extra tunic."

When the one-legged man mentions a preacher named Charles Blackwell in Bayou Boutté, Louisiana, E. F. takes it as a sign that he is to meet with this man and found a new church. As Sonny explains his mission to an initially cautious Blackwell, another biblical parallel is touched upon. Sonny explains that he has been in every state "except Alaska," and has visited several foreign countries, always founding churches. In this, of course, Sonny's self-description reminds us of the career of Paul, who spent much of his life traveling the Roman world founding Christian churches.

In Bayou Boutté Sonny is given a dilapidated and disused church in which the Reverend Blackwell preached for many years before his retirement, a church far more humble than the megachurch he previously ran in Texas. While his work to restore the church—repairing the roof, cleaning the interior, and painting the exterior—and his restoration of an ancient bus to transport his small congregation can be understood as outward symbols of his attempt to atone for his sins and renovate himself, the film avoids a sentimental narrative of perfect redemption. Although Sonny is concerned about his ailing mother and deeply laments the loss of his family, he shows little if any actual guilt over the attack upon

Horace, even when he is informed by Joe that Horace has died of his injury. Similarly, despite his lamentation over his estranged wife, Sonny quite early in his stay in Bayou Boutté develops an interest in Toosie, the pretty secretary at the radio station at which he begins broadcasting his energetic Pentecostal sermons in an attempt to expand interest in his church services. It is important to note, given the link Sonny has himself previously made between his evangelical passion and his more carnal interests, that he first asks Toosie to have dinner with him immediately following his initial broadcast. Toosie, who exclaims that she has never seen preaching like Sonny's, is clearly impressed by his passionate and energetic performance, and she agrees to the date. Sonny's response to her reaction, "You won't find the frozen chosen," serves again to underscore, in its advocacy of warm-blooded enthusiasm, the connection between religious and sexual transport, carnal and spiritual love. At the same time, however, this emphasis on Sonny's passionate nature reminds us of the scene at the baseball game in which he attempted to pull Jessie away by the hair and delivered the ultimately fatal blow to Horace.

Sonny's passion, expressing itself in religious enthusiasm and the desire to evangelize but also in an intense sexuality and propensity for violence, can be disturbing for viewers of the film. In teaching *The Apostle* we have found that a significant number of students, discouraged by Sonny's behavior, come to consider him a hypocrite and a fraud. Yet, it is useful to note how often the film contrives for the audience to attend to Sonny's private prayers, to speech, that is, in which he has no need for any dissimulation. Each time he addresses God, when going to sleep on his first night in Sammy's house, during his self-baptism, and on a number of other occasions, Sonny reveals a sincerity of purpose. However much Sonny may be the instrument of his sexual desire and aggression, he reveals in these instances of private communication a sincere desire to achieve his other passionate purpose, the founding of his church and his dedication to the apostleship he has assumed.

It is thus this paradox that the film explores through Sonny: that love and violence, religious passion and terrible aggression arise from the same source, the powerful emotional depths of human nature. In the central confrontation between Sonny and the unnamed local who threatens to bulldoze the church, the film suggests the power of religion to transform negative passions and human violence into their opposites. We first see the unnamed local as he enters the church one evening during a service and his feigned politeness quickly gives way to barely restrained anger, apparent resentment, and racial slurs. In Sonny's rapidly increasing anger at the behavior of the visitor we are again reminded of his capacity for violence. Almost immediately, Sonny invites the heckler outside for a fight that he wins without apparent difficulty. Sonny's quick and accurate appraisal of the visitor's purpose and his willingness with little hesitation to fight serve to emphasize the similarities between the antagonists. Sonny, fighting the visitor, fights a version of himself, an opponent given to the same violent impulses. It is worth noting as well that from the perspective of this later event we are given a further understanding of Sonny's attack upon Horace in which Sonny, an admitted adulterer himself, does violence to the man who has committed adultery with Jessie. If Horace through his lack of self-control does harm to Sonny's marriage and family, this is no more than Sonny has himself done in his own adulteries.

This pattern of mirroring between Sonny and his antagonists suggests of course Sonny's own struggles with himself. For this reason the final confrontation between Sonny and his antagonist has emphatic significance. Following the fight, he promises to return, and he does so during a church fundraising picnic, entering the scene aboard a bulldozer with a holstered pistol mounted beside the seat, a weapon that reminds us of the pistol Sonny places on the dashboard of his car on the night he discovers Jessie at Horace's house. If Sonny has lost his Dallas church at least partially as a result of his own behavior, he is in this scene threatened with the second loss of a church he has founded and loved at the hands of an antagonist who is in significant respects his double. The bulldozer driver's conversion, his breaking down and acceptance of Jesus as Savior, enacts with only the slightest touch of irony the utopian possibilities of religious faith. If we are tempted to smile at the hyperbole of the radio announcer's description of the conversion as "absolutely incredible," we nevertheless witness a moment of transformation in which hatred and potential violence give way to a sense of redemptive possibility. We have no way of knowing whether this angry and violent man will achieve a permanent change. He may, after recovering from the emotional impact of the moment, simply become again the angry, hate-filled man he was. Yet, this is perhaps the point. Our knowledge of human behavior suggests that such radical transformations are fragile at best. After all, we have seen Sonny's surrender to negative and destructive impulses. Yet, in recognizing that in the passionate, emotional aspects of human nature lie the roots of both the best and worst of our impulses, the film maintains a faith in the necessity of the struggle between these impulses, one aided by religious commitment.

# Vignettes

## *Saved* (2004)

Set in a Pentecostal Christian high school, this film provides a light-hearted look at how, even among those participating in relationship with Jesus, human concerns rather than divine dedication often come to the fore. About to start her senior year, Mary thinks life is perfect and looks forward to serving the Lord with her friends. But instead of everyone living perfect lives, they descend into scandal. Although the characters are as innocent and naïve as most high school kids, there are a surprising number of scandalous acts, and their consequences, in the film.

Before the year begins, Mary learns her boyfriend is gay and his parents have sent him to the Mercy House institution for de-gayification—but not before Mary becomes pregnant with his child. Then her best friend's wheel-chair-bound brother takes up with the school's poster girl for bad behavior, the one Jewish student. Both, in their own way, are scandalous: she for her outrageous behavior attempting to get herself expelled, he for his refusal to let his crippled body dictate his desire to live his own life. It also seems that Mary's widowed mom is having an affair with the school's preacher-principal, who would be divorced except that he seems more interested in obeying rules ("divorce is not part of God's plan"). And then there is Hilary Faye, the "perfect" Christian girl, who commits the only crime in the film, and frames Mary and her friends for it.

The film may lack the violence and murder of this chapter's main films, but it still explores the coexistence of belief and scandal, innocence and crime—with a nod in the direction of *Grease*. The film suggests that the Christian community around the school deals with scandal by getting rid of it, but that this strategy fails because the pillars of the community are those who are most scandalous.

## *Leap of Faith* (1992)

If *The Apostle*'s Sonny is a flawed minister who nonetheless serves God and creates a community of believers, then the "Reverend" Jonas

Nightengale of *Leap of Faith* is a conman who uses the appearance of serving the Lord to enrich himself from the community he invades. Jonas does not believe in God, and the entire revival show that he brings to the small town of Rustwater, Kansas, is designed to separate the "suckers" from their money through huckstering, fake miracles, and claims that Jonas is a conduit for God's power. For three nights, Jonas's show mesmerizes and flimflams a growing audience of farmers desperate for rain and out-of-work laborers desperate to feed their families. If the question for *The Apostle* is whether God can work through a flawed servant, then the question for *Leap* is whether God can work through a fraud who does not serve him at all.

Through most of the film, it is clear that the revival show is a fake, for the film revels in showing the details of how each scam is set up and carried out. But on the last night a real miracle takes place: the crippled teenager Boyd is healed. Faced with an "authentic" work of God, Jonas is personally overwhelmed. He refuses to take credit for the healing and runs away—in a reverse echo of *The Music Man* he manages to escape—realizing perhaps that although he can run a fake revival show, he knows nothing about handling one where God is truly present.

Although the community of believers gathered around the revival tent lose the human center around which they have gathered, since Jonas has never really been there in spirit or intention that does not prevent a second, more important miracle from occurring. The scandal of course is that the "Reverend" is not a Christian, but he ministers to the people anyway. The main question is whether they received the blessings he claimed (and faked), even though in many ways he is a less-suitable vessel than even Sonny. When the religious leader is a fake, does that mean that the religious experiences had by the congregation are also fake?

# Suggested Reading

George M. Marsden, *Understanding Fundamentalism and Evangelicalism* (Grand Rapids, Mich.: Wm. B. Eerdmans, 1991).

# CHAPTER 12

# The Religion of Baseball

Christopher Evans has pointed out that it has "become fashionable to speak of baseball's significance in American popular culture as analogous to an institutional religion" (Evans, p. 35). He argues that baseball, more than any other sport, reveals an alliance with the "distinctive liberal-Protestant theological worldview" that arose in the progressive and optimistic post–Civil War period of the late nineteenth and early twentieth centuries.

> In an era defined by a variety of social-reform initiatives, baseball became a symbol of postmillennial liberal-Protestant zeal that contributed to the personal and social uplifting of all Americans. Turn-of-the-century Protestant church leaders preached a gospel of a new millennial civilization, where the faith of God meant faith that the virtues of an Anglo-Saxon civilization would spread the Gospel and lead to unprecedented social advancement in the Western world. In short, baseball encapsulated Protestant hope to usher in the kingdom of God in America. (Evans, p. 37)

Evans enumerates what were regarded as the virtues of baseball in the service of this millennial hope. Ballparks introduced the pastoral space of the country into the American city, places to embody the "rural virtues" of closeness to nature and healthy recreation that encouraged physical exercise and "youthful zeal." Furthermore, the game of baseball taught the moral virtues of sportsmanlike, gentlemanly competition, and the desire to win through hard work and team cooperation, and it emphasized "the virtues of male ruggedness and Protestant piety" (Evans, pp. 39-40). Most important, Evans explains, baseball "served as an illustration of how Americans from different class and ethnic backgrounds could work cooperatively to build a better society—striving for a shared vision of the kingdom of God" (Evans, p. 40). The game thus embodied the cooperative and democratic ideals that for liberal Protestants lay at the heart of America's millennial promise as a redemptive power in the world.

The millennial significance of America's special promise has been articulated again and again, in various forms, in American popular film. This is also true of the baseball films we will discuss here. *The Natural* was released in 1984, near the end of Ronald Reagan's first term as president. *Field of Dreams* appeared in 1989, near the end of his second term. The Reagan presidency famously promised in its dedication to conservative politics a return to what Reagan felt were the traditional American values of small government, free enterprise, and unabashed patriotism. His presidency was announced as a return to "Morning in America," the rebirth of the values that Republican conservatives felt had been eroded by liberalism. Reagan's conservative presidency declared its intention to restore a vision of American redemptive promise that had been damaged by the discouraging events of the sixties and early seventies. The long trauma and disastrous end of the Vietnam conflict, the Watergate scandal and the resignation under threat of impeachment of President Richard Nixon, the Iranian hostage crisis during the administration of President Jimmy Carter—these and other events had severely tested many Americans' faith in the course of American history. As early as 1974, in a speech before the Republican National Convention, Reagan had made emphatic use of the puritan idea of America as the New Jerusalem, filled with millennial promise and serving as an example to the world by quoting John Winthrop's famous characterization of the New World enterprise: "We will be as a city upon a hill." Reagan would go on to become one of the most popular presidents in American history, one whose vision of American promise would inspire millions and at the same time appall and discourage those for whom the sixties had been a period of renewed liberal hope, of a return to another vision of "traditional American values" quite different from those espoused by Reagan conservatives.

# The Wounds of the Game

*The Natural* (1984), the first of our films, is based upon the 1952 novel by Bernard Malamud. The film eliminates the book's ironies and pes-

simism to develop a full-blown vision of American heroism as a redemptive force of mythic significance and power. Malamud's novel makes use
for ultimately ironic purposes the myth of the quest for the Holy Grail
that had been reactivated in the most famous and influential poem of the
twentieth century: T. S. Eliot's *The Waste Land*. For those unfamiliar with
the poem and the medieval works from which it draws its materials, here
is a brief summary of the grail quest legend.

The poem begins with a world in profound crisis, a wasteland suffering
from drought and disease and ruled over by a figure called the Fisher King.
The Fisher King is in a state of perpetual illness and suffering brought
about by an unspecified wound that will not heal. It is of crucial importance to the myth that we understand the link between the state of the
king and the condition of the land; the illness of the king is mirrored in
the condition of the land over which he rules. Herein lies the purpose of
the quest. The knight assigned to the quest is to search for the Holy Grail,
water from which is the only means of restoring the health of the Fisher
King and thus the land. In the discovery of the grail, the quest hero provides the means whereby the king and thus kingdom are returned to
health and vitality.

Long before Roy Hobbs actually plays professional baseball, we are
alerted to the mythic interests of the film when he has his ultimately
unfortunate meeting with Harriet Bird on the train to Chicago. Harriet
asks Hobbs if he has ever read Homer who, she informs him, wrote about
gods and heroes, and she asserts "would have had it in mind to write
about baseball had he seen you out there today."

This indication of the mythic underpinnings of *The Natural* are reinforced when Hobbs, years after his near-fatal shooting by Harriet, shows
up as a newly hired, middle-aged player for the Knights. The scene is
filled with references to the grail myth. The team manager is Pop Fisher,
who "rules" over a wasteland in that the Knights are suffering from a long
dry period without any games won. The Knights, as we catch glimpses of
the disastrous game they are playing, reveal themselves to be dispirited,
infected with losing. Indeed, in a subsequent scene, a hypnotist hired by
Fisher to help the team reverse their losing streak informs the assembled
Knights that "losing is a disease." Even small details reinforce the message. Pop Fisher, for example, underscores the wasteland motif when he
complains about the foul, undrinkable water in the ballpark. That the
film is set in the 1930s during the period of the Great Depression extends
the wasteland reference and alerts us to the film's social and political

interests as the crisis of the thirties stands in for the more recent crises faced by American society.

If, as Christopher Evans explains, baseball was thought in the progressive era to embody the rural virtues central to a redemptive American identity, we are provided with a vision of an edenic rural America in the film's opening sequence as we watch Roy, encouraged by his father, practice the skills of the game and hone his obviously great talent on a farm somewhere deep in the American heartland. It is, of course, Roy's leaving the farm that precipitates his crisis. Roy, under the spell of the murderous Harriet Bird, forgets his promise to his fiancée and is nearly killed by Bird in the scandalous circumstances of his visit to her hotel room. Due to his injuries and his shame, Roy is out of the game before he even tries out for the majors. Roy's exile from the game is an interruption of a narrative forecast in his youth, that of his great personal success in the game, and at a symbolic level the interruption of the narrative of continual social progress embodied by baseball according to the millennial expectations of liberal Protestantism. Thus, when the film moves sixteen years into the future with Roy's return to baseball as the newest player for the Knights, he enters a world in decline. The Knights, far from representing the positive virtues of teamwork and commitment to winning celebrated in the vision of baseball as an embodiment of American values, are a dispirited, losing team, and what is more, a team infected by corruption. It is not long before we hear of the wager between Pop Fisher and the Judge, the new owner of the Knights. The Judge, who literally resides in darkness in his office overlooking the field, and Pop Fisher have agreed that if the Knights fail to win the pennant, Pop will sell out his remaining shares and the Judge will own the team entirely. The Judge has bribed several members of the Knights, most notably Bump Bailey, and has hired Roy believing that this over-the-hill, middle-aged player will further reduce the team's hopes of success.

For the Judge, baseball has merely an economic significance, and his desire wholly to own the team suggests a struggle between the progressive and democratic idealism of the myth of baseball and America, and the corruption of that myth by greed and personal interest. For the Judge and his allies, the game serves merely as a means of satisfying selfish ambitions. He is surrounded by characters like Max Mercy, the sportswriter intoxicated with his own power to "make and break" players; Gus Sands, the gambler who benefits from the corruption of the players willing to throw games; and Paris, Pop Fisher's niece, who is used by the Judge and

Gus Sands in an attempt to convince Roy to aid the Judge in his plans to win his wager and take over the team. In this welter of corruption and greed the very dream of progress as the reward of such virtues of democratic cooperation, manly zeal, and fair play has been lost, and baseball has become the embodiment of all that has diverted America from its early promise.

In its depiction of Roy's return to the game, bringing with him an incorruptible heroism and dedication to fair play, *The Natural* would seem to be the archetypal Reagan-era film, featuring Roy as a hero who, like the president born in rural Illinois, arrives from the American heartland to restore what has been lost. Yet the film, unlike *Field of Dreams*, which we will discuss later, remains ambiguously related to the historical realities shaping its context. Whereas one may indeed see in Roy a type of Reaganesque hero, the film's condemnation of the Judge and the wealthy interests he represents may also be understood as a condemnation of the Reagan administration's dedicated support of big business and corporate interests, as most famously reflected in what has been called "Reaganomics." In brief, the Reagan government believed in what is termed supply-side economics, the idea that a healthy economy was maintained by supporting the business and owner classes who are the creators of wealth. By lowering taxes, the Reagan administration believed, business would be invigorated, and the wealth thus created would "trickle down" through the economy. Although *The Natural* reflects the Reagan-era rhetoric of a return to traditional rural heartland, it also employs a Frank Capra-like narrative of the common man defeating the corrupt interests of big money. It is after all not the Judge and his associates who create financial success for the team, but the players/workers, who see little of the money the team generates. Indeed, the Judge is characterized as especially stingy toward his players to whom little wealth "trickles down," no matter how filled the stands become with the team's success.

Roy's return to the game is the means by which the film enacts a return to the American narrative that baseball embodied for its early celebrants. The interrupted story can, the film asserts, be resumed through the reinvigoration of its initial values. It is worth noting, however, that Roy as the embodiment of these virtues has had himself to mature into their full realization. When the audience sees Roy as a boy in the opening of the film, he is a gifted innocent (indeed, one of the meanings of the word "natural" at the time the novel was written was "rube, hick"). He has great skill and promise and a sense of justice as illustrated in his anger at Mercy's and The Whammer's mockery of Sam, Roy's alcoholic coach and agent. Yet, he is blind to the mythic significance of the game he plays so well. When Harriet Bird evokes Homer and Arthurian legend, Roy reveals an ignorance of both, and when asked by Harriet what he hopes to gain from playing, he tells her that he wants to "walk down the street and hear people say 'There goes Roy Hobbs, the best there ever was.'" Harriet responds, "It that all?" For the young Roy, the desire for personal fame is paramount, and he cannot imagine baseball as affording the sort of participation in an enactment of American myth imagined by its early proponents. In fact, although we are told that Roy has played baseball in school, we do not see him engaged in any team activity. We watch as he practices catching and pitching with his father on the farm, and that's all. For Roy as a young player, the goal of baseball is personal glory. He wishes to be the best, to be regarded as a living monument. Yet, the very idea of such monumental fame is to a degree subverted by the episode dealing with Bump Bailey's death. We are given a close-up of Bump's brass memorial plaque as his ashes are dumped over Knight's Field. The service over, the game begins.

# Return of the Caring Father

Roy, of course, is a much better man than the corrupt Bump, yet the point remains: baseball should be devoted to continuity, to the passing along of skills and values from one generation the next, not to the achievement of fame. Now returning to the game, Roy no longer seeks fame as an end. If once, to cite 1 Corinthians 13, Roy "reasoned like a child," he has now "put an end to childish ways." The older Roy who returns to baseball after years of exile is concerned not with personal glory but rather with participation as a member of a team. He wants to "get back in the game" and this means to devote himself to the good of the team rather than merely to personal success. He will provide the inspiration for the team to win the pennant for Pop Fisher and thus preserve the values Pop represents as opposed to the corruption of the Judge and his cohorts. As Roy says when the Judge, attempting to discern his new, unexpectedly successful player's susceptibility to bribery, offers him a raise, "Raise or not, I play to win." When Paris, unable to convince Roy to join in the Judge's plan, poisons him to bring to a near fatal condition his old bullet wound, the symbolism is clear: the corrupting poison represented by the Judge will not defeat Roy. Indeed, the image of Roy's bleeding side as he struggles to succeed in his final game asserts his Christlike determination to sacrifice himself for the good of the team and, thus, a powerful representation of baseball as the arena for the manly spiritual values of honesty and effort admired by its early religious enthusiasts.

That Roy is inspired to heroic action by the presence of his son at the final game places Roy within a pattern of continuity and paternal responsibility that the film celebrates as the supreme values of baseball as an American religious practice. When we recall that the word "religion" is derived from the Latin verb *relegare*, to bind together, the point is made clear. Baseball—by providing a set of rituals and values, by giving its fans heroes to be admired and emulated and tales of defeat and victory, of suffering and success—is precisely a means of binding together, of creating a community of shared faith and involvement. This binding also requires an historical coherence linking generation to generation, father to son, not merely the discourse of records or the rituals of the game, but the depiction of virtues to be emulated: skill, a sense of fair play, and democratic team cooperation.

If Roy's narrative of participation in baseball has been interrupted, it is important to recall that his narrative of fatherhood suffers the same discontinuity. In fact, until late in the film Roy is unaware that he is a father. In an episode following those depicting Roy's training and encouragement by his own father, Roy's son is conceived on the very evening Roy receives the call to try out for the majors. Following Roy's wounding and disappearance, Iris is left to raise the boy on her own. As absent father, Roy symbolizes the discontinuity and lack that has infected the game of baseball as symbol of American virtue and hope. Roy has not been present to instruct his son as his father instructed him. This absence, the film asserts, is as damaging as the other sort of paternal "absence" symbolized by the likes of Bump Bailey, Gus Sands, and the Judge. As corrupters of the game, these characters have replaced the honest, virtuous father whose role is enacted by the proper athlete hero that Roy will become. Emphasizing the crucial importance of baseball as uncorrupted sport, Evans quotes Kenesaw Landis, the first commissioner of major-league baseball: "'[B]aseball is something more than a game to an American boy. It is his training field for life work. Destroy his faith in its squareness and honesty, and you have destroyed something more—you have planted suspicion of all things in his heart'" (Evans, p. 41).

Throughout the film Roy is associated with children: he signs autographs and gives advice (not forgetting to include a young girl), and in each game sequence the camera is careful to include multiple shots of children watching raptly his performance and cheering him on. Roy also encourages Bobby Savoy, the team bat boy, helping him make a bat like Roy's own handmade wonderboy. If Roy's dangerous relationship with Paris threatens to repeat the disastrous alliance with Harriet Bird, it is his reconnection with Iris, the mother of his son, that saves him. It is she who, as the "woman in white," inspires Roy's recovered powers after they have been sapped by the Delilahlike, Paris. Most significant, it is she who readmits Roy into the narrative of paternity. Having been informed by Iris that the son he did not know he had is present, Roy is able to summon the strength he needs to achieve his heroic victory in the final game and thus to provide both his actual son and all his symbolic children in the stands with an enduring example of courage and honesty. It is during this sequence, too, that the theme of generational continuity is underscored in another way through the image of the "Iowa farm boy" brought in to pitch to Roy in his crucial time at bat. The pitcher, young and blond, recalls the young Roy of the film's beginning and implies that what Roy represents is being handed off safely to the next generation. In the same way, the final shots of the film show us Roy, married to Iris and reunited with his son, Ted, back on a farm. As Roy and Ted play catch, the boy falls into the high grass and emerges holding the ball in his hand. This rising of the young player, ball in hand, ends the film with a symbol of the "natural" emergence of young players from the rural Eden of the American heartland, depicts the promise of a new generation to carry on all that has been represented by Roy as a heroic figure who has himself emerged from and returned to the virtuous environment of the heartland. Roy's son, like the young Iowa farm-boy pitcher, embodies a continuity of benevolent influence, the continued power of baseball to inform American culture with what its early enthusiasts approved: the manliness, honesty, and cooperative spirit that recommend the game as the national sport. Roy, like the successful grail knight who restores health to the Fisher King and fertility to the wasteland, reinvigorates a threatened idealism.

# The Prophet of the *Field of Dreams*

This motif of baseball's origin in and perpetuation of the virtues of an edenic rural America is emphatically asserted in *Field of Dreams* (1989).

The protagonist, Ray Kinsella, has returned with his wife, Annie, and young daughter, Karin, to Annie's home state of Iowa to run the family farm. While Ray walks in his cornfield on a late summer afternoon, he hears a voice saying, "If you build it, he will come." It is not long before Ray, in a demonstration of his virtues of faith and spiritual intuition, comes to understand that what the voice instructs him to do is plow over a portion of his corn crop and build a baseball field. Having been all his life fascinated with the story of Shoeless Joe Jackson, the great player for the Chicago White Sox who, on the grounds of his alleged participation in the fixing of the 1919 World Series, was eventually banned for life from the game, Ray believes that the "he" the voice refers to is Jackson. With the support of his wife and to the bemused disbelief of his rural neighbors, Ray proceeds to build the field, complete with lights, and awaits the arrival of Jackson.

Ray and Annie's seemingly absurd belief in the veracity of the voice and its prediction is, obviously, an important aspect of the film. Ray, in the face of these bizarre events, never for a moment doubts their reality, and Annie is happily willing to share her husband's unquestioning faith. It is this emphasis on such faith in what to most others seems utterly absurd (and the miracles that result) that promotes the film's characterization of Ray as a kind of religious prophet (not unlike Neary in *Close Encounters of the Third Kind*). We are clearly meant to see, in Ray's hearing and faithful acting upon the directives of the voice, analogues to a variety of visionary religious experiences in the history of religion. We may think of Saint Paul on the road to Damascus; of Muhammad; or in more recent history, the visions of Joseph Smith. Interestingly, Ray's experience has much in common with such famous visions of the Virgin Mary, at Lourdes, for example, or Fatima. Like the children involved in these Marian visions, Ray has a direct and personal encounter with the sacred, with the *mysterium tremendum*. He is directed to build what amounts to a shrine, and he is promised miracles in reward for his obedience. Furthermore, Ray's baseball diamond becomes the venue for what amounts to a religious celebration and a renewal of faith—a reference to the long historical tradition of Protestant religious revivals. Ray's baseball field, erected in rural Iowa and which will draw the faithful to a renewal of faith, thus recalls the familiar image of the revivalist tent.

*Field of Dreams* thus insists, forcefully and unapologetically, upon the religious significance of baseball. After building the field, Ray, like the New Testament faithful who are instructed "to watch and wait" for the return of Jesus, sits at his window each evening in expectation. His faith is rewarded when one summer evening Shoeless Joe, in an image recalling the final scene of *The Natural*, emerges from the high corn at the edge of the field. He is soon followed by a number of the most famous baseball players in history whose games Ray, Annie, and Karin watch each afternoon. But neither Ray's banker brother-in-law; nor his wife, Annie's sister; nor Annie's mother can see anything on the field watched so attentively by Ray and his family. They are thus without faith and imagination, having lost the capacity for childlike wonder retained by Ray and his family. That the viewers of the film can see Shoeless Joe and the other players locates them immediately within the community of the faithful that the film constructs. This ability to see invites, of course, a strong identification with Ray in his difference from the brother-in-law for whom money is all-important, and who constantly complains to Ray of what he sees as the financial idiocy of turning profitable farmland into a baseball field. That Ray's relatives and neighbors cannot see with the eyes of faith and mock what is for them his absurd enterprise suggests that here—in the very green fields of the American heartland, the cradle of baseball and all that it signified about American virtue and promise—the faith has been lost, and a revival is required.

If the liberal Protestant celebrators of baseball saw the game as promoting America's millennial and democratic potential, *The Field of Dreams*—like *The Natural* made five years earlier—laments the weakening and potential loss of that potential. The materialist perspective of Ray's brother-in-law who cannot see the miraculous in front of his face suggests part of the reason for this spiritual decline. More important, though, the film depicts the growing power of a rigid, repressive political conservatism as the major threat to the American potential symbolized by baseball. In an early scene Ray and Annie attend a school board meeting at which several of their rural neighbors advocate the banning of a number of "subversive" books from the school library. Her right-wing opponent in the meeting makes clear the link between what Ray's field represents and Annie's liberal values by demanding the removal of "subversive" books from the library and mocking Ray for "plowing under his corn to build a baseball field," and she demands that Terence Mann's books be removed from the school. According to this "right thinking" conservative, Mann's books advocate "promiscuity, godlessness, the mongrelization of the races, and disrespect to high ranking officers of the U.S. Army." Annie defends Mann's work and calls him a "voice of reason" in the troubled sixties, adding, "If you had experienced even a little bit of the sixties, you might feel the same way too." Having convinced many of her neighbors to resist this call for censorship, Annie gleefully tells her husband that she has stopped the "rise of neo-fascism in America."

# A Second Chance

Annie's passionate criticism of right-wing sentiments reflect the liberal distaste for Reagan conservatism that had by the late eighties become further encouraged by the actions of the White House. By the end of Ronald Reagan's second term his administration had been troubled by a growing list of scandals, most notably the Iran/Contra affair, which resulted in a protracted congressional investigation and ultimately the conviction on felony counts of several members of the administration. Such troubling revelations of government corruption are reflected in the film's treatment of corruption in baseball early in the twentieth century.

The fixing of the 1919 World Series becomes in the film a symbol of a disastrous loss of innocence in which the game (by which is implied not merely baseball but America's initially progressive and hopeful millennial promise) has been terribly compromised. Much as in *The Natural*, then, the corruption of baseball serves as a symbol of lost national direction and virtue. In each film, this corruption takes the form of game fixing, in which baseball becomes essentially a means of making money for gamblers who have no interest in the values the game is meant to display and conserve. Roy, we know, refuses to submit to this corruption. The case of Shoeless Joe is more complicated. Kinsella, who has studied Joe's play in the infamous World Series, refuses to believe that his hero played with anything less than his usual skill. "He did take their money," Ray says, but "nobody could ever prove that he did a single thing to lose those games." Nevertheless, Joe was tainted by the corruption, and made a scapegoat by more powerful forces that escaped discovery and censure.

It is thus not surprising that, as in *The Natural*, *Field of Dreams* makes symbolic use of its characters' state of exile from baseball. Just as Roy Hobbs has been for eighteen years self-exiled from the game he loves and whose positive values he personifies, Shoeless Joe Jackson, in death as in life, has been barred from participation in the game he loves. It is, of course, with Ray's building of the field/shrine that Shoeless Joe can once again play the game to which he devoted his youth. Ray's father, failing to make it in professional ball, lived his life in a regret and resentment that he attempts to overcome through his son, who he trains up as a skilled player. This insistence, of course, angers Ray, who, in a paradigm of sixties rebellion, turns against his father, leaves home, and fails even to attend his father's funeral.

But one more figure needs to be on this lineup. Like Ray, his father, Shoeless Joe, and the other players who return to play on Ray's field, Dr. Archie "Moonlight" Graham, whom Ray is directed to find, has left the game. After playing only one inning in the major leagues, Graham suffered an injury. No longer able to play, he became a physician and lived out his life serving the people of a small Minnesota town. To find him, the film gives Ray a helper, Terence Mann.

To emphasize, as its early admirers had done, an association between baseball and American progressive potential, *Field of Dreams* brings in another character alienated from the game: the sixties novelist Terence Mann, whose work has inspired Ray, Annie, and thousands of other counterculturalists and whom Annie defends at the school board meeting. Mann, disgusted with the failure of the sixties to bring about any significant change, went into seclusion, quit writing, and maintains a defensive, sardonic contempt for all that the sixties once stood for. It is he that the voice, with the words, "Heal his pain," commands Ray to find. Mann, as a psychologically wounded "Fisher King" to be redeemed by the efforts of the visionary Ray, marks a significant thematic connection between *Field of Dreams* and *The Natural*. Ray, researching Mann's career, discovers an interview in which the author relates his youthful passion for baseball and his youthful dream to play at Ebbits Field. Even though the field is long gone, Mann says in the interview, "I still dream and dream," but when Ray locates Mann in Boston and announces that he has come to take him to a baseball game, Mann shows no interest and denies that he has ever been a lover of the game. In this parallel between Mann's disavowal of both baseball and the socially activist, inspiring novels he has written, the film again insists upon the link between the game and visionary political engagement. That only Ray and Mann can see the instructions to find Graham written in light upon the scoreboard in Boston makes the point: the true meaning of the game is still available to those few who can yet read its bright, visionary message. In a sense, given the site of the message's appearance, the film suggests that only Ray and Mann really "know the score."

Thus, in that the message appears only to Ray and Mann, even though they are surrounded by thousands of other fans at the game, *Field of*

*Dreams* expresses a sense of widespread American loss of direction. Like Ray's rural neighbors in Iowa who mock the absurdity of his field and consider banning books from the school library, the crowd in Boston can no longer *see*. It has lost the vision Ray hopes to recover. Again, it is difficult not to discern in this representation of loss of vision a criticism of the Reagan years. Reagan's conservative, antiprogressive message, presented as a return to traditional American values, was of course embraced by millions of "common Americans," especially in what we have come to term the "red states," representative of the rural America from which baseball arose and in which rural, democratic, and progressive values were once believed to inhere. To counter this loss of direction in the heartland and among common Americans, the film presents a series of images whose symbolic import could hardly be plainer. Ray hears, right in the middle of his cornfield in rural Iowa, the voice that instructs him to build the baseball field. Shoeless Joe and the other resurrected players emerge from and return to the deep corn surrounding the field. The games played there, which bring together in one place baseball heroes from many times, can only be seen, like the sign's message in Boston, by the faithful and the young—like Ray's daughter Karin, who delights in watching the heroes perform every day. Those who have faith and vision observe a spectacle literally springing up again, like a summer crop, from the heartland. The characters who can see the miracle are those who have, like Ray and Annie, never lost sight of the liberal values of the sixties; or who, like Mann, recover that faith; or those with childlike innocence, like Karin. Ray's "crop" consists of the risen players who restore the glory of baseball to the heartland, and in this he is like the planter in Matthew 13:24, who "sowed good seed in his field." In terms of the film's explicit criticism of the conservatism that during the Reagan years exerted a powerful, anti-progressive tone to American culture, it is worth recalling more of Matthew 13, which goes on to say, "But while everybody was asleep, an enemy came and sowed weeds among the wheat." In a metaphor that would have appealed to the liberal-Protestant sensibility that saw baseball as reflecting the saving virtues of an enlightened democracy, *Field of Dreams* imagines the growth again of the "good seeds" of American progressivism.

That such seeds remain vital in the American heartland is again demonstrated in the story of Dr. Graham, the player Ray and Mann are directed to by the message at the ball field in Boston. When the two arrive at the small Minnesota town that Graham served for decades as a physician, they learn that the doctor has been dead for some years. They also learn from the townspeople they speak to about Graham's deep humanity and his self-sacrificing dedication to the welfare of his small-town neighbors. Graham never became wealthy but rather earned the love and respect of generations of patients. Ray experiences himself the doctor's kindness when he meets Graham's spirit on the streets of the small town where he served as a physician for many years and speaks with him in his office. Graham, he finds, has never regretted the direction of his life. Although glorying in his one inning in professional baseball, the doctor does not regard his leaving the game as a tragedy. As he explains to Kinsella, not to have become a doctor would have been the tragedy.

Although Ray and Mann, who meet the young "Moonlight" Graham on the road to Iowa, allow the boy once again to play baseball with the others in the wondrous field, Graham leaves the field's precincts, knowing that he cannot return, to save the life of Karin when she falls from the bleachers. In this characteristic act of self-sacrifice and humane concern for others, Graham becomes perhaps the most moving character in the film. The emotional weight given Graham in the narrative serves its central point, that the doctor who played baseball for so short a time in his youth was drawn to and inspired by the game because of the cooperative, democratic values it reflects. *Field of Dreams* therefore finds in baseball what its initial progressive admirers found, the image of an ideal America worth the participation of its citizens. Graham, coming from the game to the small American town he serves for decades, is a "good seed" whose quiet, dedicated life provides the film with an example of American heroism.

We have seen that, like *The Natural*, *Field of Dreams* makes use of the motif of lost participation in the game of baseball. Yet following the example of Doc Graham, whose life as a dedicated self-sacrificing member of his community represents the values of the game sustained in life beyond the limits of the playing field, the image of return achieves its full significance. Doc's return to his calling as a physician as he steps from the field to aid Karin makes the point with symbolic economy and clarity. It is the baseball field, peopled with heroes and charged with true American virtue, that made men like Graham. The radiant, visionary space Ray has reconstructed contains the hope for a revival of such virtue. Thus, in the final shot of the film we are given an aerial shot of the Iowan landscape surrounding Ray's farm. On the road is a long line of cars driving toward the field like pilgrims approaching a shrine, their headlights shining.

# Suggested Readings

Christopher H. Evans and William R. Herzog II, *The Faith of 50 Million: Baseball, Religion, and American Culture* (Louisville, Ky.: Westminster John Knox Press, 2002).

Joseph L. Price, *Rounding the Bases: Baseball and Religion in America* (Macon, Ga.: Mercer University Press, 2006).

# World Religions in Film

# CHAPTER 13

# American Dharma

Immigrants from Asia—Japan, China, India, Korea, Vietnam and even Tibet—have been coming to the United States for more than two centuries. At different times, they have been more, or less, welcomed; but the families of those who stayed found a place in American society. These immigrants brought their religious beliefs with them, but they often kept those beliefs to themselves, seeing no need to propagate their religions outside their own circles. To oversimplify, they wished to maintain their traditions, not to bring others from the American populace into their beliefs. They had enough difficulties fitting into American society; they saw no need to complicate matters by trying to introduce their religions as well.

From this perspective, it seems that America has no place for religions like Hinduism, Buddhism, or Daoism. Given the predominance of Christianity in this country, there seems to be no place for nonchristian religions, especially those of Asia. Asians may become Americans, but why would non-Asian Americans—especially those of European origins—follow Asian religions?

This chapter's two films address this question. In their own way, each film suggests that the reality of an Asian religion is already in America; it has just gone unrecognized.

*The Legend of Bagger Vance* applies a Hindu view of the nature of cosmos—that found in the *Bhagavad Gita*—to a game of golf. When the film's central character integrates this view into his play, he manages to overcome his difficulties and triumph in the big tournament. The film's point is that even though Christians and other non-Hindus do not recognize it, the Hindu worldview still governs the laws of nature. Hence, that view applies in America just as it does in the rest of the cosmos.

*Little Buddha* takes a more aggressive approach. Although the connection between Tibetan Buddhism (i.e., Vajrayana) is established through evangelism—Tibetan monks are in America to set up a Dharma center to teach Buddhism—the movie unveils a link between America and Buddhism that is at once more subtle yet more powerful. The film's premise is that an American boy of European descent is the reincarnation of the deceased Tibetan religious leader, Lama Dorje. The film's narrative logic is if the lama can be reborn as an American, then America can become a home to Buddhism.

Both movies work out their perspective by adhering to American film standards. Despite the difference in religious orientation, these films are made for release to an American popular audience and use major American actors in key roles. *Little Buddha* is by far the most didactic of the two, but each suggests the applicability of Asian religious insights to modern American life.

The World Parliament of Religions in 1890 in Chicago formally introduced Buddhism and Hinduism to the American religious community. Neither religion, however, has been particularly successful in gaining American converts, although intellectual forms of these religions (Zen, Vedanta, Vajrayana) have appealed to some American artists and intellectuals. Vedanta, for example, was taken up by British writers living in Los Angeles (e.g., Aldous Huxley and Christopher Isherwood), while Zen Buddhism had a wider appeal among American artists. This was largely due to D. T. Suzuki, whose numerous books introduced Zen Buddhism to an American audience.

Another popularizer of Hindu and Buddhist philosophy was Alan Watts, who published many books lucidly explaining aspects of both Buddhist and Hindu belief and practice. Their writings were particularly influential during the 1960s when alternative systems of belief held an attraction for many young people seeking to escape what they saw as the overly restrictive dogmas and traditions of middle-class America. More recently, an interest in Buddhism in particular has been evidenced by such Hollywood figures as Richard Gere (an active advocate of Buddhism), Steven Segal, and Keanu Reeves, among others. Although the films discussed here were hardly major commercial successes, each testifies to a continuing interest in Eastern religions among culturally influential segments of the American population.

# *Little Buddha* and the Discovery of Impermanence

The narrative of *Little Buddha*, in telling the fictional story of Jesse Conrad, a young Seattle boy whom a group of Tibetan monks believe may be the reincarnation of a recently deceased Tibetan lama, provides the means through which the film pursues its two entwined purposes. The first of these is to provide Western, and particularly American, viewers with an introduction to Tibetan Buddhism. The second is to argue that Buddhism, however exotic it may at first appear, provides a viable spiritual option for modern Americans. First, and most obviously, the selection of Jesse Conrad, the young American, as the reincarnated Lama Dorje symbolizes the movement of Buddhism from East to West, a goal that, as we are told, inspired Dorje to come to Seattle to spread the Dharma (i.e., Buddhist teachings). Indeed, the opening sequences of the film accumulate examples of the movement of Buddhism from East to West. The film opens in the exotic locale of a Buddhist monastery in Nepal, where Lama Norbu instructs a number of young students of about Jesse's age in a principle of the Dharma: "No animal shall be sacrificed." Information whispered in his ear tells Norbu about the possibility that Dorje has been reincarnated in Seattle, and, armed with Dorje's begging bowl, he sets out on his quest. Thus Norbu and his assistant monks repeat the East to West movement first made by Dorje. We recall as well that in his dream of Dorje, Kempo Tenzin sees the lama dressed in jeans like a typical American, although in life Dorje "always dressed in robes." Finally, Lama Norbu brings for Jesse a children's book in English, *Little Buddha, The Story of Prince Siddartha*, an act which reinforces the emphasis of the passage of Buddhist thought from Asia to America.

It is during the American visit of the monks that the film seeks to reduce the perception of Buddhism as an alien, "exotic" religion by suggesting that it is not dramatically different from Christianity. When Jesse leads Norbu to the statue of Buddha in the art museum, Jesse asks if Buddha is a god. Norbu responds (albeit with a simplification of Christian theology) that Buddha was a man, "not unlike Jesus." Arriving with his mother at the Dharma center, Jesse says that the building is like a church. In this, the film aligns itself with other popular works, such as the book by the famous Vietnamese Buddhist, Thich Nhat Hanh, *Living Buddha, Living Christ*.

As Jesse reads and is read to from *Little Buddha*, we see the structural importance of the book to the film's narrative and didactic purposes. The book serves not only to instruct Jesse and his family (as well as the audience) concerning the basic tenets of Buddhism, but it also argues for the universal applicability of Buddhism by bringing the lives of Siddhartha and Jesse into parallel. As the narrative intersperses into Jesse's story that of Siddhartha's early sheltered life, his discovery—despite his father's precautions—of the facts of aging, disease, and death, and his search and ultimate attainment of enlightenment, we are invited to see the resemblances between the two. If Siddhartha is a privileged prince, kept within his palace walls and by his father's design unaware of suffering, Jesse is himself a child of privilege. His father is a successful architectural engineer and his mother a schoolteacher. But the upper-middle-class life provided Jesse only seems to protect him and his family from the inescapable facts of existence, from the suffering that Buddhism recognizes as providing the motivation for enlightenment. Jesse reads and the film presents Siddhartha's discovery outside his father's protective walls of the ill, the aged, the dying, and the dead. This discovery, of course, underlies the first of Buddhism's Four Noble Truths—that life is suffering. When the film returns to Jesse's narrative, we learn of the suicide of Evan, one of his father's business partners. Thus, as in the life of Siddhartha, the inevitability of suffering and death is dramatically emphasized in Jesse's life. Indeed, it is following Evan's suicide and funeral that Jesse's father, clearly unnerved by the tragedy, reverses his initial resistance to the idea that Jesse travel to Nepal to further explore the possibility that he is the reincarnated Dorje.

As *Little Buddha* clearly aims to demonstrate, suffering in life is the constant that transcends time and place, and to recognize this fact can be the first step in a consideration of Buddhism as a means of understanding and ultimately escaping the wheel of pain and loss. The film even implies that, because Americans like Jesse and his family live at a level of comfort that buffers them from much of the privation and suffering common in the world, they, like the sheltered and privileged Siddhartha, may find in trauma an especially powerful motive to seek enlightenment. When for example Dean learns of Evan's death, he pulls over his car and stands on an overpass looking down at the cars speeding along below in the twilight. In context, this image of ceaseless passage powerfully suggests, in a particularly American image, a central tenet of Buddhism: that of impermanence, to which the film will repeatedly return. In fact, we have a subtle allusion to this image when later in the film Lama Norbu explicitly instructs Jesse concerning impermanence. Again it is twilight, and Norbu asks Jesse to look at the hundreds of persons—a traffic of people—walking the streets of Katmandu beneath the gaze of the Buddha eyes painted on the immense *stupa*. "In a hundred years," Norbu explains, "all these people will be dead. That is what is meant by impermanence." We are in this scene invited to recall the earlier image of rushing traffic at which Jesse's father gazes immediately after learning of Evan's suicide.

What is implied in the link between the images is the possibility of learning through an understanding of Buddhism another, powerful way of looking upon the world of impermanence and death. Dean's initial despairing gaze downward upon the cars may become the detached and peaceful gaze of the Buddha, embracing impermanence as the very means of grasping enlightenment. This downward gaze is again repeated near the end of the film as Lama Norbu, who has just died, is seen by Jesse and his companions looking down at them from a balcony in the monastery as he repeats the famous lines from the end of the *Heart Sutra*: "Form is empty; emptiness is form. No eye, ear, nose, body, mind. . . . " Thus, the film subtly depicts the passage from ignorance to enlightenment by tracing the movement from a gaze of despair to that of enlightened understanding. Furthermore, the links between these images again underscore the applicability of Buddhism to American experience by providing a Buddhist perspective for understanding the profoundly American image of rushing traffic. At the same time the images of moving crowds as emblems of impermanence, first in America and then in Nepal, returns to the film's allied insistence that the insights of Buddhism are not restricted to the "Asian mind," but are instead everywhere and always of profound significance.

# The Journey Toward Emptiness

*Little Buddha* adopts a strategy of transformed perception in its focus throughout on the theme of emptiness. Emptiness, the nonexistence of things, and the allied doctrine of *anatman*, the nonexistence of the self, are concepts central to Buddhism that the film repeatedly emphasizes. Together these are known as *sunyata*. During the depiction of Buddha's enlightenment we see the famous moment when Siddhartha, realizing the illusory nature of the ego, declares, "Architect, finally I have met you.

You will not build your house again. . . . Oh lord of my own ego, you are nothing but illusion." When Siddhartha recognizes the "architect" as the power of ignorant desire seeking to sustain the illusion of the ego, we are once again invited to grasp a link to earlier sequences in the film. We recall that Jesse's father, an architectural engineer, has built the house in Seattle to which Kempo Tenzin leads Norbu, and we should recall the exact words Tenzin uses. He says that Dorje led him in a dream to an "empty site." And then describes finding that site, the "empty spot" and discovering that a house has been built upon it. We see the sudden dreamlike appearance of the house out of nowhere. When Norbu and associates enter the house on their initial visit, Norbu praises its emptiness as Lisa explains that the family has not finished moving in. Lisa repeats Norbu's word to Dean when he arrives home: "They were just admiring the emptiness of the room," she tells her husband. Again, when Jesse and Norbu are on the way to the museum where they see a statue of the Buddha, Jesse points out a skyscraper, saying, "My father built that building . . . but it's always empty." When we later hear the word "architect," we understand how carefully the film has prepared us. The moment of Siddhartha's enlightenment serves as a potential revelation for the careful viewer as well in that the early repeated references to the emptiness of the house, the building, the characterization by Tenzin of the lot as the "empty spot," and the sudden appearance of the house on that lot combine into a significant pattern. Such empty buildings symbolize the empty nature of the ego, its illusory nature sustained by ignorance and craving. As with the imagery of the downward gaze, the images of empty buildings assume significance in retrospect, after we have been presented with the depiction of Siddhartha's enlightenment in which he becomes the Buddha through the power of his achieved understanding.

In the early references to emptiness, especially as they are colored by Evan's suicide, the American viewer is likely to supply a conventional meaning to the term, to understand this evocation of "emptiness" as a familiar criticism of an American obsession with material wealth and comfort. Evan's bankruptcy and suicide suggests, from this perspective, the spiritual emptiness of American culture, its "meaninglessness." Yet, we come to understand that the film intends merely to use this conventional criticism as the basis for a depiction of possible transformation of perspective. The negative despair signaled by the first meaning of "emptiness" is transformed through the depiction of Buddha's enlightenment into a new understanding. To grasp the meaning of *sunyata*, the Buddhist term for the essential emptiness of all phenomena including the ego, is to obtain the means of enlightenment.

Through the paralleled narratives of Jesse and Siddhartha, the movement toward enlightenment becomes the focus of the film after Jesse begins his journey to Bhutan. We see Siddhartha, troubled by the suffering he has witnessed, vow to find a solution to the pain of human existence. Just as Siddhartha leaves his family behind to begin his quest, Jesse (although accompanied by his father) leaves his mother to travel to Bhutan. His mother, worrying about the trip, says, "he has never spent a night without me." Siddhartha, when leaving his father's palace, finds that everyone has fallen into a deep sleep; only he and Channa remain awake. This singular wakefulness, the voice-over assures us, prefigures Siddhartha's final and compete awakening, his becoming the Buddha, "the awakened one." Jesse's wakefulness, shared only by Norbu, on the flight to Bhutan insists upon the Siddhartha/Jesse parallel. Having found his father asleep, Jesse sits in front of Norbu and asks if he is sleeping. "No, I'm meditating," replies Norbu, who goes on to give Jesse an initial lesson in the art of meditative detachment. The implication of course is that Jesse, like Siddhartha, has begun the process of awakening with this initial lesson from Norbu.

Later, Jesse and the two other candidates sit under a tree "very much like" the one under which Siddhartha became the Buddha, the "enlightened one." They "see" through the power of Norbu's storytelling the unfolding of that event. When in the ritual staged at the monastery it is revealed that all three of the children are reincarnations of Lama Dorje, Jesse learns another lesson concerning impermanence: that there is in fact no "self" to be reincarnated, and that Dorje's various attributes (*skandhas?*) may be separated from one another and continue independent from the person in whom their combination gave rise to the appearance of a unified selfhood. Finally, it is following the death of Norbu, when Jesse and the other children see him standing upon the balcony reciting the *Heart Sutra*, that Jesse achieves, if not complete enlightenment, a joyful understanding of that part of the Buddhist message. As Jesse paraphrases the *Heart Sutra* to his father, "No Jesse, no Lama . . . no death and no fear."

When we see Jesse back in Seattle, about to release the ashes of Norbu contained in his begging bowl into the ocean currents, we do not learn whether he plans to return to Bhutan or remain in America. But clearly he has been powerfully affected by his experience of Buddhism. The theme of the promise of an American Buddhism is reinforced.

Throughout the film, Director Bertolucci has suggested the differences between Buddhism in Bhutan and America through the use of a color scheme in which bright, warm reds and oranges predominate in Bhutan, while Seattle is shot in shades of cool blues and grays. In this final scene, however, Jesse's pregnant mother's clothing, her red sweater and blue jacket, signify the conjunction of Bhutan and America, of Buddhism and the West. Indeed, the fact that his mother is pregnant suggests the possibility that Norbu may himself be reincarnated into Jesse's family.

# Hinduism and *The Legend of Bagger Vance*

*The Legend of Bagger Vance* (2000), unlike *Little Buddha*, is far from explicit in its use of Asian religion, in this case several ideas central to the *Bhagavad Gita*. The *Bhagavad Gita*, the most popular Hindu religious text, is a long poem inserted into the massive epic, the *Mahabharata*, at a point just before the climactic battle in which most of the combatants are killed. Informed viewers of the film, however, will recognize that the name of the film's protagonist, Rannulph Junuh, or R. Junuh, an odd and oddly spelled name indeed, draws attention to itself as a echo of the *Gita's* main character, namely, Arjuna. It is Arjuna who throughout the Hindu poem is instructed by Krishna in religious truth and the means of achieving enlightenment.

The *Gita* depicts in eighteen chapters of verse the god Krishna's revelation to the warrior Arjuna. Central to the *Gita* and to the film is the focus upon the problem of human action. The problem is that action entails liability for the action—or *karma* in Hindu belief—but that one cannot cease acting. In the opening book of the poem, its main human character, the warrior Arjuna, contemplates the battle he is about to enter. Knowing that many of his relatives are fighting on the other side and aware of the terrible loss of life the battle will bring about, Arjuna loses his nerve, telling his charioteer, the god Krishna, that he will not fight. It is this refusal that inaugurates Krishna's spiritual education of Arjuna. In the opening books of the poem, Krishna's theme is that of action properly understood and undertaken. Krishna begins by informing Arjuna that it is sheer ignorance to believe in the illusions of killing and death. The self, he explains, is eternal. The body is born and dies, but in each body resides an eternal spiritual essence that has never been born and will never die.

The wise grieve neither for the living nor for the dead. There has never been a time when you and I and the kings gathered there have not existed, nor will there be a time when we will cease to exist. . . . One man believes he is the slayer, another believes he is the slain. Both are ignorant; you were never born; you will never die; you have never changed; you can never change. . . . [W]hen the body is worn out a new one is acquired by the Self. (*Gita* II:12-13)

The *Gita* is not a philosophical treatise; its ideas are to be found distributed among several formal schools of Hindu philosophy with significant disagreements. Since *The Legend of Bagger Vance* is our focus here, we will follow its lead in selecting what elements of the poem are to be emphasized and how they are interpreted. The film's perspective is essentially that of the Vedanta school of philosophy. Vedanta is resolutely non-dualist in perspective. That is, it maintains that all of reality is in essence One, and that the apparent perception of difference, of objects and individuals, is in fact *maya*, illusion. The two terms essential to our discussion are these: *Brahman* and *atman*. Brahman refers to the divine Self, the unified reality of the universe outside of which nothing whatsoever falls. Atman refers to the innermost core of human subjectivity, what we might call the "self." The point of the spiritual practice of Vedanta is to produce the insight that the self and the Self are one, that atman is Brahman. To use a typical analogy, think of a bottle of water afloat in a lake. Although separated from the water outside by the glass of the bottle, the water within is not different from what surrounds it. To extend the analogy, the glass stands for ignorance, the false beliefs that maintain the illusion of difference and individual identity. This idea, as we shall see, is central to the narrative of *Bagger Vance*.

When Krishna upbraids Arjuna for his belief that he can kill or be killed, it is this eternal identity that he refers to. The individual is an illusion; the unborn and undying Self, Brahman, is all that really exists. It is this truth that underlies Krishna's insistence that Arjuna act, that he fight in the battle to come. The connection between action and enlightenment is this: right action, as Krishna explains, is action not selfishly concerned with action's outcomes and rewards. Such action is therefore not at all interested in or even aware of any imagined benefits to the illusory "self" as an individual, but is action serving the Self—Brahman. Thus, in every enlightened action, the identity of atman and Brahman is realized. "The awakened sages call a person wise when all his undertakings are free from anxiety about results. . . . [The wise,] [f]ree from all

expectations and all sense of possession, with mind and body firmly controlled by the Self, . . . do not incur sin by the performance of physical
action" (*Gita* IV:19-21). What Krishna means here is that to act without
the slightest trace of self-interest is to allow the Self—Brahman/atman—
to act without impediment. Thus Arjuna, in his refusal to act, is committing the worst of mistakes. All must act. "Even to maintain your body,
Arjuna, you are obliged to act," says Krishna, and he adds, "Every selfless
act . . . is born from Brahman, the eternal, infinite Godhead. He is present in every act of service" (*Gita* III:15-16).

Thus, in action without interest in the fruits of action, the illusory self
is deprived of the very mechanism by which its apparent reality is maintained. In acting in concert with the One, the performer acts as the One,
and illusion is dispelled.

# R. Junuh Realizes the Oneness of the Cosmos

These are the insights of the Gita that are most emphasized in the film.
Junuh, once a promising young golfer from Savannah, Georgia, engaged
to the beautiful Adele Invergordon, experiences the horror of World War
I during a disastrous attack from which he emerges as the sole survivor of
the Savannah regiment. After this trauma, he becomes a disillusioned
drifter, eventually returning to his hometown to live alone, withdrawn
from life in his dilapidated family home. In terms of the Gita's emphasis
on service, it is of course important that the film is set during the Great
Depression in the 1930s. The magnificent resort built by Adele's father as
the premier golf club in the South has been left unsuccessful by the rav-
ages of the Depression, and the town fathers hope to buy the property
cheaply and resell it to developers at a profit. Adele's plan to save the
resort by staging a great golf tournament featuring the best players of
the period—Bobby Jones and Walter Hagan—is approved reluctantly by the
town leaders, but they wish the inclusion of a local player, one who will
represent the city of Savannah itself. The difficulty Adele has in convincing Junuh to play marks the parallel between him and Arjuna. Like the
protagonist of the Gita, Junuh is stalled in inaction and requires an
enlightened explanation of action if he is to serve the interests of his
city and the South. Just as Krishna teaches Arjuna, Junuh is instructed

by a modern version of the god charioteer. Suddenly, as Junuh attempts with bleak results to regain his once magnificent golf swing, Bagger Vance (*Bhagavad Gita*) appears. As Junuh's caddy, Vance will instruct Junuh in the reality of the One, and in the secret of regaining an "authentic swing."

Bagger Vance's mystical authority is nicely illustrated in the film on several occasions. One of these occurs at night as Vance and Hardy Greaves, the young boy who idolizes Junuh and who serves as assistant caddy, "walk the course" before the morning match. Carrying a lantern that bathes one of the course's greens in an almost supernatural glow, Vance instructs Hardy on the necessity of immersion into reality as a seamless unity. As Bagger's voice echoes on the sound track, the film inserts into the scene a montage depicting details of the nocturnal world surrounding the green, a set of images that interweaves the action as Hardy attempts to putt with his eyes closed into the immensity of "all there is." Again, attempting to restore to Junuh his authentic swing, Bagger describes that swing, the perfect unity of player and game, man and world, as arising from the ability to "see the place where the tides, the seasons, and the turning of the earth all come together, where everything that is becomes one."

Throughout the tournament this immersion of the player into the unity of the One is emphasized in a series of images. When Bagger explains to Junuh that he must be aware of the "field" if he is to regain his swing, we are given another montage, interweaving images of the surrounding world into the action on the course (see *Gita* 13). The implication of this imagery is that to play the game, which by this time we understand to be the game of life represented by the game of golf, we must comprehend our inclusion in the whole of reality and abandon the illusion of separation from that whole. Several times therefore, we are presented with close-up images of the flag on the first green, the white one displayed upon a bright red background. In an especially effective representation of unity, Junuh experiences the disappearance of the spectators, the silencing of all sound as he concentrates upon the distant flag bearing the one. Suddenly, in a telephoto zoom shot, the distance between Junuh and the faraway green collapses in a visual metaphor of the dissolution of distance and difference, of the collapse of *maya* in the recognition of unity.

Just as Krishna informs Arjuna that every selfless act is born from Brahman, Bagger tells Junuh that the perfect, authentic swing awaits within. All one has to do is "get the hell out of the way." It is important to note that, for Junuh as for Arjuna, the key to enlightened performance of action depends upon motive. Junuh, alienated and depressed by the horror of combat in the war, resists the opportunity to act despite the pleas of Adele and the city fathers. It is only when Bagger arrives on the scene that Junuh reconsiders and agrees to play. The link between the two events is subtly made. As Junuh tests his abilities with a driver and several golf balls the night he has turned down the city's request that he play, he finds that he cannot even hit a straight drive. It is at this point that Bagger arrives to tell him that he has lost his swing. Junuh's opportunity to act on behalf of Savannah is an opportunity to act beyond self-interest for the good of others. It is this opportunity offered and refused that leads to the appearance of Bagger. The point is clear: the means to the recovery of the swing is the game played to benefit Savannah, ravaged by the effects of the Depression, and to save the beautiful golf course, which the film depicts throughout as a place of natural beauty preserved from loss. To play is thus for Junuh to act on the behalf of the people of Savannah and, in a particularly modern American aspect of the film, to help preserve the natural beauty of the course from being lost to developers. Early in the film he panics and attempts to leave Savannah before the match. He comes, though, upon crowds of the city's inhabitants (significantly, many of them from among the poor and underprivileged), who cheer him and wish him well. Junuh, unable to deprive them of hope, turns back. It is in his actions taken on the behalf of Savannah that Junuh encounters the possibility of recovering his swing.

When Junuh, not yet fully accepting Bagger's advice, plays badly, Bagger explains, "Right now my player is still a little confused about who he is. He still thinks he's Rannulph Junuh." The mayor of Savannah, overhearing, responds, "He *is* Rannulph Junuh!" Bagger replies, "He is and he isn't." In this apparent paradox, of course, Bagger indicates the supreme lesson of the Gita. From the enlightened perspective, the self is the Self, and disinterested action allows the Self to act beyond the fears and desires of the deluded individual who believes himself to be separate from the impersonal unity of the universe.

Thus, although Junuh exhibits a desire to act on behalf of others, he must work to escape an egotistic involvement in the match while Bagger's advice enables him to play with immense skill. After a few magnificent shots, Junuh is taken with his success and his egotism emerges. He begins to refuse Bagger's advice. " I hope you're all paying customers," he says to the crowd as he attempts an impossible shot against which Bagger has advised. He fails miserably. After Junuh, filled with self-importance, describes to Adele his plan to win the tournament in the quickest possible way, his play further deteriorates. It is only when Junuh is able to rise above an egotistic interest in winning the game to achieve personal glory that he is able to play with genius and genuine joy.

In the final sequence of the film, Junuh decides to call a stroke on himself when his ball rolls after he clears away some dry grass. It is notable that in doing so he refuses to lie, even though a lie would probably win him the game. The advice of the other players, sympathetic with Junuh's plight, becomes in the context of the film's emphasis upon seeing without illusion, subtly significant. They ask Junuh if he might not be mistaken, if the ball might have moved before he removed the grass and twigs, and remind that "sometimes a ball will shudder and settle back again." Hagen says that the ball "might not have moved at all," reminding Junuh that the "light plays tricks." Junuh is here tempted to doubt his clear perception of what has occurred, to grasp the chance to win by accepting that he has been misled by an illusion. That he will neither accept this proposition nor pretend to in order to win the game is of course a testament to Junuh's ability to subdue with admirable sportsmanship his egotistic interests. Equally important, though, is his resolute insistence upon what he has seen, his certainty that he has not succumbed to illusion. To see without illusion is of course the point of Krishna's lessons to Arjuna in the *Bhagavad Gita*, and the illusion most necessary to escape is that of separation from the all-encompassing unity of the universe as Brahman. In adding this stroke to his score, Junuh loses his chance to win the match, but neither does he lose it. He ties with Hagan and Jones. In this tie, winning and losing—and therefore self and other—become meaningless terms in a unity beyond which none of the players lies.

# Vignette

## *Why Has Bodhidharma Left for the East?* (1989)

For those interested in further films dealing with Buddhism, we recommend *Why Has Bodhidharma Left for the East*, a Korean Buddhist film of great subtlety and beauty. Set in a remote mountain monastery in Korea, the film deals with three characters—Hyegok, an old monk; Kibong, his young student; and Haejin, an orphan boy to whom the old monk has given a home. The film gives its viewers a sense of the process of enlightenment from the perspective of Zen Buddhism. Although difficult to follow due to its numerous flashbacks and minimal dialogue, *Bodhidharma* repays close attention.

Through the experiences of the young orphan, we are presented with issues of loss and desire central to Buddhist doctrine. It is such experiences, unavoidable in life, that led Buddha to the role of impermanence in suffering. Humans are tortured by desire, but even to gain the objects of desire leads to pain since everything is impermanent. In a particularly moving sequence the young boy seeks to assuage his loneliness by capturing a bird, who eventually dies and decomposes. In his horrified discovery of the bird's remains, Haejin has a profound experience of impermanence, and in the forlorn calls of the bird's mate we are given a heartbreaking representation of the desire and sense of loss that may be transformed into enlightenment.

The film reveals that Kibong, the young monk, has left his impoverished city existence, abandoning his sister and blind mother to seek enlightenment—an act that fills him with guilt and leads him to question his commitment to self-liberation. The old monk, whose strenuous dedication to an austere, meditative life has severely damaged his physical health, serves both to inspire Kibong and to increase his questions about the validity of his choice in life.

In the most powerful of the film's sequences, Kibong must burn the body of his deceased teacher. As Kibong observes the funeral pyre throughout the night, we realize that his vigil provides the means to his enlightenment. We are invited to understand that the body he watches burn represents the self it is the purpose of Zen to extinguish as the most profound of illusions. Watching the dissolution of the body, Kibong realizes his own nonexistence and achieves a liberation wonderfully depicted when the monk disappears between one shot of the film and the next. The film implies that the child Haejin, as the only person remaining at the monastery, will continue along the path to enlightenment himself.

The film's beautiful photography in long sequences without dialogue traces with great sensitivity the concrete particulars of the monastery and the wild natural landscape in which it lies. One of the film's most engaging features, this photography suggests throughout the Buddhist idea of "suchness," the enlightened experience of the world observed without judgment or clinging, seen merely as it is.

Students of the film should be familiar with the famous *Ox Herding Pictures*, a traditional series of images that traces the process of enlightenment through the metaphor of the search for an ox. The sequence of Haejin's interaction with the ox draws from them.

# Suggested Readings

*Bhagavad Gita*, Ecnath Easwaran, ed. (Tomales, Calif.: Nilgiri Press, 1985).

Kim Knott, *Hinduism: A Very Short Introduction* (New York: Oxford University Press, 2000).

Dalai Lama, *The World of Tibetan Buddhism: An Overview of Its Philosophy and Practice* (Wisdom Publications, 1995).

Steven Pressfield, *The Legend of Bagger Vance: A Novel of Golf and the Game of Life* (New York: William Morrow, 1995).

Huston Smith and Philip Novak, *Buddhism: A Concise Introduction* (San Francisco: HarperSanFrancisco, 2004).

R. C. Zaehner, *Hinduism* (New York: Oxford University Press, 1983).

CHAPTER 14

# Jewish Films: Finding the Path Between Torah and Modernity

R eligions present themselves as eternally true, thus implying that they never change. But of course religions change constantly. The impetus for change usually comes from the society in which a religion exists. When the culture of a society changes in particular ways, then a religion within that culture may respond to those changes. Often the changes are relatively minor. The increasing popularity of rock-and-roll music in 1960s America led to the incorporation of that music into Christian worship, while one result of the women's rights movement is the use of gender-inclusive language in Bible translations. Sometimes, the changes are large and dramatic, like the attempt of Cromwell's Protestant forces to drive out the Catholics during the English Civil War, or Hitler's success in killing six million Jews during World War II. Both of these events essentially eliminated the living presence of the attacked religion in those areas.

Sometimes the largest changes in religions stem not from sudden, dramatic cultural changes, but from deep transformations that take place over generations or even centuries. The European Enlightenment is one such transformation. Beginning in the seventeenth century, the collection of processes and changes identified as the Enlightenment moved Europe from a continent where Christianity was dominant to one in which, by the twentieth century, human reason and secularism—often referred to as modernity—became the reigning social paradigm. This shift robbed religions of their power and their immediate validity; religion was no longer part of the power of government.

Although Judaism in Europe and America was never part of the governing structures, it existed within those societies and thus faced a similar set of challenges at the onset of modernity. These challenges comprise the focus of the two films featured in this chapter, *The Chosen* (1982) and *The Quarrel* (1990). These films transfer major social and religious alterations onto the central characters and let their personal interaction provide a platform for wrestling with the ramifications of the larger questions.

*The Chosen* is a coming-of-age film featuring two teenage Jewish boys in New York during World War II. One boy, Danny, is the son of a Hasidic *rebbe* and his life has been lived almost exclusively within the Hasidic community. He dresses like his ancestors did generations earlier in Europe and has been educated solely within the community. He has remained within Judaism by keeping out the modern world. The other, Reuben, is the son of a university professor who is an expert in rabbinic literature, especially the Babylonian Talmud. Although Reuben, like Danny, studies Talmud regularly, he lives a typically American life. He dresses like other Americans, goes to a typical high school, and even plays some jazz piano. He blends his Judaism with elements of modernity.

The film follows their unlikely friendship, showing how each boy influences the other. Over the course of the film, each boy changes. Danny the Hasid reveals his fascination with psychology and ultimately leaves the community to attend Columbia University to study it full-time. Reuben, who has grown up in a freer environment, decides to deepen his commitment to Judaism by becoming a rabbi. The film thus shows that the modern world is one of possibilities, movement, and change. This change takes place not just away from religion toward increasing secularism, but also toward increasing religious activity. Judaism encompasses both directions.

If *The Chosen* presents two boys making the choices that determine their adult lives, then *The Quarrel* presents two adults looking back on the moment in their youth where their different choices and actions defined the directions that led them to their present circumstances. It is perhaps a post–coming-of-age film. The protagonists are Hersh and Chaim, the former a rabbi of an Orthodox yeshiva, the latter a secular Yiddish writer—a poet, a novelist, and a journalist. The defining moment of their youth occurred when Chaim left the yeshiva of their youth—where the two men had been best friends—giving up Torah study to immerse himself in the study and composition of literature. Hersh, seeing his friend forsaking God, had tried to stop him. Rather than bringing him back, his actions led to his friend's total estrangement.

When these two (ex)friends accidentally meet in a park, they spend the afternoon talking, trying to bridge their differences. The differences are not merely the personal ones, but are also those of a traditional Judaism that has rejected modernism versus a "Judaism" that has embraced it. To complicate matters even more, these differences are viewed through the unforgiving lens of the Holocaust, in which both men lost their entire families—their parents, their wives, and their children. In the end, they can reconcile their hearts but not their minds. They part friends, but not having budged from their rigid positions vis-à-vis Judaism, God, and the modern world.

Both *The Chosen* and *The Quarrel* spend most of the film emphasizing the differences between the central characters and thus between their views of Judaism and modernity. These differences range from relatively superficial choices over dress, music, and entertainment to fundamental and irreconcilable differences over the role and even the existence of God. Neither film favors one approach to Judaism and modernity over another. Instead, both accept the legitimacy of the different forms of Judaism. In other words, they favor the unity of the Jewish people over the separation imposed by the different approaches to religion.

# Responding to Cultural Context: The Problem of Judaism's Changes

In *The Quarrel*, the main character Chaim left the yeshiva as a young man. In Hersh's view, he forsook his roots to become part of the modern world. This perspective reveals how Orthodox Judaism views its more modernized counterparts. Not to put too fine a point on it, the modern forms of Judaism have deserted the original. Orthodoxy denies members of these forms of Judaism standing as God's Chosen People—their special character that called upon them to separate from the nations and to be devoted to God only. For Orthodoxy, this special character is to be expressed through study of and devotion to the Torah.

The historical reality is more complex than that. First, study and reverence of the Torah as a central religious activity expected from all males was formalized not in biblical times, but later, in the Rabbinic Period, which began at the end of the first century CE. The Hebrew Bible (=Old Testament) enjoined the people Israel to worship God at the Jerusalem Temple with sacrifices, offerings, and song. Following the leadership of the priests and practicing the moral and ritual laws constitute the most important activities. During the Rabbinic Period following the Temple's destruction, rabbis replaced the priests as the most important leadership figures. Without a Temple, study of the sacred texts replaced the importance of sacrificial offerings. By the time the Babylonian Talmud was composed in the sixth century, Torah rather than Temple had become Judaism's central religious focus, a focus that supplied the basis for European Judaism. The practices attached to Torah study were refined and reshaped in different ways in different communities of European Jews.

The specific character of Judaism that appears in Orthodoxy and Hasidism stems from the response of Jews to Christian oppression during the late Middle Ages that continued into the nineteenth century, and even the twentieth century, in areas of Eastern Europe. It arose from the Christian rejection of the presence of Jews among them. The Christian rulers prevented Jews from living among the Christian population and instead restricted them to living in specific areas known as ghettos and shtetls. Jews were also limited to following only a few occupations, prevented from owning land, and restricted in their associations with Christians to business activities. The Christian-enforced isolation of the Jews promoted the development of forms of Judaism that did not need to take into account the outside world on a daily basis. Thus, traditional Judaism—in both its Orthodox and Hasidic forms—could focus inward upon the religion and the Jews' relationship to God. Their Torah reverence did not need to take into account the outside world. Orthodoxy emphasized intellectual study and knowledge of Torah, while Hasidism added the importance of "feeling" to it.

Second, when the Christian world began its Enlightenment transformation, Jews in the ghettos and shtetls saw it as something happening outside of them. Any Jewish interest in it was therefore an interest in foreign ideas, not in matters relevant to Judaism. But the Enlightenment resulted as much from Jewish thinkers as from Christians, relatively speaking. Some of the key figures were Jews, such as Moses Mendelssohn and Benedict Spinoza. The Enlightenment was a product of people whose origins lay in Judaism as well as Christianity. It was not totally imposed from outside, even though that is the standard perception.

The most fundamental achievement of the Enlightenment was the transformation of the understanding of human nature. Prior to the Enlightenment, humans were largely defined in Europe by their religion. Truth came from religious faith. Those who belonged to the correct faith were accepted because they knew the truth; the rest were not. While this led to religiously inspired wars between the Protestants and the Catholics during the Reformation, both sides saw the Jews as outsiders. The Enlightenment redefined truth as stemming from reason. All humans capable of reason were accepted, were seen as the same. Since Jews had reason, they became accepted.

The next step of social transformation did come from outside. Just as the Christian world had pushed Jews into their restricted lives, so now the governments informed by Enlightenment principles lifted those restrictions during the nineteenth century. In Germany, France, and other countries, Jews became free to live wherever they could find suitable housing. As societies changed, Jews could increasingly enter a broader range of occupations, seek higher education, and so on. They even became citizens of the countries in which they lived. Of course, some restrictions were slow to lift, in part due to remaining anti-Jewish prejudice among Jews' fellow citizens.

But this prejudice simply added more fuel to Jews' desire to integrate. Where Jews were barred from joining fraternities and private clubs, for instance, Jews created their own. If Jews were banned from universities, they built their own colleges. Sometimes these colleges, like Hirsch College in *The Chosen*, combined the study of traditional Jewish subjects with the disciplines of the modern academy. Throughout the nineteenth century and into the twentieth, Jews took aspects of modernity and wove them together with aspects of their own backgrounds and religion. In this way, they created new types of Judaism—now known as Progressive, Reform, and Conservative. These types of Judaism not only took on some of the features found in Christian churches but also developed their theology and their worship practices in line with notions of religion put forward in Enlightenment thought.

Not all Jews favored this adaptation of Judaism to the increasing cultural dominance of modernity. They argued that the new forms of Judaism betrayed those that God had established. The new forms of Judaism in turn argued against the backwardness of Orthodoxy, which refused to engage with the advantages of the modern world. Thus, Jewish adaptation to modernity—a seemingly outside, non-Jewish development—

created a rift within Judaism itself. The anger and sense of betrayal, which these changes brought about, became so virulent that at times the two camps of Judaism seemed to fight each other more than they did non-Jews.

Of course, reason, Enlightenment, and Emancipation did not always produce enlightened tolerance and acceptance for Jews in Europe. The twentieth century found such equality and acceptance on the wane. The Dreyfus case in France revealed the prejudices of the military, ruling classes, and the masses. English anti-Semitism was also high between the two World Wars, especially among certain segments of the aristocracy. But it was Germany's so-called Final Solution—the elimination of all Jews—that brought the curtain down on acceptance of Jews in Europe. The Nazis' successful murder of more than six million Jews, called the Holocaust, gave Jews and indeed the world a monumental example of humans' cruelty to each other. It is the rumination on these circumstances that gave rise to the two films discussed below.

# *The Chosen*

*The Chosen* begins by panning through a cityscape, finally settling on a group of American boys warming up for a baseball game. One suddenly cries out, "Here they come," and a second group of boys appear, dressed in black suits and hats of a type that had been stylish in Eastern Europe a couple of centuries earlier. The narrator's voice-over (Reuben Maulter, one of the boys already on the field) makes it clear that these newcomers are as strange to him as they are to the audience. They "would keep to themselves and that was fine with me." They are Hasidic Jews.

Reuben's internal monologue relates how playing baseball in 1940s New York provides a way for Jews to show themselves strong, physically fit, and part of American society. Reuben's team of Jewish boys, dressed in American street clothes and looking like any other bunch of American boys, is certain they will win easily. The Hasids bat first, and after their team has been through the batting rotation once, Reuben's team realizes they are about to get beaten badly. The coach puts in Reuben as pitcher and the rivalry between the teams suddenly takes on a personal character as the new batter, Danny Saunders, faces him. They glare at each other with mounting tension as Reuben throws balls and strikes, one of which Danny catches and tosses back. When the next throw goes over the plate,

Danny slams it, and the ball flies straight into Reuben's face, smashing his glasses and pushing broken glass into his eye. Reuben wakes in a hospital. Despite this inauspicious beginning Reuben and Danny become friends, and the struggle to define themselves as Jews in modern American society becomes the film's central focus.

A reading of the film's structure readily reveals that the relationship between Judaism and modernity is flexible. It can take several forms, and people can move from one relationship to another. It does not have to be fixed and rigid.

At the film's beginning, Reuben's relationship to modernity is clear. He lives within it and likes it. He dresses like his non-Jewish contemporaries, goes to the movies (the most technologically advanced form of entertainment), and plays jazz piano. Although he is obviously Jewish—he even studies Talmud regularly—his relationship to Judaism is somewhat unclear. The film never presents him at worship or prayer, except when he is with Danny. When Reuben graduates from high school, he attends Hirsch College, where he studies both Jewish and secular subjects. Toward the film's end, he decides that he wants to become a rabbi, in particular a rabbi for "today's world." So he moves closer toward Judaism, becoming more involved and more committed to the religion.

Danny by contrast has lived his life in a Hasidic community. There he has become an expert in Judaism, but has gained little exposure to the modern, non-Jewish world. Despite this, he has read Freud's writings and has developed a keen passion for psychology. But how can he negotiate his way out of the expectations of his father and the Hasidic community? At first, it looks like he might be able to imitate Reuben's path, for he persuades his father to permit him to attend the same college. In the end, however, Danny is unsatisfied with Hirsch. He wants to study psychology and does not like the way it is done there. Ultimately, he is admitted to Columbia University and gains his father's permission to study psychology there. He shaves his forelocks, exchanges his Hasidic black clothes for a stylish American suit, and moves across the river to be near the university. Note that Danny's interest in psychology stems from reading the works of Sigmund Freud. Even though Freud serves as the symbol of non-religious modernity in the film, Freud's Jewish origins show through in many of his writings. Freud's own journey from his Jewish origins to psychology suggest a similar trajectory for Danny.

From a structural viewpoint, then, one boy starts closer to modernism and then moves toward Judaism, while the other boy starts almost isolated within Judaism and moves further toward the modern, secular society than the other ever was. The crossing of their paths makes an "X". *The Chosen* indicates that modernism provides a choice about how to be Jew. This choice is flexible; it enables movement and change.

This structural approach enables quick insight into the film's overall shape. But it provides little in the way of showing how the film's details support that structure. In particular, it does not seem to enable a deeper analysis to explain why the boys move in these directions. One question stands out: why does psychology so fascinate Danny and become the central point of nearly all his interest in the modern world? To answer that question, we need to refocus and analyze the film from a slightly different approach.

## Danny Saunders Is *The Chosen*

If we ask who fills the title role—who is chosen?—the immediate answer is Danny. He has been chosen to succeed his father, Reb Saunders, as the leader of the Hasidic Jewish community. This comes with the enormous weight of his father's expectations and his father's guidance and education to meet those expectations. Danny must find his way between this intense Jewish experience and the modern world from which he is largely isolated and has little time to experience.

In *The Chosen*, Danny struggles not just with modernity but also with his father's decision that Danny lacked compassion. The strong intellectual abilities with which he was born did not appear to be accompanied by an instinctual concern for the suffering of others. Reb Saunders decided to take steps to instill compassion in him by relating to him through silence only. This means that from the age of about four, except during the times they study together, Reb Saunders has not spoken to his son. Even when his son speaks directly to him or asks for advice or permission, he does not respond. Although this seems cruel from the perspective of a modern, western audience, Danny's father is doing this out of love and concern for his son. Since his son has been chosen to succeed him, he must have compassion.

From the perspective of Danny's father, Reb Saunders, Danny's struggle focuses not on how to weave a path between the past—that is, the traditional practices and beliefs of this Hasidic community—and modern America, but on how to become compassionate. Since Danny is to succeed his father, he needs the same skills as his father. Compassion is necessary, but knowledge of modernity is, from Reb Saunders's view, essentially irrelevant. His perspective stems not from a senseless rejection of the modern world, but from the view that the modern world, like other characteristics of life outside Judaism, is seen to be dangerous. This view comes from the experience of Reb Saunders and the Hasidic community with non-Jews earlier in his life. As Danny tells the story:

> They're proud of my father! Reuven, back in Russia my father saved his whole community. Bands and gangs of Cossacks attacked the little town we lived in. They killed everybody. They left him for dead with a bullet wound in his chest. Well, once he recovered, he announced to his people, They were done with Russia. They were going to America.

This experience apparently taught Reb Saunders that the outside world was dangerous. America may be safer than Russia, but it remains irrelevant to the inner life of his Jewish community. Danny's father has great compassion for the people of this community—and he expressed it by saving them from the danger of Russia—but his compassion is largely limited to this community. It has to be for his leadership to work.

From his childhood, this has been the model given to Danny for how he will lead his life as an adult. It is wholly focused on the Hasidic community he will lead and contains nothing of the outside world. By the time the audience learns of this plan for Danny—at the Sabbath evening when Reuben meets Danny's father—they already know this plan will not work for him. He is too interested in, indeed too passionate about, psychology. But even as the film lays out this course for Danny, it undermines it in a traditional Jewish fashion.

Reb Saunders sets the scene. After the Sabbath service, Danny, Reuben, Reb Saunders, and the men of the Hasidic community are gathered around the dinner table. Reb Saunders gives a "little talk" about the importance of Torah as a link to God. After telling a story that likens God giving the Torah to humanity to someone throwing a drowning man a rope, he concludes, "Only through the Torah can you lead a full life. Only then will the Master of the Universe hear your words." Afterward, he turns to Reuben and asks him whether he thinks this view is correct. Rather hesitantly, Reuben answers that Torah should be combined with work and good deeds. Reuben's answer is based on a passage in one of the earliest rabbinic texts, Mishnah Abot, which reads,

[Simeon the Righteous] would say, "On three things the world stands: upon the Torah, upon work, and upon deeds of loving kindness." (Mishnah Abot 1:2)

Reb Saunders approves Reuben's response to his question, loudly saying, "It is good!" The symbolism of Simeon's three points is clear. Torah is the study and practice of the Torah (i.e., the revered and sacred texts of Judaism); for Reb Saunders this would further imply in the context of the Hasidic community. "Deeds of loving kindness" stands for compassion. Finally, "work" stands for the world, for working out in the world. Reb Saunders fulfills the first two points, but not the third; he is not out in the world or having contact with it. Danny, as his successor, has no need for it either. This, at least, is the view of Reb Saunders.

Danny sees the matter differently. His father's decision to raise him in silence has pushed him toward the modern world, in particular, toward psychology. True, he has gained compassion. But his understanding of compassion comes from silence. The experience of silence is one of suffering, of being separated from his father. He did not have the expressive, joyous experiences of his father that he sees his younger brother, Levi, having. Instead, he suffered in loneliness. This experience of suffering has enabled him to see suffering in others and to have compassion for them. He has learned to listen to his heart. But he has also discovered that he does not understand his heart, his feelings. His intellect gives him a desire to know this too. But perhaps having compassion is enough. Danny should learn to express his compassion in a modern, yet Jewish, way.

Reuben and Reuben's father, Professor Mautner, both provide models Danny could follow. Professor Mautner provides the most secular model. He underwent suffering at the death of his wife. When he sees the suffering that the Jews experienced in the Nazi death camps, and the continuing difficulties they face in the Displaced Persons camps, he has compassion for them and expresses that compassion by working to provide them a homeland. The scene where he and Reuben hear the United Nations vote on the Partition Plan marks the success of this approach.

Reuben has also suffered in his life. Not only did he lose his mother, but we see throughout the film the healing of his eye, which is followed by the silent treatment from Danny, which his father imposes. Because of this Reuben decides to become a rabbi himself—not in the model of Reb Saunders or any other rabbi he knows, but a "rabbi for today's world."

Both Reuben and Professor Mautner, then, constitute foils for Danny. They suffer and learn compassion. They find ways of combining that compassion with a blend of modernity and Judaism. Like the model of his father, they represent choices open to Danny. But Danny will not take them. All three choices modeled in the film represent ways of helping people with external forms of suffering, the suffering of body and danger to the physical body, even death. Danny's experience with suffering through the silent treatment has attuned him to the suffering of the heart, the internal experience of deprivation instead of the external experience of hard conditions of life. So, he will pursue a different path.

Danny's attraction to the modern world comes from psychology. This is not an obvious attraction. He actually does not seem to be attracted by anything else, other than baseball. Reuben tries him out on movies and art; in the giddy exuberance at the war's end Danny is suddenly kissed by a woman, an experience that upsets him more than attracts him. What is the interest, then, that makes psychology Danny's passion? The short answer is that, for Danny, psychology provides a window into a person's heart. But to explain why that attracts Danny, we follow the clues placed in the film.

First, in the conversation that forms the beginning of their friendship, Danny tells Reuben, "My father believes that words distort what a person really feels in his heart." A person cannot accurately explain or understand what is in their heart by speaking with words. Danny's experience with silence has brought home the truth of this observation and so his intellect causes him to want to understand the heart.

Second, in their next meeting, Danny helps Reuben memorize parts of William Shakespeare's play *Hamlet*. The line "perchance to dream" impels Danny to ask Reuben about his dreams, and suddenly Danny makes the most un-Hasidic remarks about dreams. Although Hamlet's remark implies that dreams are to be avoided because they are nightmares, Danny's comments point to the welcome importance of dreams for, as Freud argues, they give access to an individual's unconscious mind.

> But don't you see the importance that the symbols in our dreams can have. Reuben, deep inside of us there's something. It's called the unconscious. It makes us do and feel things without us ever being aware of it. It's filled with things that, that (*sic*) we are afraid to tell ourselves. It is only by interpreting the symbols in our dreams that we can find out about what is really going on inside of us.

For Danny, Freud's unconscious is the Jewish notion of the heart, as articulated in his comment about his father's belief. If words cannot express the heart, then the symbols of dreams can. Danny follows up this remark by giving a talmudic interpretation of a dream of Reuben's, talking about the interplay of letters indicating the role of mind and heart. (His interpretation shows, at this point, that he has not yet learned fully the lesson of compassion.)

Third, it is the importance of understanding feelings and actions that drives Danny, as indicated by his concern about his feelings toward Reuben at the baseball game. Although he seems truly sorry about the injury he caused Reuben, he is also profoundly puzzled by the feelings he experienced when as a batter he faced Reuben pitching. He does not understand where his desire to hit Reuben with the bat, to kill him, came from, and he is rightly disturbed by that desire. Although not made explicit in the film, Danny apparently sees Freud's interpretative use of dreams as a way to understand where these feelings came from. Such feelings caused suffering in two ways. First, they resulted in serious injury to Reuben, from which he suffers and for which Danny feels remorse. Second, Danny's knowledge that these feelings came from within him frightens him a bit. He fears he does not know himself as well as he should. In other words, he suffers because of them.

Therefore, psychology for Danny becomes the means for understanding the cause of people's internal suffering. Such suffering in turn causes people to act in ways that cause other people suffering. Danny's driving passion, then, is to understand psychology better, so that he can relieve the suffering of others before that suffering leads them to cause suffering in others. It is here ultimately where his intellect and his compassion meet.

In the end, Danny's desire to study psychology—his passion and his compassion—lead him to attend Columbia University. The film's final scene shows him shorn of his forelocks, dressed in a modern suit, and going to live near the university. Our structural interpretation of the film saw this change as suggesting that of all the film's characters, Danny goes the furthest toward modernity and away from Judaism. But this interpretation is too simplistic, for Danny's move has the blessing of his father, who could not condone any abandonment of Judaism on Danny's part. So how should this change be understood?

The key lies in Reuben's observation earlier in the film, that Torah should be combined with work and deeds of loving-kindness. Now all three elements of the symbolism fit Danny. Work again should be seen as the world, although it should also be seen the "work" of psychology, in the service of all humanity (i.e., the world). Danny is going out into the world for this specific work. Deeds of loving-kindness represents the compassion, the driving force of concern for other's suffering, that leads Danny to pursue this path. The meaning of Torah, in this formulation, has changed, but only slightly. Danny will still follow "ritual Judaism," the regular prayer and study and practice of Orthodox/Hasidic Jewry. However, he will leave the enclosed "life of Torah" that the Hasidic community practices to live surrounded not by Torah but by the world.

One last piece remains in this puzzle. When Reuben returns at the end to meet Reb Saunders and Danny, Reuben becomes the conduit by which Danny and his father resolve their separation and Danny enters into his adult status. As Reb Saunders indicates that Danny has his permission and approval to attend Columbia, he says that he is not afraid. The reason for this lack of fear is that he has realized that his son Danny is a *tzadik*, a righteous man. "But you see now I am not afraid. I have no fear, because my Daniel is a *tzadik*, he's a righteous man. And the world needs a righteous man."

The declaration that Danny is a *tzadik* represents in this scene the recognition that Danny is now his own person. He no longer remains under his father's authority as a child, but has matured into a man. Indeed, he is a righteous man. It is the final remark that is in many ways the most significant: "the world needs a righteous man." Reb Saunders sends Danny out into the world to be a *tzadik* for the world. A *tzadik* is a bridge, as Danny told Reuben in an earlier scene, a bridge between God and his people. To declare that the world needs a righteous man, then, is to recognize that all humans are God's people and that they need their bridge to God. Through psychology, Danny will become that bridge, a bridge that will relieve people's internal suffering.

What then does it mean to be a Jew in the modern world? *The Chosen* provides four models—models presented by Danny, and Reuben, and their fathers. The film neither rejects nor criticizes any of the four. They are all accepted as valid options. The film's resolution to the question of how to combine Judaism and modernity, then, is that one must be a Jew with compassion. Any combination of Judaism and modernity is acceptable, as long as one remains a Jew whose life expresses compassion for others.

# Debate after Destruction, *The Quarrel*

Like *The Chosen*, *The Quarrel*'s main conflict centers on whether and to what extent Judaism and Jews should interact with the modern world,

which the film portrays as entirely non-Jewish. This conflict is represented—through the memories of the adult Chaim and Hersh—as the
time when the youthful Chaim left the orthodox world of the religious
yeshiva to pursue a life of literature and writing. The attempts by the
young Hersh at that time to keep Chaim within that world exacerbated
the situation, leading the adult Chaim to recall Hersh before their accidental meeting as his best friend "and bitterest enemy."

Unlike *The Chosen*, however, *The Quarrel* places the debate over this
issue into the highly charged arena of the Holocaust's aftermath instead
of the safe streets of immigrant New York. Indeed, the Holocaust and the
impact it had on Jews seemingly towers over the entire film. But however
difficult the personal pain and tragedy the Holocaust caused these two
men, the quarrel of their youth keeps breaking through. In the end, the
differences of their early manhood keep them apart, while ironically the
terrors and the perniciousness of the Holocaust serve to unite them.
Although the Holocaust provides the experiences over which the two
men debate—often in a classic yeshiva style—and adds immediacy to the
debate, it is the relationship to Judaism and to the modern world that in
the end remains irresolvable. It is modernity, not the Holocaust per se,
that divides the two men.

The magnitude of the Holocaust's horror and inhumanity is difficult to
convey in a short space. One could easily devote this entire chapter or
even this entire book to it and not do it justice. But *The Quarrel* cannot
be even partially understood without at least a brief introduction to this
catastrophe.

After World War I, the Nazi party attempted to unite the defeated
German nation by propagating the belief that the German people were
the only pure descendants of the Aryan race. As Germany began to conquer other nations during World War II, Hitler and his administration
decided to purify the German nation of non-Aryans, the largest group of
these being the Jews. Even as German armies fought on the Eastern and
the Western fronts, the security apparatus put into effect the Final
Solution. It began with rounding up all Jews and imprisoning millions of
them in what came to be known as Death Camps. In these camps, most
of the Jews were put to death in gas chambers. Before the end of the war,
over six million Jews had been murdered simply because they were
Jewish. The hatred of the Nazi leaders' anti-Semitism was so virulent that
even as they were losing the war they continued to divert huge resources
of manpower and materials into this effort.

The numbers of Jews killed in the Holocaust is so huge that it is difficult to grasp the human significance of this tragedy. But *The Quarrel* gives us an insight into it as Hersh and Chaim share their experiences and their knowledge of what happened to others. Both men lost their entire families: their parents, their wives, their children, and apparently, nearly all other relatives as well. Both lived with enormous guilt about their relationships with those who had been killed: Hersh over not having forgiven his father, and Chaim over having left his family to their fate and not being able to ask their forgiveness. They compare notes over friends who were killed, and laugh over the few who were spared. It is clear that both are alone. Despite their argument and their differences, they are closer to each other than to anyone else still alive.

The shared Holocaust experience—from imprisonment or escape to the murders of family and friends—provides *The Quarrel* with an egalitarian approach. Both sides to the modernism debate present their cases in their own terms. This is in sharp contrast to *The Chosen*, where Reuben's internal narration filters the more traditional view represented by Danny and the Hasidic community.

# The Three Questions

*The Quarrel* provides Hersh and Chaim with a common source of information on which to stage their argument. The Holocaust—both their experiences of it and their knowledge of what happened—provides the grounds for their discussion. It also refocuses the formulation of the question of Judaism and modernity from one of generalities to a specific debate. This debate addresses three questions. The first question asks whether God exists. The second question asks, if God does exist, how do we explain what happened to the Jews in the Holocaust? The third question focuses on the present and the future. How should Jews treat each other now? Hersh and Chaim agree on none of these questions.

The question of God's existence is the first question Hersh and Chaim address, and they immediately lay out opposing views. During the Holocaust, Hersh's youthful faith—so willing to believe yet so plagued with doubts and temptations—became strong and solidified, solid as a rock. His faith in God not only enabled him to pray and to rescue those in danger, but to establish a yeshiva while still in the camps and then to bring all the boys in the yeshiva to safety in Canada. As he declares,

"If my faith was on the same level as before it would be an insult to the martyrs."

Hersh believes that even in the midst of tragedy and catastrophe God works miracles. Indeed, he says, his own rescue was a miracle. At this point Chaim cannot stand it anymore. He breaks in and asks, where were the miracles for our wives and children? "Now you see why I find it difficult to believe in [God]." This short statement is the logical outcome of Hersh's belief in his own miraculous rescue by God—an outcome that Chaim sees even if Hersh does not. Chaim's view is this: If God rescued me, then he could have rescued my wife, but he chose not to do so. Is that a just God, a God worth believing in? Because of this Chaim does not believe in him.

Chaim is not radical in his refusal to believe; he is not on a crusade to eradicate all belief in God. His disbelief is more subtle. While Hersh thinks the question of God's existence and belief in him is life's fundamental question, Chaim does not. The set-piece debate in the shed during the rain shows Chaim's disbelief is more carefully formulated. Hersh starts the debate by setting out his own terms. Which is the basis for morality, belief in God or belief in reason? Despite the arguments of philosophers over the millennia, Hersh says, reason too easily leads to the Nazi destruction of people not like them and to the acquiescence of others in that destruction. True morality stems from a power in the universe higher than human beings; otherwise it is simply a matter of opinion. "If there is no Master of the Universe, then who is to say that Hitler did anything wrong?"

Chaim counters Hersh's argument not by taking the side of reason, which by implication would ally him with the Nazis, but by changing the terms of the argument. He responds:

> If you ask me what makes people moral, it is neither God nor reason. It is a faith. Your faith that God wants you to do good. That old woman's faith, that human beings must help each other. This is my faith too. Human beings must help each other, for our good and for our survival. For people who have this faith, it does not matter whether they believe in God or not. And for people who do not have that faith, that belief, they'll use their brain to justify whatever they want.

For Chaim, the question is not whether one believes in God, but whether one believes that human beings should help each other. People who believe in God and people who do not will act to help others if they believe they should. If they do not believe this, then they will not help, whatever their position on God. If people believe they should help others, then they will, Chaim responds, whether or not they believe in God. Personally, Chaim does not, but he does not see the need to persuade others that they should adopt that position.

Having made his position clear, Chaim is willing to accept the existence of God for the purposes of his discussion with Hersh. This does not provide any common ground with Hersh about the second question, for he differs significantly from Hersh on his understanding of God's relationship with the Jews.

For Hersh, the Jews are the Chosen People, and the Chosen People are to be separate from the world. As at the Covenant that Moses and the Israelites made with God at Mt. Sinai, God chose the Jews to be a people who would worship him only and thus no longer mix with the other nations of the world. In answer to Chaim's charge that God broke the Covenant with the people Israel at Auschwitz, Hersh responds, "The Germans were entirely guilty, but the Jews were not entirely innocent. We wanted to be like other nations and so we broke our covenant." Chaim's exclamation brings out the implication here, "Is punishment for assimilation death by gas?" Although this is clearly a rhetorical accusation beyond Hersh's intended meaning, it lays open his underlying assumption. In Hersh's view, the Jews are the Chosen People. In keeping with the original Covenant at Sinai, Jews are supposed to be separated from the other people of the world for this special relationship. To abandon the study of Torah for the pursuit of secular interests in the modern world—such as the study and composition of literature—is to join with the nations and to forsake one's status as the Chosen People. To become modern, then, is to abandon one's status as Chosen People. God is thus justified in punishing the Jews because they broke the Covenant to which they agreed.

Chaim rejects this view utterly. He says, "My leaving the yeshiva did not kill your family, cause the Nazi destruction. There were no sins that were foul enough to cause the Holocaust." He rejects the idea that adopting aspects of post-Enlightenment modernity is the rejection of God. It is just a different approach to God. As he says later, "I was on a different path. Honoring God in my own way."

Chaim does not limit himself to speaking about the Jews and whether or not they are culpable in their own deaths. He twice reverses the responsibility and places it on God. When Hersh emphasizes the special character of the Jews as being chosen by God, Chaim responds, "Yes, God chose us to be persecuted, to be slaughtered, to be hanged." Elsewhere Chaim goes so far as to claim, "God abandoned us. No. He humiliated us."

From Chaim's perspective, the problem with Hersh's claim that the Jews were punished by God because they were not entirely innocent is that to punish the Jews as a group, God killed many innocent individuals. When Chaim challenges Hersh over the number of religious Jews who were killed, Hersh admits he does not know how to answer. Then Chaim turns to the question of the children. "He humiliated us. Six million people. One million children. The children did not abandon God, Hersh! How can we ever forgive him for not saving the children?" Again Hersh does not have an answer. The unstated implication is that if God used the Holocaust as a punishment for Jews straying from him, then approximately one-sixth of the individuals he punished were too young to even understand the issue or be responsible for their actions. If this is the case, then God would be unjust, even to his Chosen People. It is not surprising, then, that Chaim would choose not to believe in God than to believe in one who unjustly causes the death of children.

The third question, that of how Jews should treat each other now, is also a vexed issue for the two men in *The Quarrel*. Both see the question as asking whether Jews should be unified. They cannot agree on God, they cannot agree on being chosen, but they both believe that Jews should be unified, that they are one people. The problem is that they do not agree on the conditions of unity.

Hersh believes that the Jews are one people. He says explicitly, "All Jews are bound to one another." This sounds like a great sentiment, but a further detail comes out as he is challenged over why so many religious Jews were killed in the Holocaust. His answer is that he, Hersh, is guilty because he did not change the assimilating Jews. For Hersh, unity means for all Jews to join under the Orthodox banner, and that the Orthodox should take steps to bring other Jews back to Orthodoxy. Chaim sees this as stemming from his leaving the yeshiva as a youth and Hersh's attempts to "change" his mind, to stop him. These attempts by Hersh not only separated Chaim from all his friends, but even from his own family.

Hersh's views on unity have a second caveat, namely, that should attempts to bring others into the Orthodox fold fail, then they should be separated out, rejected. This becomes clear in a scene following the discussion in the hut that seemed to have brought Chaim and Hersh to an understanding—a truce perhaps—on religious questions. The rapprochement is shattered by one of Hersh's students, who happens to find them and, upon being introduced to Chaim, berates him for leaving the yeshiva and deserting Judaism. His knowledge about Chaim can only have come from Hersh, and the anger reflects what Hersh has been teaching his students. This leads to the following realization by Chaim:

**Hersh:** Chaim, Chaim, I should have stopped him. He's a very young boy. . . . You should forgive him.

**Chaim:** Forgive him? You are the one who filled his heart with hatred!

**Hersh:** It's not hatred, Chaim, it's distance. I have to teach them this way or we won't survive.

**Chaim:** If this is all that you have to offer, it's better that we not survive.

**Hersh:** Better for whom? Hitler murdered 6 million. Now you want to finish the job for him.

**Chaim:** You are crazy. You hear that? You are crazy and cruel.

**Hersh:** . . . In Bialistok maybe I could have taught that the Torah had 70 faces of truth; each face a different reality. But not now.

**Chaim:** Yes now. We are a devastated people. This is precisely why we should turn to treasure each other like you would treasure a rare jewel. Be tolerant.

**Hersh:** These children are our last hope to save what we once had in Bialistok.

**Chaim:** I don't want any part of your vision. The world on one side, we the Chosen People on the other.

To understand Hersh's point we must focus his notion of "distance." He means distance from non-Orthodox Jews, from Jews like Chaim. Why? In Hersh's words, the answer is to "survive," by which he means "to save what we once had in Bialistok." What does Hersh mean by these words? Hersh clearly believes that the assimilating of Jews to modernity, to the world around them, constitutes the reason for the Holocaust. God brought on the Holocaust to punish the Jews for forsaking their Covenant with him and becoming like other nations. This explains both the death of non-Orthodox Jews and Orthodox Jews—the non-Orthodox because they were being punished for their apostasy and the Orthodox because they did not prevent it. The non-Orthodox thus caused the death of the Orthodox.

There are only two ways to prevent this from happening again. The first is to bring the assimilated Jews back to Orthodoxy. This has failed, and the film shows how Hersh is clearly failing with Chaim. The second way to prevent this is through "distance," that is, for the Orthodox to separate themselves from the non-Orthodox. In this way, they define the other Jews as no longer part of the Chosen People; they are ex-Jews and part of the nations of the world. In this way, Hersh and those like him preserve the Orthodox heritage of Bialistok—the European yeshiva culture—and the Covenant they have with God. For him, remaining a member of the Chosen People requires one to forgo any involvement with the modern world because, by definition, it is not Jewish. As Chaim observes, "The world on one side and we the Chosen People on the other."

Chaim, of course, does not buy this view in the least. His view is that the Jews are united; they are, or at least should be, one people, no matter what. Jews "should turn to treasure each other like you would treasure a rare jewel." What he means is that Jews should treasure the variety they represent. No matter what their stance vis-à-vis modernity, Jews should accept each other as Jews. It is their relationship to each other that is important, not their relationship to God. If Jews like Chaim no longer believe in God—and thus no longer believe in the idea of the Chosen People—they should be accepted as Jews anyway. It is the unity of the people, of their Jewish brothers and sisters, that should have ultimate priority. All that is required is the acceptance of modernity, to which of course the Orthodox cannot accede.

*The Quarrel* ends with the parting of Hersh and Chaim as friends. Chaim says twice in the closing minutes of the film: "You are my only friend, Hersh," and "You are a good friend, Hersh." They remain unified at the heart even as they are divided in everything else: God, the intellect, modernity, and their understanding of Chosen People. At the end, Chaim will not—perhaps cannot—even pray the afternoon prayer with Hersh. Instead he lights up a cigarette—that symbol of the modern world—and walks away.

Their friendship—indeed, their brotherhood—remains and keeps Hersh and Chaim united, even though everything else in their lives pulls them apart. As the voiceover at the end indicates, "But until his brothers came, Joseph was alone." Hersh and Chaim represent not only themselves, but the variety of Jews today. They may be fixed in their differences; they may not change their beliefs to be more in line with each other; they may even quarrel. But at some deep level, a level that some do not perhaps recognize, they are brothers. They are one people.

In the end, what we see in *The Quarrel* and *The Chosen* are two films that wrestle with the problem of whether and how modernity should influence Jews and Judaism. *The Chosen* provides in its main characters four different possibilities and shows how those characters can change as they live their lives. *The Quarrel* shows only two possibilities, in some ways more extreme than the options presented in the other film. These two men prove themselves fixed in their positions; they do not budge an inch toward each other. They are fixed and immovable in their beliefs about God and the Jewish people. *The Quarrel*, like *The Chosen*, does not evaluate their positions or indicate that one is superior to the other. Both are valid. So in these two films, we see six different positions on how modernity and Judaism could mix (or not). All are accepted as valid, even though some of these positions do not recognize the validity of other positions.

*The Quarrel's* reference to Joseph indicates that despite their rigid differences, Hersh and Chaim—representatives of Orthodox Judaism and secular Yiddish Jews, respectively—remain brothers and recognize each other as such. One cannot pray with the other, even though he had prayed in a *minyan* earlier in the day. The other cannot accept the one's refusal to believe in God without putting "distance" between them. Despite this, they are bound together and are alone without each other. *The Quarrel*, and to a lesser extent *The Chosen*, emphasizes that Jews are Jews—they are a unity—whatever they think of each other.

# Suggested Readings

Yehuda Bauer and Nili Keren, *A History of the Holocaust*, rev. ed. (Franklyn Watts, 2002).

Nathan Glazer, *American Judaism*, 2nd ed. (Chicago: University of Chicago Press, 1988).

Irving Howe, *World of Our Fathers: The Journey of the East European Jews to America and the Life They Found and Made* (New York: Galahad Books, 1994).

Jacob Neusner, *Death and Birth of Judaism: The Impact of Christianity, Secularism and the Holocaust on Jewish Faith* (New York: Basic Books, 1987).

Jacob Neusner, *The Way of Torah: An Introduction to Judaism*, 6th ed. (New York: Wadsworth, 1997).

Richard L. Rubenstein, *After Auschwitz: Radical Theology and Contemporary Judaism* (New York: Macmillan, 1966).

Elie Wiesel, *Night* (New York: Bantam, 1986).

C H A P T E R   1 5

# Islam and Fanaticism: Only in the Eye of the Beholder?

Since the destruction of the World Trade Center on September 11, 2001, by Islamic terrorists, Islam has been on Americans' minds. The men who flew the planes into the twin towers, to their own deaths, were not just terrorists, but religious fanatics willing to kill themselves for their cause. Americans have pondered the relationship between fanaticism and Islam since that day, wondering about the extent to which these fanatics represent the rest of the Muslim world. Even though the question's immediacy may recede from Americans' minds, it comes to the fore with every new terrorist event, from the train bombings in Madrid to the subway and bus bombings in London to the suicide attacks of the Iraqi insurgency.

The same question has been on the minds of Muslims themselves, for violent extremists using Islam as the justification for their actions have lived within Muslim societies for decades. Whether it is the Muslim Brotherhood of Syria and Egypt, Hamas in Palestine, Hezbollah in Lebanon, or the different "resistance movements" in Indonesia, Islamic societies have had to wrestle with their presence and the meaning of that presence. While the governments and police forces of those nations have been condemnatory, the response of the populace has been more varied. Sometimes these groups have been condemned, but at other times they have been embraced—as modern Robin Hoods even—by segments of the population.

These differences over the place of not only terrorists, but also those with active adherence to extreme religious views—that is, fanaticism—have led to debates within the Islamic world over their role in Islamic society and over the effect their presence has on normal, everyday life. Unfortunately, few Muslim countries meet the conditions for free speech and unfettered debate. Most nations of the Islamic world—from North Africa across the Middle East to Indonesia—are governed by strong men or other forms of nondemocratic governments with strong internal security apparatuses. Direct criticism of society, government, and social conditions can be dangerous. Furthermore, the presence of fanatics willing to use violence and murder against people who speak against them makes average citizens leery of speaking too loudly, if at all.

In this environment, ideas must be debated through indirection. Television, films, books, and other forms of mass communication often speak of one subject on the surface but of another at a deeper level. This approach provides a level of safety for the work's creator by allowing them to speak on a safe topic, while communicating their ideas to those who understand through metaphor, analogy, and symbolism.

The 1997 film *Destiny*, an Egyptian film by the accomplished director Youssef Chahine, takes just this approach to the question of Islam and fanaticism. Set in twelfth-century Islamic Spain, the film follows the struggles of the great philosopher Averroës and his friends as they try to preserve their open society against a growing threat from a group of fanatics led by Sheik Riad who are used as a tool in his goal to become politically powerful. In the end, the fanatics subvert the ruling Caliph's son, intending him to assassinate his father so the Sheik can seize ultimate power. Despite the excitement of this plot line, the key goal of the film is to show how fanaticism destroys normal life and its pleasures, namely, family, friends, music, dancing, and romantic love (mostly within marriage). Most significantly, fanaticism subverts the devout search for the true interpretation of Allah's word, the Koran, replacing it with mindless adherence to an imposed interpretation masquerading as the inherent and obvious meaning of the text.

The use of *Destiny*—an Egyptian film made for the Middle East market and distributed in the USA with English subtitles—may seem odd in this book, which has focused so exclusively on American-made films in English. The reason for the choice is that films dealing knowledgably with Islam are not yet made in the American market. This is true for nearly the entire English-language market, although England is home to a minor film genre that focuses primarily on the problems of the Muslim immigrant experience in Britain. These include films such as *My Beautiful Launderette* and *East Is East*. This chapter will end with a brief discussion of the most religiously oriented of these films, *My Son the Fanatic*.

For our study of *Destiny*, we begin the analysis with an introduction to the historical background to Averroës, then move to the interpretation of the film within that context, and finally to an explication of the film's message in the modern Muslim world.

# Averroës and the Medieval World

At the start of the fourth century, the Roman Empire controlled all the land around the Mediterranean Sea. When the Emperor Constantine took charge of this pagan empire in 324 CE, he ruled by favoring Christianity. By the end of the fifth century Christianity stood as the Empire's dominant religion. Many Christians thought that the Kingdom of God had arrived on earth. So when the new religion of Islam swept across the eastern and southern sides of the Mediterranean in the seventh century, the Christian lands were unprepared for the onslaught and fell to the Muslims. The Muslims took control over much of Spain as well, beginning in the south; only the northern region adjacent to France remained Christian. Although this general description held for many centuries, the Christians and the Muslims frequently fought over the border. It was not until the Christians drove the Muslims completely out of Spain in the fifteenth century that such fighting ceased.

The loss of half the Christian world in the seventh century plunged Europe into the Dark Ages. During this time, knowledge was controlled by the Christian church and essentially limited to matters and perspectives that the church thought beneficial to itself and to the people of its lands. Philosophy and rational thought was largely banned. So when *Destiny* begins with the burning of philosopher Gerard Breuil at the stake for heresy, it is not surprising to see that it takes place in the Christian city of Languedoc, France. The film then moves to Averroës and his city, Cordoba in Andalusia (Muslim Spain), where we find the philosopher enjoying his family and friends, and freely and happily engaging in philosophical study. Significantly, both Averroës and the burned Breuil study the works of the Greek philosopher Aristotle.

The link between Islam and Greek philosophy is important. When the Greek and Latin churches banned the works of Greek thinkers such as

Plato and Aristotle, the Syrian church did not concur. Indeed, they were translating these works into Syriac. After the coming of Islam to Syria, Muslim thinkers translated them into Arabic and brought them to Baghdad, then the flourishing capital of the Islamic Abbasid Empire. As interest in Greek philosophers became more common among the Muslim intelligentsia, their writings were taken west across Northern Africa into Andalusia. From there, they were smuggled into Christian France, along with many Muslim philosophical studies. In Europe, Averroës's commentaries on Aristotle were actually printed on pages opposite the work itself. Averroës was simply identified as The Commentator. The rising knowledge of Greek philosophy, which later in part inspired the European Renaissance, thus traveled a long, roundabout route to get there.

Averroës, who lived from 1126 to 1198, was only a part-time philosopher. Known in the Islamic world as Ibn Rushd, his full-time job was that of a *qadi*, a high-ranking judge in Cordoba's court system, and he was an advisor to the Caliph. During this time, Cordoba was under pressure from Christian armies trying to drive out the Muslims. In the film, the Caliph's need to ensure Cordoba's protection causes him to consider his relations with his civilian society in terms of how they will help him achieve this primary goal. This gives an opportunity for a movement of fanatics to grow and become influential in the city. It is the influence this change has on Cordovan society and religion that constitutes the primary interest of *Destiny*. Little is known about the events of Averroës's life, and so the film can create its own portrayal without worrying about historical facts.

# Family, Friends, and Fanatics

*Destiny's* plot revolves around three main groups: the Caliph and his sons, the fanatics who are led by the Emir who is in the pay of Sheik Riad, and Averroës and his friends. The Caliph's main interest is the military situation with the Christians. He has just won a major battle at the start of the film and is about to begin another at the end. In between he worries about his sons and about the people's allegiance to him. The older son, Nasser, has yet to prove his worth to him, while the younger one, Abdallah, is interested in nothing but dancing.

Sheik Riad is ambitious for power. He wants to rule Cordoba, apparently as the power behind a puppet caliph whom he installs. Through a religious leader known as the Emir, he has brainwashed a large following of religious fanatics to help him fulfill these ambitions. The fanatics interest the Caliph's son Abdallah in their religious activities and try to mold him into one of themselves to do their bidding. Similarly, the Sheik and the Emir have co-opted the Council of Theologians—the city's religious leaders—into following their lead.

Averroës, his family, his friends, and his students form a multifaceted group. The audience first sees them having a meal, laughing, joking, and enjoying each other's company. The group includes Averroës with his wife; his daughter, Salma; the Caliph's brother; and two students, including Joseph, the Christian son of Breuil. The Caliph's son Abdallah appears with food from Manuela, who the viewers soon learn is the wife in a family of gypsy entertainers, along with her husband, Marwan, and her sister Sarah. They are accomplished singers, dancers, and musicians who run a drinking establishment. They are close friends with Averroës and his family, and they serve as Abdallah's surrogate parents. Together they constitute a cross section of Cordovan society, and represent the difficulties and joys of normal life. While *Destiny's* portrayal of the Caliph, Sheik Riad, and the fanatics presents them within a limited range of activities related to their concerns, Averroës's group appears in a wide variety of settings and activities, from the drinking house entertainment to tender family moments to lovers' interludes to judicial investigation and judgment to teaching, writing, and manuscript copying, and to medical interventions (Averroës also being a doctor). All the song-and-dance numbers take place among this group. They are the only ones who evidence the range of normal human activity, compassion, and emotion.

# The Trouble with Fanatics Is . . .

Under the guise of fanatical devotion to Islam, the Emir's followers actually fail to follow the precepts of Islam. In society, they show disrespect to their elders and other fellow citizens. They disrespect their families and make no friends outside the group. Most important, from the perspective of *Destiny*, is that their "faith" in Islam is actually a blind following of a leader who guides their activities for political gain. They do not seek true understanding of the religion, but think themselves superior because they have memorized a few verses of the Koran.

A large group of active fanatics like those in *Destiny* can wreak havoc on the society in which they are located. Because their view of permitted activities is narrowed by their extreme religious beliefs, their rejection of all social ties except for those linking them to the group, and their obedience to the dictates of their leaders, they come into conflict with the society. Indeed, they set themselves the task of disrupting normal social activities. Some disruptions appear petty. They interrupt Averroës's teaching by walking out of his talks in twos and threes. They sit at taverns and do not drink. Other incidents are more major. Since they do not approve of light music—"Good Muslims don't sing!"—they attempt to murder the singer Marwan. Borhan, the agitator, comments to Abdallah while resting after the desert hike, "Every throat I cut takes me one step closer to Paradise." This suggests that murder is a common mode of operation for the fanatics.

More important than these, however, is the disruption of the family. Borhan says to Abdallah, "We are your true family," as he works to subvert Abdallah's loyalty to his father. The family to which he refers is the cult, a collection of young men with no interest in marriage or in holding down jobs—as the audience learns from the mother of Marwan's assailant. They are to direct their devotion to the Emir and nowhere else. Because of this, we know they show no respect for their parents.

Nor do they participate in normal social interaction. The fanatics hang together by themselves. They never talk to women in the film, young or old. The only interaction with older men occurs when Borhan challenges Averroës in the mosque. They seem to be interested in young men outside the group only to recruit them. When they talk to Abdallah, it is to flatter him and persuade him to come join them in their activities. There is little real interest in him as a person. The fanatics' adherence to their cult, then, cuts them off from normal social interaction, normal friendship, and normal family relationships.

Most important, however, is that even though the fanatics talk about faith in Islam, their strong devotion is not to the religion itself, but to a leader, namely, the Emir. As *Destiny* makes clear, a little knowledge is a dangerous thing. The cult teaches them enough to sound pious, but does not actually encourage study or learning. The faith they have comes not from personal involvement in Koran study or in the pursuit of knowledge of Allah, but from the brainwashing techniques of the desert walks and the nighttime dances. They do not recognize the difference.

The scene of Averroës teaching in the mosque, with the Council of Theologians watching and listening through a window, reveals the two parts to this issue. The first part focuses on how the text should be under-stood. The activity opens with Averroës teaching calmly at the mosque. His lesson mixes his own thoughts with support from the Koran and the Hadith. His treatment of the holy material shows his piety.

> A lazy fool learns two verses of the Koran and passes himself off as a pur-veyor of divine truth. Is this man pious? A true understanding of these texts requires years of reflection, research and labor.
> If we believe these self-proclaimed geniuses we disregard this Koranic verse:
> In the name of Allah the merciful: "The ignorant man, whose vain words lead astray from the way of God and take it in mockery will be met by a humbling chastisement."
> True is the word of Almighty God.
> No one can claim to know the whole truth.

Without making any direct comment, Averroës is clearly teaching about the increasing numbers of fanatics in the city. His opening point seems to be just that true understanding of the Koran comes from years of study and thought. This aims directly at the young fanatics who are not yet old enough to have studied much. He aims to undermine the authority that their pious attitude claims for them. They in turn attempt to undermine Averroës's authority in this scene by constantly leaving in twos and threes.

A sharper point is put to Averroës's observation after Borhan, the fanatic attack dog, attempts to trip up Averroës by questioning him. He fails, and a member of the Council of Theologians observes:

> Averroës says: "Revelation [i.e., the Koran] can be interpreted only by study."
> We should have answered: "The text requires no interpretation."

Here, the issue is not that Averroës is older than the fanatics and thus more learned. It is that he thinks the Koran requires study in order to be understood. The claim of his opponents—whether on the Council or among the fanatics—is that revelation bears its own inherent and obvi-ous meaning. If it requires neither study nor interpretation, then this sug-gests that anyone who finds meaning only after study is really reading his own ideas into the text.

Although Averroës, of course, does not hear this remark, later in the film when he passes judgment on Marwan's assailant he responds to this position.

Revelation is destined only to those endowed with Reason. That is, mankind. Divine law combines Revelation and Reason. It consists in determining causes and effects, means and ends. Revelation encompasses Reason and Reason encompasses Revelation.

Certain children confuse religion and ignorance. Certain adults turn ignorance into a religion. Our young defendants were led into perdition. Without realizing it, they were forced astray.

Averroës's point is clear. Since humans were endowed by Allah with the capacity of Reason, they must use that capacity when they aim to understand Allah's words. The exercise of law, of the application of justice, means that humans must not mindlessly apply divinely revealed law to the individual before them, but must through Reason seek out the causes, the effects, and indeed the entire background that led to their actions. It is only the reasonable application of revelation that results in justice.

The issue of years of study Averroës referred to before is not a question of status, but of being able to recognize the difference between religious truth and ignorance. The young assailants could not; they had been purposely misled into believing that their ignorance was true religion. They believed because they did not know; the adults who used them knew, but led them astray. The Emir, as the audience knows, told them what to believe, and they believed it. They followed a man, not a religion.

The second part of this issue focuses on the differences between the Council of Theologians and the fanatics. Although both would agree on the statement that "the text requires no interpretation," they disagree on the exact meaning the text gives. That is, since reading and hearing are at their core acts of interpretation, those who receive the text will understand different things. The fanatics take their meaning from the teachings of the Emir, who is beholden to Sheik Riad. But where does the Council's understanding come from, for Riad's planned betrayal is as hidden from them as it is from the Caliph.

The answer becomes clear from a later comment by Caliph Mansur who mentions to Nasser that the Council sides with Ghazali. This suggests that the Council is angered at Averroës more because of his position in a philosophical debate than with anything else. The debate is over the question of how the Koran should be interpreted. When Greek thinkers like Aristotle and Plato became an important part of Islamic philosophy in the ninth century, a Muslim philosopher named Avicenna wrote a book arguing that philosophical reason alone was the means by which the

Koran should be understood. He went so far as to subordinate the Koran to Reason, claiming the Koran was symbolic truth rather than demonstrable truth (i.e., philosophical truth).

Al-Ghazali attacked this position as too extreme. Although he allowed Greek rational thought, he subordinated Reason to the Revelation of the Koran. His demonstration of the superiority of the Koran was a favorite with more conservative religious theologians, especially those who saw Greek philosophy as foreign and untrustworthy. He titled this book, *The Incoherence of the Philosophers.*

Averroës's most important work, at least as portrayed by *Destiny*, was *The Incoherence of Incoherence.* This was a disagreement with Al-Ghazali in which Averroës took the middle ground between Al-Ghazali and Avicenna. He saw philosophy, theology, and law as different aspects of a unity. Reason should be seen neither as superior nor inferior to Revelation. Instead, each was necessary to the other. As Averroës says in *Destiny,* "Revelation encompasses Reason and Reason encompasses Revelation." This refutation of Al-Ghazali's work made Averroës rather unpopular with traditional Islamic thinkers.

Sheik Riad takes advantage of the antagonism against Averroës among the Council for his own purposes of political betrayal. The religious faith of the fanatics may on the surface sound traditional, but it is really a surface façade, one that hides dishonesty, criminality, and blind following of leaders willing to use faithful devotion for political ends.

# The End

*Destiny's* ending transforms the seeming loss of Averroës and the triumph of Sheik Riad in this political competition into Averroës's success and the destruction of Riad's hopes of power. Even as the *fatwa* engineered by Riad and the Council goes into effect and the burning of Averroës's books commences, with Averroës and his family ejected from his house and all his possessions loaded onto a small wagon, Riad's fall and Averroës's triumph begins.

Mansur's sons remain loyal to him, neither persuaded to play the role assigned to them by Riad and the fanatics. Instead of eliminating the Caliph to make way for Riad's plans, they remain loyal to their family head and help him send Riad and the fanatics to the front lines of the coming battle. There, presumably, most will lose their lives in defense of the city, thus ending this threat to the Caliph and to the proper order of the society.

Averroës and his constant upholding of his values has saved the day. Despite the hardships that Riad's connivance and the Caliph's complicity have caused, Averroës has remained true to his faith and has retained his integrity. Because of this, he, his friends, and his family have returned the Caliph's two sons to him, whole and strong. Despite the loss of his house and the burning of his books, Averroës retains his family, his friends, and, through the help of Nasser, his writings, preserved where they will be safe from Cordovan political machinations.

*Destiny*'s message then is that fanaticism endangers a society and its rulers. Under the guise of true religion—that which is seen as traditional—they attack and undermine the key social institutions, namely, the family and the Caliph, which means, as the Emir's last words remind the audience, the prophet Muhammad's successor. Islam is not a matter of one man's declaration of the Koran's meaning, but a reasoned and rational inquiry into it with the application of Reason.

# Destiny and the Islamic World

Like the other films studied in this book, *Destiny* speaks to the larger social and political circumstances of its day. Unlike the other films, however, those circumstances are found in the Islamic world rather than in the United States. *Destiny* addresses both the general problem of radical religious-political groups in Muslim countries and the specific problem posed by the rise of the Taliban in Afghanistan. It argues that, despite the attractiveness of some of these groups in comparison to the governments of their countries, these religious-based groups would destroy the fabric of normal Muslim life if they came to power. By the time of the film's release, the Taliban's rise to power in Afghanistan had become an obvious demonstration of the correctness of *Destiny*'s position. To unpack this observation, let us turn to a brief (and overly generalized) explanation of the political situation that *Destiny* addresses.

Prior to the mid-twentieth century, few Islamic countries had the opportunity to develop a national identity of their own. The countries around the Mediterranean Sea were part of the Ottoman Empire until World War I, and most countries to the east of that were under colonial rule until after World War II. With no tradition of self government, most of these countries at best came under some form of one-party rule, often that of a strong-man supported by a political party he controlled. A few countries went through periods of civil war and occupation. The postwar superpowers—the United States and Soviet Russia—were also involved in the region, supplying arms, money, and occasionally troops to various countries.

In the one-party states, political freedom was in short supply. Opposition parties were banned. Political expression of the people could only be achieved in the one public institution these governments still permitted to operate, namely, Islam. Although most mosques and religious schools steered clear of politics, a few became forums for a new melding of political expression and religion, with Islam's divine connections adding a veneer of otherworld authority to this-worldly goals. In some cases, this led to the formation of radical religious-political groups opposing governments. In Syria and Egypt, the Muslim Brotherhood arose, while in Lebanon and Palestine, which were occupied by Israel, Hezbollah, and Hamas, respectively, became strong.

*Destiny* does not seem to address either of these situations. In neither Egypt nor Syria was the government ever cozy with the Muslim Brotherhood. Nor does the film address the circumstance of occupied Islamic lands. Instead, it seems to be addressing the rise of the Taliban in Afghanistan. When they first appeared on the scene in 1993, the Taliban brought peace to a war-ravaged country. After years of civil war, the Soviet Union had invaded Afghanistan in 1979. Ten years and forty thousand deaths later, they went home. This left a communist government in Kabul and the rest of the country being fought over by regional warlords. The Taliban's strong military showing, its success at stamping out corruption and illegal activities, and the return of economic activity in the areas it controlled won it a strong early following among the Afghan people.

The strength of the Taliban came from its appeal to young men. The name actually means "religious students." Preaching an extreme—and often poorly understood—brand of Islam, they brought in new members with more enthusiasm than knowledge. Seeing the source of their problems as stemming from Western influence, the Taliban banned television, films, and the Internet when they took power in 1996. They also banned music and related forms of entertainment. Most seriously, however, they removed women from the workplace and isolated them in their homes, not allowing them outside unless accompanied by a male. This caused a crisis in women's healthcare as well as disruption of traditional social norms.

When *Destiny* was released in 1997, it was seen in terms of these developments. Even though the film portrayed the Caliph as more interested in military and security matters than his own sons, and more interested in his own authority than the rule of law, it argues that it is only under such authority that normal Islamic life can take place. The religious fanatics, by contrast, would disrupt normal family life, require the following of a form of Islam that was more slogans than understanding, and eliminate the pleasures and joys of daily life. Although the film did not allow the fanatics to triumph, the Taliban's strictures proved the film's thesis correct. The regular news reports in the Arab world frequently revealed this. Thus, even though Averroës himself has his life's successes destroyed, he retains his family and friends. And, more important, the normal life of society is preserved. The average person on the street can go on living their own life without the disruption the fanatics would have imposed.

# Islam and Fanaticism in *My Son the Fanatic*

In *Destiny*, the distinction between Islam and fanaticism is clear. The only thing to debate is why a fanatical approach to religion is wrong. *My Son the Fanatic* (1997) presents the two as the same thing. Whether it is Islam or fanaticism depends on who is watching. Released the same year as *Destiny*, this British-made film can be read in two ways. Western audiences identify with the father in this story and see the son's new-found interest in Islam as fanaticism. Muslim audiences identify with the son and see his return to Islamic values and practices as praiseworthy. What the West sees as fanaticism, the Muslim world sees as typical Islam.

Despite its title, *My Son the Fanatic* is less about religion than cultural assimilation—specifically, of Pakistanis who emigrated to England in the decades following World War II. The British ruled much of the Indian subcontinent for over two centuries, first as a trading power, and then, after the Great Mutiny of 1857 (known in India as the First War of Independence), through direct governmental rule from London. After World War II, the British government found it could no longer bear the cost of an empire and so in 1947 granted India its freedom. Immediately the subcontinent was divided into two countries along religious lines, with Pakistan becoming predominantly Muslim and India becoming predominantly Hindu. Because of these changes, many sought economic opportunity in England and more than two million Muslims now call Britain home. Large sections of many cities in Britain—Manchester and its environs, for example—have become predominantly Muslim. Many old churches have been converted into mosques, and new mosques have been built.

But economic and cultural integration of these newcomers has not been uniformly successful. While *My Son the Fanatic* presents the father's friend Fizzy as a prosperous businessman with a large restaurant, the father himself has not done as well. Parvez is a taxi driver who spends much of his time driving the lower classes. Despite all the father's years in England, the German visitor Schitz speaks better English than he does. Parvez aspires to the "code of a gentleman," but spends much of his time driving whores.

His son, Farid, on whom he dotes, has been more successful. He earned good grades in school, became captain of the cricket team, and is now going to university to study economics. Furthermore, the son has become engaged to a young English woman, Madeline, who is the daughter of the Chief Inspector of the police.

It is the meeting of the two sets of parents that changes Farid's attitude toward England. Farid—and the audience—sees what Parvez does not. The Chief Inspector and his wife despise Farid's family. Although they relate to immigrants on a daily basis, they find the notion that their daughter would marry one repulsive. Farid breaks off the engagement and turns to the religion of his forefathers for consolation. As he learns more about Islam, he becomes increasingly devout and observant.

Farid has a long way to go. The father first finds out about his son's religious interests when he discovers Farid learning from a recording how to pray. Apparently, Parvez never taught his son how to pray, even though praying fives times a day is a minimal expectation of Islam, one of its Five Pillars. Farid's interest in Islam apparently begins with little knowledge of it in his life prior to the film. Although he has been part of the Pakistani cultural community in England his entire life, he knows almost nothing of its religious aspects.

This is not surprising, for the film presents the older generation of the immigrant community as being uninvolved in religion. Neither Parvez nor his friend, Fizzy, show any interest in it. When Parvez follows his son and discovers that he is going to the mosque to pray, he has a brief exchange with a regular worshiper of his own generation. The man observes that the boys do not listen to their elders, but they stand for something. "We never did that," he says, the implication being that even the immigrants practicing Islam lack a spiritual fire, a religious hunger. They are unsuited to teach their children about true Islam.

The lack of religious piety in the older generation shown in the film is a condemnation of Muslims in England. They did not—perhaps could not—follow the precepts and beliefs of Islam in a foreign country. For the son and his new friends to learn about Islam, they need to import a teacher from Pakistan. True Islam can only be found among Muslims. This is not only a matter of teaching but also of life. Farid says that although he will marry, he will not raise his children in England. He thus rejects the choice his father made to come to England, as well as his own prior success within it.

As the son becomes increasingly religious, the father becomes more heavily involved in the sex trade. It starts as Parvez recommends a whore for the visiting Schitz and increases until he becomes the procurer for a sex party Schitz hosts. At the same time, he becomes increasingly involved with one prostitute in particular, Bettina. They bring a tenderness into each other's life, which neither finds elsewhere.

The film climaxes when the son and his religious friends try to drive out the whores living in their neighborhood. The father sees Farid mistreating Bettina, grabs him by the collar, and takes him home. This may prevent Farid's arrest by the arriving police reinforcements, but it is the last straw for Farid, who leaves home. This is followed by Parvez's wife deciding to head back to Pakistan, implying that she hopes never to see him again.

The closing scenes show Bettina consoling Parvez, and then his return to his now-empty house to listen to jazz while drinking a whiskey. He has chosen to remain in the culture of his adopted country, England, even though his son and his wife have rejected it.

# Western and Eastern Perspectives

Western audiences almost exclusively understand this film in one way. The destruction of Parvez's life and family is the fault of his son's adoption of radical Islam. Farid has lived his life before the film as a success in the terms of English culture. He is a success at sports, education, music, fashion, and even romance. Then he gets religion. He loses interest in all his past activities, including his fiancée. As he becomes more committed to Islam, he dresses in religious clothes, forms a new group of religiously committed friends, becomes invested in learning about Islam, and begins to practice what he learns.

The goal that he and his friends set, of ridding the neighborhood of whores, is seen as beyond the bounds of proper behavior. Indeed, it is their attempted destruction of the whore's residence that destroys the family of Parvez, Farid, and Minoo. Despite the father's involvement in the sex trade and his adultery with Bettina, at the film's end the audience's sympathies are with Parvez, and not with his son. The audience sees Islam here as fanaticism. It destroys family life and leads to the rejection of the parents.

A Muslim view of the film gives quite a different read. From this perspective, the problem is not one of adapting to a new culture, but of how to live a Muslim life in a society that is non-Muslim. The first-generation immigrants in this film have largely given up living as Muslims. Parvez and Fizzy indicate no interest in Islam, even though they both retain their cultural identities as Pakistanis. Parvez did not even teach his son how to pray. Even the man Parvez meets in the mosque recognizes in Farid and his young companions a religious commitment their older generation lacks. The first-generation immigrants cannot pass on or teach something they do not have.

Given this situation, it is not surprising that the son Farid has to learn about his religious background on his own. At the start, the audience sees him learning how to pray. He is such a religious neophyte that to learn what most five-year-old boys in Pakistan know how to do, he must take instruction from a faceless, recorded voice. Nor is praying in a mosque a sign of religious zealotry. Although one need not pray in the mosque all the time, a Muslim is encouraged to do so as often as possible. Similarly, the white clothes and cap in which Farid begins to dress are not a sign of religious weirdness, but are the traditional Pakistani Muslim equivalent of what American Christians used to call "Sunday go to meeting clothes." This represents not fanaticism, but simply typical Pakistani Islamic practices.

There are two actions that the son and his friends take that go beyond these normal practices. First, they bring in a Muslim teacher from Pakistan. This is another indication of the failure of the first-generation immigrants to look after the religious needs of themselves and their families. The film is indicating that this Muslim community has no teachers for the young. True Islam cannot be found in England, it must be brought in from home. It is, of course, notable that the teacher introduces traditional social practices into Parvez's home, such as the separation of the sexes at mealtimes. Yet, these are not fanatical changes, but simply traditional practices followed prior to the changes introduced into the Muslim world by Western influence.

Second, Farid and his friends take steps to drive the whores out of the neighborhood. This escalates toward violence, but the climactic scene shows more anger, frustration, and noise than violence. Someone uses the anonymity of the crowd to throw an incendiary device into the house and it starts a fire, but the face-to-face encounters between the prostitutes and crowd members are little more than shoving matches. Parvez is angered by Farid's encounter with Bettina not because Farid is beating or kicking her (he isn't), but because he spits in her face; he violates the "code of the gentleman."

The action against the whores certainly violates their right to live where they choose, but prostitution is illegal in Britain. Legally, they should not be plying their trade there. It is clear from the beginning of the film that no one in the community welcomes their presence. The young men are essentially carrying out the will of the community in trying to rid the neighborhood of them. They are doing what the police themselves should have done. Although the action is confrontational, it is an act of purification rather than fanaticism. In the United States, Christians would not stand for a whorehouse around the corner from their church, why should Muslims have to put up with a similar situation?

When watched through Muslim eyes rather than Western ones, *My Son the Fanatic* portrays not fanaticism but little more than expected Muslim behavior. The attempt to rid the neighborhood of whores would be seen not as an extreme action, but as an attempt to make the neighborhood more livable for the residents.

If the portrayal of the son's return to Islam is seen by Muslim viewers as essentially an attempt to return to Islamic normalcy, the English society from which he returns is portrayed as decadent and immoral. It is riddled with drugs and alcohol, which are forbidden by Islam. The film portrays the Pakistani cabbies drinking in the bar, where Parvez calls them "very low class types," although the main difference between them and Parvez is that Parvez does his drinking alone at home. But it is the sex trade that truly represents Western immorality. One group of whores have changed the character of this neighborhood. In the film's portrayal they are everywhere. As Farid observes to his father when dining at Fizzy's, "They say integrate, but they live in pornography and filth, and tell us how backwards we are."

The difference between the two cultures is so great that when Parvez asks Farid whether he ever kissed Madeline—apparently trying to determine whether his son is gay or "normal"—Minoo his wife responds, "Normal is not perverted as it is in your mind." The father's question comes from typical English practice, while Minoo's comment reflects her more traditional Muslim approach. She is scandalized that an engaged couple would kiss.

In the end, it is Parvez's involvement in the sex trade that destroys the family. Not only does the son know about the sex party Parvez arranged, but Minoo and everyone else knows that he is seeing Bettina. Parvez is committing adultery. In Muslim eyes, then, *My Son the Fanatic* shows that the destruction of the family comes from immoral behavior brought by the father's involvement in the decadent character of Western society. He prefers a whore to his wife.

*My Son the Fanatic* has one more trick to play. Most Western viewers of this film identify with the father rather than the son. Parvez is the one who has been mistreated, and they are glad for the suggestion that he will rebuild his life with Bettina. They have no sympathy for the son and his religious interests. This confirms the Muslim view of Western society, that it is corrupt and immoral. Whether the West is seen as secular or Christian, the identification of Western audiences with a man who destroys his family for a whore shows that they fit the Muslim characterization of the West. It is not just that the film portrays the immorality of the West, but that Western audiences themselves affirm that portrayal. They show themselves as immoral because they identify with the film's immoral character rather than with the one who tries to follow a moral search for God.

\* \* \*

These two films, *Destiny* and *My Son the Fanatic*, were both released in 1997, but they take opposite positions on the question of whether Islam and fanaticism can be distinguished. The difference lies in part in the films' intended audiences. *Destiny* was made for the Muslim world. Muslims can identify the difference between "normal" Islam and the practices of fanatics, and the threat they bring to Muslim societies and their families. My *Son the Fanatic*, by contrast, was filmed for a Western audience. That audience knows so little about Islam that they cannot recognize even the most elementary features of Muslim practice and belief. The film plays on this and causes the audience to identify the son's first attempts at learning to pray as an increasing commitment to fanaticism.

# Suggested Readings

Karen Armstrong, *Islam: A Short History*, rev. ed. (Modern Library, 2002).

Frederick M. Denny, *Muslims in America* (Oxford: Oxford University Press, 2006).

S. H. Nasr, *Islam: Religion, History and Civilization* (San Francisco: HarperSanFrancisco, 2002).

# Appendix

## Targum Neofiti to Genesis 2–3: The Adam and Eve Story

Translation by Martin McNamara

### Genesis 2

1. And they completed the creation of the heavens and the earth and all their hosts. 2. And on the seventh day the Memra of the Lord completed his work which he had created and there was sabbath and repose before him on the seventh day from all his work which he had created. 3. And the Glory of the Lord blessed the seventh day and hallowed it because on it there was a great sabbath and repose before him from all his work which the Glory of the Lord had done in creation. 4. This is the genealogical pedigree of the heavens and of the earth when they were created. On the day that the Lord God created the heavens and the earth, 5. none of the trees that are on the surface of the field had as yet existed on the earth and none of the herbs that are on the face of the field had as yet sprouted on the earth, because the Lord God had not as yet caused rain to fall, and as yet Adam had not been created to till the earth. 6. But a cloud used to go up from the earth and watered all the surface of the earth. 7. And the Lord God created Adam (out of) dust from the ground and breathed into his nostrils the breath of life, and Adam became a living being endowed with speech. 8. And the Lord God had planted a garden in Eden from the beginning and he placed there the first Adam

299

whom he had created. 9. And out of the ground the Lord God made grow every tree that was nice to see and good to eat, and the tree of life within the middle of the garden, and the tree of knowledge of which anyone who would eat would know to distinguish between good and evil. 10. And a river went out from Eden to water the garden and from there it was divided and turned to become four heads of great rivers. 11. The name of one of them is Pishon. It is that which surrounds and encircles all the land of India, from where the gold comes. 12. And the gold of that land is good. From there comes bdellium, and precious stones and pearl. 13. And the name of the second river is Gihon. It is that which surrounds and encircles the land of Cush. 14. The name of the third river is Tigris. It is that which surrounds and encircles Assyria to the east. And the fourth river is the Great River, the river Euphrates. 15. And the Lord God took Adam and had him dwell in the garden of Eden to toil in the Law and to observe its commandments. 16. And the Lord God commanded Adam, saying: "From all the trees of the garden you may surely eat; 17. from the tree of knowledge, however, from which anyone who eats would know to distinguish between good and evil, you shall not eat of it because on the day that you shall eat you shall surely die." 18. And the Lord God said, "It is not proper that man should be alone; I will make for him a partner similar to himself." 19. And from the ground the Lord God created every beast that is on the surface of the field and all the birds of the heavens; and he brought them to Adam to see what he would call them. And whatever Adam called a living creature in the language of the sanctuary, that was its name. 20. And Adam gave their names to all the cattle and to the birds of the heavens, and to all the wild beasts that are on the surface of the field; yet for Adam he did not find a partner similar to himself. 21. And the Lord God cast a deep sleep on Adam, and he fell asleep. And he took one rib of his ribs and placed flesh in its stead. 22. And the Lord God perfected the rib he had taken from Adam into a woman and he took her to Adam. 23. And Adam said: "This time, and never again, is a woman created from man, as this one has been created from me, bone from my bone and flesh from my flesh. It is fitting that this one be called woman because it is from a male that this one has been created." 24. For this reason shall a man separate his couch from that of his father and that of his mother and adhere to his wife. And the two of them will become one flesh. 25. And both of them were naked, Adam and his wife, and as yet they did not know what shame was.

# Genesis 3

1. The serpent was shrewder than all the beasts that are on the surface of the field which the Lord God had created. And he said to the woman: "So, the Lord has said: 'You may not eat of any of the trees of the garden.'" 2. And the woman said to the serpent: "We may eat of the fruit of the trees of the garden; 3. but of the fruit of the tree that is in the middle of the garden, the Lord has said: 'You shall not eat of it and you shall not draw near to it, and (thus) you shall not die." 4. And the serpent said to the woman: "You certainly shall not die; 5. because it is manifest and known before the Lord that on the day you eat of it your eyes will be opened, and that you will be like angels before the Lord, knowing to distinguish between good and evil." 6. And the woman saw that the tree was good to eat and that it was a desirable to the eyes, and that the tree was suited to have one acquire wisdom by it. So she took of its fruits and ate and she also gave to her husband with her and he ate. 7. And the eyes of both of them were opened; and they knew that they were naked and sewed fig leaves for themselves and made for themselves girdles. 8. And they heard the sound of the Memra of the Lord God walking within the garden at the breeze of the day; and Adam and his wife hid themselves from before the Lord God within the trees of the garden. 9. And the Lord God called Adam and said to him: "Behold, the whole world which I created is manifest before me; darkness and light are manifest before me. And do you reckon that the place within which you are is not manifest before me? Where is the precept that I commanded you?" 10. And he said: "I heard the sound of your Memra in the garden and I was afraid because I am naked, and I hid myself." 11. And he said: "Who told you that you were naked? Have you, perchance, eaten from the tree from which I commanded you not to eat?" 12. And Adam said: "The woman that you have placed with me, she gave me from the tree and I ate." 13. And the Lord God said to the woman: "What is this you have done?" And the woman said: "The serpent deceived me and I ate." 14. And the Lord God said to the serpent: "Because you have done this, you will be more accursed, O serpent, than all the cattle and than all the wild beasts that are on the surface of the fields. On your belly you will crawl and dust will be your food all the days of your life. 15. And I will put enmity between you and the woman and between your sons and her sons. And it will come about that when her sons observe the Law and do the commandments they will aim at you and smite you on your head and kill

you. But when they forsake the commandments of the Law you will aim and bite him on his heel and make him ill. For her sons, however, there will be a remedy, but for you, O serpent, there will not be a remedy, since they are to make appeasement in the end, in the day of King Messiah. 16. And to the woman he said: "I will greatly multiply your pains and your pregnancies. In pain you will bring forth children and to your husband you will turn and he will have authority over you, whether to remain just or to sin. 17. And to Adam he said: "Since you have heeded the voice of your wife and have eaten of the tree concerning which I commanded you, saying: 'You shall not eat of it,' the earth will be cursed on your account. In pain will you eat the fruits of its harvest all the days of your life. 18. Thorns and thistles shall it bring forth for you, and you shall eat of the herbs that are on the surface of the field." Adam answered and said: "Pray, by the mercy (that is) before you, O Lord; let us not be reckoned as the cattle, eating the grass that is on the surface of the field. Let us stand upright, I pray, and labor; and from the labor of my hands let us eat food from the fruits of the earth. Thereby shall he distinguish the sons of man from the cattle." 19. "You will eat bread from the sweat from before your face until you return to the earth, because from it you were created; because you are dust and to dust you are to return. But from the dust you are to arise again to give an account and a reckoning of all that you have done." 20. And the man called the name of his wife Eve because she was the mother of all the living. 21. And the Lord God made for Adam and for his wife garments of glory, for the skin of their flesh, and he clothed them. 22. And the Lord God said: "Behold, the first Adam whom I have created is alone in the world as I am alone in the heavens on high. Numerous nations are to arise from him, and from him shall arise one nation who will know to distinguish between good and evil. If he had observed the precept of the Law and fulfilled its commandment he would live and endure forever like the tree of life. And now, since he has not observed the precepts of the Law and has not fulfilled its commandment, behold we will banish him from the garden of Eden before he stretches out his hand and takes of the fruit of the tree of life and eats and lives forever." 23. And the Lord God banished him from the garden of Eden to till the earth from which he had been created. 24. And he banished Adam; and he had made the Glory of his Shekinah dwell from the beginning to the east of the Garden of Eden, between the two cherubim. Two thousand years before he created the world he had created the Law; he had prepared the garden of Eden for the just and Gehenna for the wicked.

He had prepared the garden of Eden for the just that they might eat and delight themselves from the fruits of the tree, because they had kept precepts of the Law in this world and fulfilled the commandments. For the wicked he prepared Gehenna, which is comparable to a sharp sword devouring with both edges. He prepared within it darts of fire and burning coals for the wicked, to be avenged of them in the world to come because they did not observe the precepts of the Law in this world. For the Law is a tree of life for everyone who toils in it and keeps the commandments: he lives and endures like the tree of life in the world to come. The Law is good for all who labor in it in this world like the fruit of the tree of life.

# Filmography

2001: A Space Odyssey (1968)
Agnes of God (1985)
Apostle, The (1998)
Bad Santa (2003)
Barabbas (1962)
Ben Hur (1959)
Brother Sun, Sister Moon (1972)
Charlie Brown Christmas, A (1965)
Chosen, The (1982)
Christmas Carol, A (1951)
Close Encounters of the Third Kind (1977)
Clueless (1995)
Conquest of Space (1955)
Day the Earth Stood Still, The (1951)
Demetrius and the Gladiators (1954)
Destiny (1997)
Dr. Seuss' How the Grinch Stole Christmas (2000)
E.T. (1982)
Earnest Saves Christmas (1998)
Exorcist, The (1973)
Field of Dreams (1989)
Fifth Element, The (1997)
Fisher King, The (1991)
Godspell (1973)
Greatest Christmas Pageant Ever, The (1983)
Greatest Story Ever Told, The (1965)
Harry Potter and the Prisoner of Azkaban (2004)
Harry Potter and the Sorcerer's Stone (2001)

*Home Alone* (1990)
*How the Grinch Stole Christmas!* (1967)
*It's a Wonderful Life* (1946)
*Jesus Christ, Superstar* (1973)
*Jesus of Nazareth* (1977)
*King of Kings* (1961)
*Last Temptation of Christ, The* (1988)
*Leap of Faith* (1992)
*Legend of Bagger Vance, The* (2000)
*Life of Brian, The* (1979)
*Little Buddha* (1993)
*Matrix, The* (1999)
*Miracle on 34th Street* (1947)
*Mr. Magoo's Christmas Carol* (1962)
*Muppet Christmas Carol, A* (1993)
*My Son the Fanatic* (1997)
*Natural, The* (1984)
*Nightmare Before Christmas, The* (1993)
*Olive, the Other Reindeer* (1999)
*Omen, The* (1976)
*Passion of the Christ, The* (2004)
*Polar Express, The* (2004)
*Quarrel, The* (1990)
*Quo Vadis* (1951)
*Robe, The* (1953)
*Rosemary's Baby* (1968)
*Rudolf, the Red-Nosed Reindeer* (1964)
*Saved* (2004)
*Scrooge* (1970)
*Scrooged* (1988)
*Ten Commandments, The* (1956)
*Them* (1954)
*Thing, The* (1951)
*Towering Inferno, The* (1974)
*When Worlds Collide* (1951)
*Why Has Bodhi-Dharma Left for the East?* (1989)
*Winnie the Pooh and the Honey Tree* (1966)